Reconstructing Climate Policy

Reconstructing Climate Policy

Beyond Kyoto

Richard B. Stewart and Jonathan B. Wiener

The AEI Press

Publisher for the American Enterprise Institute

WASHINGTON, D.C.

2003

Available in the United States from the AEI Press, c/o Publisher Resources Inc., 1224 Heil Quaker Blvd., P.O. Box 7001, La Vergne, TN 37086-7001. To order, call toll free: 1-800-937-5557. Distributed outside the United States by arrangement with Eurospan, 3 Henrietta Street, London WC2E 8LU, England.

Library of Congress Cataloging-in-Publication Data
Stewart, Richard B.
    Reconstructing climate policy: after Kyoto / Richard B. Stewart and Jonathan B. Wiener
        p. cm.
    Includes bibliographical references and index.
    ISBN 0-8447-4186-8 (pbk.: alk. paper)
    1. Climatic changes—Government policy. I. Wiener, Jonathan Baert, 1962–
II. Title.

QC981.8.C5 S753 2002
363.738'7456—dc21   2002042672

ISBN 0-8447-4186-8 (pbk.: alk. paper)

1 3 5 7 9 10 8 6 4 2

Printed in the United States of America

Contents

Foreword

This volume is one in a series commissioned by the American Enterprise Institute to contribute to the debates over global environmental policy issues. Until very recently, American environmental policy was directed toward problems that were seen to be of a purely, or at least largely, domestic nature. Decisions concerning emissions standards for automobiles and power plants, for example, were set with reference to their effect on the quality of air Americans breathe.

That is no longer the case. Policymakers increasingly find that debates over environmental standards have become globalized, to borrow a word that has come into fashion in several contexts. Global warming is the most prominent of those issues: Americans now confront claims that the types of cars they choose to drive, the amount and mix of energy they consume in their homes and factories, and the organization of their basic industries all have a direct effect on the lives of citizens of other countries—and, in some formulations, may affect the future of the planet itself.

Other issues range from the management of forests, fisheries, and water resources to the preservation of species and the search for new energy sources. Not far in the background of all those new debates, however, are the oldest subjects of international politics—competition for resources and competing interests and ideas concerning economic growth, the distribution of wealth, and the terms of trade.

An important consequence of those developments is that the arenas in which environmental policy is determined are increasingly international— not just debates in the U.S. Congress, rulemaking proceedings at the Environmental Protection Agency, and implementation decisions by the states and municipalities, but opaque diplomatic "frameworks" and "protocols" hammered out in remote locales. To some, that constitutes a dangerous surrender of national sovereignty; to others, it heralds a new era of American cooperation with other nations that is propelled by the realities of an interdependent world. To policymakers themselves, it means that familiar questions of the benefits and costs of environmental rules are now enmeshed with questions of sovereignty and political legitimacy, of the possibility of large international income transfers, and of the relations of developed to developing countries.

In short, environmental issues are becoming as much a question of foreign policy as of domestic policy; indeed, the Clinton administration made what it called "environmental diplomacy" a centerpiece of this country's foreign policy.

AEI's project on global environmental policy includes contributions from scholars in many academic disciplines and features frequent lectures and seminars at the Institute's headquarters as well as this series of studies. We hope that the project will illuminate the many complex issues confronting those attempting to strike a balance between environmental quality and the other goals of industrialized and emerging economies.

CHRISTOPHER C. DEMUTH
ROBERT W. HAHN
American Enterprise Institute
for Public Policy Research

Acknowledgments

For very helpful discussions and comments, the authors thank David Bradford, Carlo Carraro, Lakshman Guruswamy, Robert Hahn, Henry Jacoby, Robert Keohane, Benedict Kingsbury, Jonathan Ocko, Michael Oppenheimer, Annie Petsonk, Richard Revesz, Richard Richels, Philippe Sands, William Schlesinger, Jane Bloom Stewart, David Victor, and participants at workshops at New York University and the University of Colorado. For invaluable research assistance, the authors thank Tyler Roozen at NYU and Mark Axelrod and Zheng Zhou at Duke University.

1

Introduction and Summary

As of early 2003, global climate policy appears to be in an awkward spot. The Kyoto Protocol has been ratified by the European Union and its member states and by Japan, and ratification seems likely (though not guaranteed) by the Russian Federation, Poland, and other industrialized countries with economies in transition.[1] If those countries ratify the Kyoto Protocol, it will enter into force, probably in early 2003.[2] Even if the Kyoto Protocol enters into force, however, it would cover less than half of global greenhouse gas emissions. The United States, responsible for about a quarter of all greenhouse gas emissions,[3] remains on the sidelines, with no current intention of ratifying the protocol and few signs of engaging in global climate policy efforts. Although President George W. Bush has proposed a set of tax credits and voluntary measures intended to reduce future emissions intensity (emissions per dollar of gross domestic product), few concrete steps have been taken to implement those proposals, and he has repudiated regulatory limitations on emissions.[4] Further, the Kyoto Protocol includes no emissions limitations on developing countries, whose greenhouse gas emissions are increasing rapidly and will surpass those of the industrialized countries by 2020 or so; China's emissions alone already account for over 13 percent of the world total carbon dioxide emissions.[5] Developing countries have staunchly opposed any limitations obligations; they have asserted (with considerable justification) that the current buildup of greenhouse gases in the earth's atmosphere is largely the responsibility of the wealthy countries, which have emitted much greater amounts of greenhouse gases in the course of industrialization and which currently maintain far more greenhouse gas–intensive lifestyles.

But without the participation of the United States and major emitting developing countries, which together account for over half of global

1

greenhouse gas emissions, the Kyoto Protocol (or any other international effort to address the risks of climate change by curbing greenhouse gas emissions) is doomed to fail.[6] Ratification of the Kyoto Protocol will be a largely symbolic victory unless all major greenhouse gas–emitting countries join in some form of effective international regulatory regime in the relatively near future. And in addition to the Kyoto Protocol's limited coverage, its design, while embodying several salutary elements, has significant flaws—most notably the failure to set regulatory targets in accordance with emissions pathways that appropriately balance relevant costs and benefits. Yet adverse effects from climate change are a serious enough prospect to warrant some well-designed, cost-effective regulatory measures. Accordingly, ways must be found to build a new and more inclusive architecture for global climate policy, through fundamental modification of the current Kyoto Protocol structure, by developing alternatives outside the Kyoto Protocol structure, or both.

We examine how the present situation in climate policy arose and the potential steps forward from the current impasse. We summarize the current state of information regarding the extent of warming that would be caused by increasing uncontrolled greenhouse gas emissions, the impacts of warming, and the costs of emissions limitations. We explain why participation by all major greenhouse gas–emitting countries is essential to curb future emissions and also note the significant obstacles to obtaining such participation. We argue that it is in the national interest of the United States to participate in such a regime, provided that it is well designed. We then discuss the elements of sound climate regulatory design, including maximum use of economic incentives, the comprehensive approach, and other flexibility mechanisms; participation by all major emitting countries including developing countries; regulatory targets based on longer-term emissions pathways that aim to maximize net social benefits; and effective arrangements to ensure compliance with regulatory obligations by nations and sources. We evaluate the successes and failures of the Kyoto Protocol in light of those elements. Finally, we propose a series of U.S. initiatives at both the international and domestic levels, with the aim of engaging the United States and major developing country emitters such as China in the global greenhouse gas regulatory effort and correcting the remaining defects in the Kyoto Protocol design. Although several alternatives to the current Kyoto Protocol regime have been proposed,[7] we argue that the best approach for surmounting the current global climate policy impasse is a new strategy that would lead, sooner or later, to simultaneous accession by the United States and China (and other major developing country emitters) to a modified and improved version of the Kyoto Protocol agreement.

Greenhouse gases are generated globally by many different human activities in many different sectors through the use of more or less deeply embedded technologies and practices. Although some substantial limitations in greenhouse gas emissions may be achieved in the near term at low (or perhaps even negative) cost, significant limitations will require major changes in production and consumption technologies, investments, and practices; those structural changes can only be accomplished over a longer time scale. The transition from a high– to a low–greenhouse gas economy will not be a free lunch. But if the transition is managed wisely by enlisting all major emitting countries and using the most cost-effective and efficient means (including comprehensive coverage, sinks, and global emissions trading) to achieve soundly designed targets over appropriate time scales, there should be no major adverse effect on economic growth. Successful technological innovations and institutional reconstruction will allow high standards of lifestyles to be maintained. Over the longer term, prosperity does not require ever expanding use of fossil fuels and ever rising greenhouse gas emissions. Indeed, if the adverse effects of climate change are or may be large, then intelligent climate policy along the lines we advocate will *enhance* total well-being by reducing the risk of significant climate damages at moderate cost.

Climate Policy Today

Following the entry into force of the 1992 Framework Convention on Climate Change, the Kyoto Protocol to the convention was concluded in December 1997. Responding to a 95 to 0 vote in the U.S. Senate against ratifying any climate treaty lacking meaningful participation by developing countries,[8] the Clinton administration, which had signed the Kyoto Protocol, never submitted it to the Senate.[9] Further multilateral negotiations on implementing the Kyoto Protocol hit a stalemate at The Hague in late 2000. In March 2001 President Bush announced that the United States would no longer pursue the Kyoto Protocol; so far, he has not proposed an alternative. By June 2001, many informed observers expected the Kyoto Protocol process to fall apart.[10] Yet it did not. At the 2001 negotiating sessions in Bonn and Marrakech, the other countries of the world reached a compromise to enable implementation of the Kyoto Protocol regime, without U.S. participation and without emissions limitations on developing countries.[11] In February 2002 President Bush reiterated his decision to stay out of the Kyoto Protocol and not to seek any domestic regulatory limitations on U.S. greenhouse gas emissions.[12] Nonetheless, a substantial number of countries and the European Union have ratified the Kyoto Protocol, and it appears likely that there will be sufficient additional ratifications for the protocol to enter into force in early 2003. What should the United States—and the world—do now?

Ironically, the agreements reached at Bonn and Marrakech in 2001 to implement the 1997 Kyoto Protocol were in important respects a success for U.S. climate policy; the U.S. delegation was a wallflower at its own victory party. For both environmental and economic reasons, the United States has long advocated two key elements: a comprehensive approach to limiting net greenhouse gas emissions (including methane and all other major greenhouse gases, not just carbon dioxide, and also sinks such as forests); and international greenhouse gas emissions trading.[13] Those two ideas were formulated and proposed in the first Bush administration and championed in the Clinton administration,[14] often against opposition from Europe. At U.S. insistence, the Framework Convention on Climate Change and the Kyoto Protocol adopted both those ideas, and in Bonn and Marrakech the participating countries agreed on rules to implement them (subject to certain restrictions) despite U.S. rejection of the protocol as a whole. So why would the United States not sign on? Although further liberalization of emissions trading and wider authorization for sink credits are important, the major stumbling blocks to U.S. participation have been the absence of any emissions limitations obligations for major developing countries and the arbitrary character of the Kyoto Protocol emissions limitation targets. We propose steps to solve those defects and thereby to promote accession by the United States and major developing countries to an efficient cap-and-trade regime.

Since the Bush administration abandoned the Kyoto Protocol process in early 2001, a number of U.S. domestic developments have suggested possible future movement on climate policy. In 2001 a National Academy of Sciences panel convened at the request of President Bush issued a report confirming that projected increases in unregulated greenhouse gas emissions would likely cause significant warming. In February 2002 President Bush proposed a package of climate measures that announced a voluntary program for limiting greenhouse gas emissions with a goal of reducing U.S. greenhouse gas intensity by 18 percent by 2012 (versus a projected 14 percent reduction by that year on the basis of current trends). He proposed to strengthen current arrangements for voluntary registration of greenhouse gas reductions with the possibility of earning tradable credits against future regulatory requirements for businesses that achieve demonstrated real reductions. Bush also proposed tax and other nonregulatory incentives and measures to reduce greenhouse gas emissions. He argued that setting targets based on greenhouse gas intensity rather than on aggregate emissions was a better way of balancing environmental and economic goals and suggested that such an approach might be of interest to developing countries. At the same time he proposed new legislation using a three pollutant strategy to reduce, over a fifteen-year period, power plant emissions of nitrogen oxide, sulfur dioxide, and mercury, but not carbon dioxide and other greenhouse gases, through a cap-and-trade system. Other domestic political actors, however, have recently shown greater willingness to initiate limitations on greenhouse gas emissions. The Senate Environment and Public Works Committee has (narrowly) reported out a bill using a four pollutant strategy that would include regulatory limitations on carbon dioxide from power plants, Senators John McCain and Joseph Lieberman have prepared a bill to cap and trade U.S. greenhouse gas emissions, and a number of influential senators have called on the administration to reengage in international climate negotiations.[15] In June 2002 the Environmental Protection Agency submitted a U.S. climate report to the Framework Convention on Climate Change secretariat that stated that warming due to projected emissions would cause significant adverse effects. Notwithstanding those developments and vocal criticism from Europe and elsewhere of the U.S. position, the administration has declined even to discuss either a domestic U.S. or international greenhouse gas regulatory regime. Meanwhile, several states, including California, New Hampshire, Massachusetts, and New Jersey, are adopting their own emissions control requirements.[16]

The terrorist attacks of September 11, 2001, seem likely to have conflicting influences on the climate policy process. On one hand, they are reminders of the interconnectedness of U.S. and international affairs and have spurred new enthusiasm for multilateral strategies to address common global ills. They may also encourage moves to reduce U.S. dependence on foreign oil, which might or might not mean reductions in greenhouse gas emissions.[17] On the other hand, the terrorist attacks have raised a new threat that is more immediate than climate change and that may understandably divert the attention of governments (especially the U.S. government) and the public from climate protection, at least for a while.

It thus remains unclear where the United States will go in the climate policy arena in the years ahead. We suggest that the two most frequently heard options—join the Kyoto Protocol in essentially its current form now or stay out of any international agreement for the indefinite future—are both unsatisfying. Instead, we suggest a proactive but alternative approach: the United States should engage China (and other major developing countries) in a parallel regime and then jointly seek to enter a suitably modified version of the Kyoto Protocol. The modifications to the Kyoto Protocol should include the participation of developing countries on appropriate terms, the removal of unjustified restrictions on the comprehensive approach and international emissions trading, and the adoption of emissions limitation pathways based on maximizing net social benefits. Such measures would be good for the United States and for the world.

The Kyoto Protocol's Persisting Flaws

As originally negotiated in 1997, the Kyoto Protocol treaty contained several salutary features, including emissions trading and a comprehensive approach. But it also had three basic flaws: it set emissions limitations for the industrialized countries without clarifying the means for achieving them; it failed to provide any emissions limitation obligations for developing countries, even in principle, now or later; and the limitations that it established for the industrialized countries were short-term and arbitrary. The negotiations at Bonn and Marrakech have partially remedied the first flaw, but the second two flaws remain and must be addressed to build a sound global climate regime.

First, the Kyoto Protocol established emissions limits without clarifying the means—and hence the costs—of compliance, including the role of sinks and the scope of emissions trading. For example, Kyoto Protocol Article 17 authorized emissions trading in two short sentences that left many open questions. In the post–Kyoto Protocol negotiations, countries and interest groups that opposed those flexibility mechanisms sought to block their elaboration and derided every attempt to implement flexibility as a "loophole" or a "weakening" of the treaty. If the flexibility mechanisms had been well defined at the outset, such obstructionism would have been deflected, and countries would have been better able to forecast the actual costs of agreeing to targets. Explicitly authorizing wide use of the flexibility mechanisms would have ensured significant reductions in the costs of compliance and thereby would have attracted participation. European opposition to U.S. advocacy of sinks and emissions trading was the main reason for the deadlock in the talks at The Hague, after which the United States was understandably dubious about joining the Kyoto Protocol.

Surprisingly, however, at Bonn in July 2001 (with the United States on the sidelines), the European Union and developing countries gave Japan and Canada much of what they had refused to give the United States at The Hague: broader use of sinks (although subject to quantitative restrictions) and of emissions trading (with no quantitative restriction on the use of trading based on "supplementarity," but with a new "reserve requirement" on sellers). In October 2001 the European Union proposed to create its own internal greenhouse gas emissions trading system. And at Marrakech in November 2001, the European Union agreed to give Russia almost twice as large a quantity limit on credit for sinks as Russia had requested in Bonn. What explains the European Union's shift toward accepting sinks and trading? Does it reflect a newfound appreciation for flexibility, or does it reveal a consistent symbolic politics of using the climate issue to shame the United States—first criticizing U.S. advocacy of flexibility as a loophole and then quietly embracing cost-saving flexibility once the United States could be denounced for staying out of the treaty altogether? Whatever the explanation for belated European openness to flexibility, it bears reminding that the Bonn and Marrakech accords still retain some restrictions on both sinks and trading. Those restrictions should be significantly eased or eliminated. Further, work should begin now on actually implementing emissions trading on the international level through a comprehensive approach.

The Bonn and Marrakech accords failed to address the second basic flaw in the Kyoto Protocol: the omission of developing country participation in emissions limits and trading. The United States has long sought to include major developing countries in the global emissions limitations regime. All major emitting countries must participate for the treaty to address climate change effectively and avoid shifting emissions from participants to nonparticipants. The full cost savings to be gained from international emissions trading also depend on the inclusion of major developing countries such as China. Further, competitiveness concerns in U.S. politics—the fear that U.S. firms subject to emissions limitations will be undercut by developing country firms not subject to any controls—make meaningful participation by China and other major developing countries a prerequisite to U.S. treaty ratification. Yet in an abrupt departure from prior global environmental agreements, the Kyoto Protocol provides no regulatory obligations for developing countries, now or in the future. The Marrakech accord agreed only to consider in a year's time how to frame the issue for discussion a year after that. Worse, the United States is now out as well. Thus, the Kyoto Protocol now omits the United States and China—the world's two largest greenhouse gas emitters—as well as other major developing countries. As a result, the Kyoto Protocol now omits more than half of global greenhouse gas emissions, and that omission will worsen over time because it excludes the countries whose emissions are growing fastest. If those omissions are not repaired, the Kyoto Protocol will prove a costly environmental failure. Accordingly, it is imperative to create incentives to engage participation by major developing countries and, correlatively, to engage the United States.

Third, the Kyoto Protocol adopted, and the Bonn and Marrakech accords accepted, a single, short-term set of emissions limitation targets established in an essentially arbitrary way. The treaty calls for industrialized countries to reduce their aggregate emissions by the first commitment period (2008–2012) to an average of 5.2 percent below their levels in 1990, the base year selected in the 1992 Framework Convention on Climate Change. Those Kyoto Protocol arrangements do not represent sound target setting or equitable burden sharing. As a result of economic growth, emissions in many industrialized countries, especially the United States, have grown rapidly since 1990, even though greenhouse gas intensity (greenhouse gas emissions per unit of GDP) has generally declined. "Business-as-usual" emissions (emissions in the absence of regulatory controls) are projected to continue to grow substantially between now and 2010 (and much more for some countries than for others). As a result, various studies estimate that the Kyoto Protocol targets would require industrialized countries, as a group, to cut their aggregate emissions by between 16 and 24 percent below the business-as-usual level in 2010.[18] Some individual countries, including in particular the United States, would be required to make even greater reductions. Those very sharp reductions were not based on and cannot be justified by an analysis of the socially desirable pathway of emissions controls. As discussed below, they are significantly more stringent than either the restrictions implied by the least-cost path to stabilize global greenhouse gas concentrations at various plausible levels or the restrictions implied by an emissions limitations pathway that balances regulatory costs and benefits and seeks to maximize net benefits to society.

The European Union has nonetheless accepted the Kyoto Protocol targets, in part because of the availability of unrestricted internal EU emissions trading and the fact that the United Kingdom and Germany have experienced dramatic reductions in carbon dioxide emissions since 1990 for nonenvironmental reasons: changes in UK energy policies and the economic rationalization of the Eastern sector of Germany following reunification. Thus, the European Union faces much lower emission reduction burdens than those imposed on the United States and a number of other industrialized countries under the Kyoto Protocol targets. For example, the United States, whose Kyoto Protocol target is 7 percent below its 1990 level by 2008–2012 (seemingly only slightly more stringent than the average required reduction of 5.2 percent below the 1990 level for all industrialized countries as a group), has experienced and is predicted to continue high emissions increases over the 1990–2010 time frame. Those increases are largely due to economic growth (the United States also has admittedly done little to curb greenhouse gas emissions, but so have most other countries). As a result, the United States would be required to reduce its emissions below the business-as-usual level in 2010 by a whopping 31 to 33 percent. The U.S. share of all of the industrialized countries' reductions required under the Kyoto Protocol would be between 50 to 80 percent.[19] That high relative burden and concerns about its impact on the competitiveness of U.S. industry help explain U.S. resistance to joining the Kyoto Protocol. Although the use of a comprehensive approach and international emissions trading would greatly reduce the costs of meeting the Kyoto Protocol targets for all nations, the United States would still be saddled with a heavily disproportionate burden. Further, the Kyoto Protocol says nothing about developing country emissions.

A better approach would be to endorse the principle of setting emissions limitations based on maximizing the net social benefits of climate regulation (balancing costs and benefits). That principle would then be used to develop and refine appropriate time paths of global emissions over several decades, starting gradually and tightening over time, and adopting and adjusting regulatory targets in relation to those pathways and new information. Those targets might be expressed in emissions intensity as well as emissions.

Moving Forward: A United States–China Strategy

The flaws in the Kyoto Protocol do not justify refusal to face up to the risks of climate change. Yet instead of proposing an alternative to the Kyoto Protocol, the Bush administration seems to have embraced a strategy of "benign neglect" in the hope perhaps that the Kyoto Protocol will collapse when the time comes to implement it, or that the climate change issue will just go away. It will not. Unchecked increases in greenhouse gas emissions appear likely to cause global warming that will, on balance, significantly adversely affect the environment and human welfare and also pose some uncertain risk of triggering fundamental, highly disruptive changes in basic climate-related earth systems.[20] Those risks warrant a well-designed global regulatory response. Further, the United States has important economic and strategic as well as environmental interests in helping to shape and participate in a sound and effective international greenhouse gas regime.

Much attention has focused on two starkly opposed options: America could stay out of the Kyoto Protocol regime altogether and thereby thwart any effective global climate policy. Or America could join the Kyoto Protocol and the Bonn and Marrakech accords as currently drafted and then work within the treaty group to promote developing country participation and better-reasoned target setting as well as to remove restrictions on the comprehensive approach and trading. The first option is contrary to the interests of the United States as well as those of the world. The second option is unrealistic; it would require an unlikely about-face by the Bush administration (but might be pursued by his successor). It is also unlikely to result in developing country participation anytime soon or to bring about any fundamental change in the existing Kyoto Protocol targets and structures. The United States is likely to have greater leverage by first seeking to develop an alternative international greenhouse gas regulatory initiative outside the Kyoto Protocol framework and later accomplishing changes in the Kyoto Protocol arrangements when they are merged into a new and more inclusive global climate regime.

Accordingly, we urge a third option: that the United States stay out of the Kyoto Protocol for now; take significant domestic actions to prepare to join an international cap-and-trade regime; insist that it will only join a regime that allows full emissions trading under a comprehensive approach, sets regulatory requirements based on sensible emissions limitations pathways, and involves developing countries; *and engage China and other major developing countries in an international cap-and-trade regime, parallel to and initially separate from the Kyoto Protocol.* The United States could implement such a strategy by reaching an agreement with China to create a joint cap-and-trade regime, possibly bringing in other developing countries as well. China already emits 13 percent of global carbon dioxide emissions; other major developing country greenhouse gas emitters include India (5 percent), South Korea (1.8 percent), Mexico (1.7 percent), South Africa (1.5 percent), Iran (1.4 percent), Brazil (1.4 percent), and Indonesia (1 percent).[21] Other industrialized countries, such as Australia and Canada, might join that regime. Once the United States, China, and other major emitters had created the new regime, economic and environmental logic would sooner or later likely lead to a merger with, or joint accession to, a modified version of the Kyoto Protocol. A virtue of such an approach is that it would allow a few nations to experiment with alternative approaches to international climate regulation, including approaches geared to the needs and interests of developing countries, and avoid the need immediately to begin a fundamental renegotiation of the Kyoto Protocol that would involve scores of nations.

Our proposed strategy would increase the likelihood that, by one or another means, the United States, China, and other major developing countries could, perhaps within a decade or less, together join an expanded and improved global emissions limitation and trading regime. As currently designed, the Kyoto Protocol cannot achieve that objective. Neither the United States nor China would likely join the Kyoto regime without the other, but joint accession would attract both. China's accession would satisfy domestic U.S. political requirements of meaningful participation by developing countries (especially if other developing countries follow China's lead), improve global environmental effectiveness, and reduce global costs through wider participation and expanded emissions trading. When coupled with the other improvements to the Kyoto Protocol that we propose, this step would meet the stated U.S. objections to the Kyoto Protocol in its present form and politically enable the Bush administration (or successor) to join the international greenhouse gas regulatory effort. At the same time, China, by joining alongside the United States (with an assignment of "headroom" greenhouse gas emissions allowances substantially in excess of its current emissions), would gain a large market for lucrative allowance sales, additional sources of foreign investment and technology transfer, and international prestige similar to that attending its recent entry into the World Trade Organization.

Further, we argue that the Kyoto Protocol parties would actually prefer the United States and China to join some version of the Kyoto Protocol together and would oppose either one joining on its own. The entry of the United States alone would drive up greenhouse gas emissions allowance prices sharply, to the detriment of other wealthy country parties to the Kyoto Protocol such as Japan and the European Union. The entry of China alone would flood the allowance market and depress prices, to the detriment of Russia and Ukraine, the principal allowance sellers under the Kyoto Protocol. The joint accession of a major buyer (the United States) and a major seller or sellers (China and possibly additional developing countries) would ensure a degree of continuing price stability in the allowance market.

As we envision the process, the United States might initially approach China alone; if the prospects were favorable, the effort might engage other major developing countries such as India, Brazil, and Indonesia. Other OECD countries that are not parties to the Kyoto Protocol, such as Australia, might join in that regime. At the same time as it was approaching China and others, the United States might also seek to develop a North American Free Trade Agreement regime for greenhouse gas emissions and trading. The European Union, Japan, Russia, and other Kyoto Protocol parties would be consulted. It is important to note that the inclusion of the United States and major developing countries (whether after an initial period of experience under one or more independent trading systems or directly) and the other improvements that we propose could be accommodated within the basic structure of the Framework Convention on Climate Change and the Kyoto Protocol. Thus, we propose that the Kyoto Protocol be improved through an evolutionary strategy of restructuring or merger rather than be scrapped and replaced with something entirely different.

We believe that such a strategy is realistic and superior to other proposals that have been made to build a better global climate policy. Our strategy is better for both the United States and the world. From the world's perspective, a more inclusive international climate regime with wider emissions trading would be far more environmentally effective and economically efficient than the Kyoto Protocol or other proposals for alternative approaches including an international carbon tax.[22] For the United States, the environmental and economic case for joining the Kyoto Protocol "as is" is not strong enough to overcome the current opposition to participation in the administration and Congress. With the addition of China and the other changes to the Kyoto Protocol that we propose (including basing regulatory targets on emissions pathways that balance social costs and benefits and removing restrictions on trading and the comprehensive approach), the net benefits would become strong enough to make the case for the United States to join an international cap-and-trade regime. (The inclusion of additional major developing countries would make the case for U.S. participation even stronger.) The United States and U.S. business firms could take advantage of the low-cost abatement opportunities in developing countries, could develop business opportunities for greenhouse gas–efficient technologies and services in those countries, and could play a significant role in designing the international trading system and providing financial and other services in the new markets that it would create.

Because it would require a number of years of negotiation and lead time before the United States and China (plus others) could together join a successor to the Kyoto Protocol by one or a combination of the methods stated above, our scenario would mean that the United States could not be held to its Kyoto Protocol limitations targets for the first commitment period in 2008–2012; the targets would have to be relaxed or postponed, with the United States, China, and others joining the cap-and-trade regime under second commitment period targets and beyond. European officials and environmental advocacy groups might resist and denounce such "special treatment" for a "laggard" United States, but our approach would be far more environmentally progressive than the current posture of permanent U.S. nonparticipation and no obligations for developing countries. In the end the environmental, economic, and competitiveness advantages of joint accession by the United States and China would likely be so overwhelming as to carry the day. Indeed, in our view, the European Union has made a strategic error over the past several years insofar as it has been focusing its efforts on cajoling the United States into joining the Kyoto Protocol while leaving China and other major developing countries out, when it was clear that the United States would not join the Kyoto Protocol without significant developing country participation. The European Union should have been working (harder) to attract China and other major developing countries and thereby to engage the United States.

China, however, may well perceive only costs from joining, not only because it would consider abatement obligations as a costly brake on its economic development but also because many forecasts of the impacts of global warming suggest that China would on balance benefit from a warmer world. If so, China will have to be "paid to play." The most cost-effective way to attract China to join the abatement regime will be through assignments of "headroom" emissions allowances that China can then sell to industrialized countries or keep as a reserve for faster economic growth—just as was done in the Kyoto Protocol and the Bonn and Marrakech accords to engage Russia and Ukraine.[23] We believe that, with China's accession to the WTO and its continued development of a market-based economy, together with the economic benefits that China could reap from selling allowances in return for foreign investments, the prospects for China's participation are good.

If China joins, other major developing countries will have both political precedent and strong economic incentives to join. Because emissions limitations may, for similar reasons, impose significant social costs on those countries and provide only modest benefits, they will also probably have to be "paid to play" via headroom allowance allocations.

The issuance of headroom allowances to China and other developing countries poses potential political problems on several fronts. Environmental interests may decry the legitimization of large increases in greenhouse gas emissions in those countries. The current Kyoto Protocol, however, condones unlimited increases in developing country emissions; our approach would establish an upward limit, while also compensating developing countries for their abatement efforts. Some critics may also oppose the expanded opportunities for firms in industrialized countries to avoid costly domestic emissions limitations by resorting to international emissions trading, but by doing so those firms would be accomplishing equal or greater emissions abatement at lower global cost (and thereby enabling their governments to join or effectively to implement the treaty). Other constituencies may resist the significant resource transfers to developing countries that are involved in purchasing allowances to meet caps on industrialized countries; yet the alternatives are either far more costly domestic abatement, far more costly methods of financing abatement in developing countries (for example through massive infusions of official development assistance), or else abandonment of any effective international greenhouse gas–limitations effort to manage the risks of climate change. Many are skeptical that a system of international emissions trading, especially one involving developing countries, can be made to work. The challenges to securing agreement on and then successfully implementing any form of a broadly inclusive global greenhouse gas regulatory regime are indeed formidable. Domestic experience, especially in the United States, has, however, demonstrated that emissions trading can work and deliver tremendous environmental and economic benefits. On a global scale, it is far superior to the available alternatives in delivering cost savings and attracting developing country participation.

* * * * *

Chapter 2 explains why the planetwide risks of climate change justify a prudent, cost-effective global regulatory program to limit the global growth of greenhouse gas emissions. Chapter 3 shows that it is essential to include all major greenhouse gas–emitting countries in such a program and also points out the significant obstacles to securing inclusive participation. In chapter 4 we argue that it is in the U.S. national interest to participate in a global greenhouse gas regulatory regime, provided that the regime's design is sound. Chapter 5 details the key elements of a sound regulatory design for global climate policy. In chapter 6 we evaluate the Kyoto Protocol relative to those elements and argue that it must be modified to include major developing county emitters, establish sound emissions limitations pathways, and remove restrictions on the comprehensive approach and trading. In chapter 7 we present the components of our proposed strategy, which includes U.S. initiatives at both the international and domestic levels to correct the Kyoto Protocol's existing flaws and to engage not only the United States but also major developing countries such as China in a mutually beneficial climate policy regime. Chapter 8 provides a brief conclusion.

2

Prudent Investment in Regulation to Mitigate Climate Change

In this chapter we briefly summarize the available information on the contribution of increases in uncontrolled greenhouse gas emissions to global warming, the resulting risks of climate change, and the costs of emissions limitations. We then summarize the essential implications of that information for climate policy. Looking at the matter from a global perspective instead of in terms of the national interest of any given country, we find that the risks of climate change due to uncontrolled increases in greenhouse gas emissions are sufficiently serious to justify initiating a well-designed global regulatory program to limit those emissions. Global investment in limiting the growth of those emissions through such a program represents prudent insurance against the risks of climate change. Such a program should use strategies to minimize the costs of limiting emissions and set realistic emissions pathway goals by balancing the costs of limiting emissions against the benefits.

The Warming Effects of Uncontrolled Emissions

Several greenhouse gases that trap solar radiation and warm the earth's atmosphere, including carbon dioxide, methane, nitrous oxide, hydrochlorofluorocarbons, perfluorocarbons, sulfur hexafluoride, tropospheric ozone and its precursors (volatile organic compounds and nitrogen oxide), and dark soot, are emitted by human activities.[1] Other emissions, including sulfur aerosols created by emissions of sulfur dioxide and particulate matter, exert a reflective cooling effect. The various gases reside in the atmosphere for different lengths of time and have different relative impacts on atmospheric temperature.[2] They arise from many diverse sources and human activities, including fossil-fuel extraction, distribution, and combustion; manufacturing; agriculture; and forestry. Some of those gases also have important sinks; for example, carbon dioxide is removed from the atmosphere by plant photosynthesis and is stored in forests, grasses, agricultural soils, and oceans. Atmospheric concentrations of those gases have increased substantially over the past century as a result of industrialization and other human activities. Economic growth, population growth, technological changes, energy alternatives, land uses, and other variables affect the level of business-as-usual emissions—the level that will occur in the absence of regulatory measures. The business-as-usual emissions are projected to increase significantly with global economic development and to raise atmospheric concentrations further.[3]

Significant uncertainties attend efforts to predict the impacts on global atmospheric temperatures of current and future greenhouse gas emissions from human activities. In estimating those impacts, climate models must deal with many complexities, including uncertainties in future economic activities and technologies; natural variability in climate; the roles of solar activity, clouds, oceans, and terrain; the impacts of copollutants emitted by the same activities that emit greenhouse gases (including the formation by copollutants of aerosols and clouds with a cooling effect); and increased growth of vegetation in the presence of increased carbon dioxide levels (which in turn removes some carbon from the atmosphere). Nonetheless, even taking into account such uncertainties, understanding has advanced sufficiently to sustain general but not unanimous agreement among knowledgeable scientists on two basic conclusions that are reflected in recent reports by the Intergovernmental Panel on Climate Change and a National Academy of Sciences panel convened at the request of the White House.[4]

First, the Intergovernmental Panel on Climate Change and the National Academy of Sciences reports concluded that rising greenhouse gas atmospheric concentrations due to human activities are already causing the earth's atmosphere to warm. Second, with respect to the future (and even if present warming is not attributable to human activities), these bodies concluded that the rate and extent of warming will increase significantly over the twenty-first century and beyond if steps are not taken to limit the growth in net greenhouse gas emissions that will otherwise occur. Forecasts suggested that business-as-usual levels will increase dramatically over the next several decades. The Intergovernmental Panel on Climate Change predicted that if measures are not taken to limit the projected growth in greenhouse gas emissions, surface temperatures will rise by 2100 between 1.4 and 5.4 degrees Celsius from 1990 levels. While somewhat more tentative in its conclusions, the National Academy of Sciences committee found that a 3 degree Celsius increase in surface temperature by 2100 is consistent with current understanding about the intricacies of climate change. The National Academy of Sciences panel also cited two other well-regarded climate change models that forecast 2.7 and 4.4 degree Celsius rises by the end of the century. The Intergovernmental Panel on Climate Change found that warming at the rate and magnitude projected is, on the basis of the available data, very likely without precedent during at least the past 10,000 years.

In considering the policy significance of those findings, which will undergo modification as scientific understanding advances, we should emphasize that global temperature is not a function of current emissions but of the total stock (concentration) of greenhouse gases in the atmosphere. All greenhouse gases stay in the atmosphere for substantial, but widely varying, periods of time. Methane, for example, resides in the atmosphere for an average of about ten years, whereas carbon dioxide can reside in the atmosphere for centuries. Emissions represent a flow into the atmospheric stock, and capture by sinks represents a flow out. The emissions from human activities that occur during a single year or even a decade are small relative to the total stock in the atmosphere.[5] Moreover, it will be difficult to alter annual emissions very much in a short period of time. These circumstances have several policy implications. Given past emissions, we are probably locked into some significant warming trend for the future, regardless of what we do now or in the future. Accordingly, investment in adaptation measures to limit adverse impacts from warming is advisable. Also, immediate steep cuts in current greenhouse gas emissions will not immediately bring about a commensurate reduction in warming because they will have only a small effect on the total stock.

Lesser reductions in the short run can, to a substantial extent, be compensated by greater reductions later. Yet earlier emission reductions will have more impact on future greenhouse gas buildup than later emission reductions and can help mitigate climate change and its consequences in the interim as well as in the longer term. Further, if reductions are postponed too long, it will be impossible or very costly to make, in a timely fashion, the reductions needed to prevent quite serious harms that may result from the buildup of the atmospheric greenhouse gas stock. Thus, decisions about the timing and magnitude of emissions limitations should be made within a decades-long perspective by taking into account the stock-flow structure and the relative costs and benefits of reductions in different periods. As a result, effective policies to limit warming should concentrate on a strategy and institutional design that is sustainable and effective over the long run. As explained below, such an approach points to a policy of beginning with broad participation in modest reductions and tightening them over time.

The Risks of Warming

Global warming at the pace predicted by the Intergovernmental Panel on Climate Change and National Academy of Sciences is likely to cause a variety of effects that, although they will vary over space and time and will include some benefits, will be adverse on balance, and will become increasingly significant and adverse over decades as climate change accelerates. The U.S. national climate policy report submitted pursuant to the UN Framework Convention on Climate Change in June 2002 appears to reflect general agreement with that view.[6]

Limited understanding of ecosystem dynamics, the potential synergistic effects of climate change (including carbon fertilization), and differing impacts by region, time frame, and geographical scale complicate the prediction of warming effects. Different countries will be affected in different ways and to differing extents. Some countries may benefit from warming in the short run, a factor that complicates the possibility of global agreement on greenhouse gas limitation measures. Nonetheless, the Intergovernmental Panel on Climate Change, the U.S. National Assessment,[7] and several independent researchers have attempted to forecast the global and regional impacts of climate change, typically based on models that predict a 2 to 5 degree Celsius rise in temperature by 2100.[8]

Although initial (gradual) warming and carbon dioxide fertilization seem likely to help agriculture in some areas,[9] the effects in other regions will likely be adverse, and the impacts of more rapid or severe warming as the business-as-usual emissions levels accelerate are likely to be adverse worldwide. Shifts in temperatures and rainfall patterns will affect crop yields and growth cycles. Impacts on human health are a particularly uncertain issue. Heat stress due to increased temperatures can lead to illness and death, but cold weather is also associated with significant morbidity. Higher populations and lengthened life cycles of disease-carrying agents such as mosquitoes could result in increased levels of disease, including the spread of tropical diseases into temperate areas. Some ecosystems, including wetlands, grasslands, forests, mountains, rivers, and lakes, are threatened because of their limited ability to adapt to the projected rate and magnitude of climate change, which leads to significant loss of biodiversity. Sea-level rise and increases in tropical storm intensity may cause increases in flooding and storm surges in low-lying coastlines. Those harms and their severity will likely grow as both warming and the rate of warming increase.

Nonlinear effects might also occur when rapid warming triggers thresholds in critical earth systems and causes far-reaching, potentially highly disruptive changes. Possibilities include the collapse of the western Antarctic ice sheets, the melting of Arctic tundra, and shifts in ocean currents.[10] The likelihood of those events' occurring and what temperature changes might cause them are not known, although most scientists think that the probabilities are low.

Those impacts from climate change would in turn affect various sectors of the economy. Agriculture and forestry will likely be the most strongly affected. Electricity supply, water supply, construction insurance, and tourism could also be significantly affected. The impacts of climate change will vary widely among different countries and regions. The most severe physical impacts will be in developing countries because of their location, climate, environment, larger share of economic activity in climate-sensitive sectors such as agriculture, and lack of resources and capacity for taking measures to adapt. Adaptation measures can reduce the adverse impact of climate, particularly in agriculture and human settlements. For example, human settlements can be relocated from low-lying coastal areas; drought-resistant crops can be developed and water storage and supply systems upgraded; public health measures can be taken to address diseases. These adaptation measures will, of course, consume social resources.[11]

Small island states are perhaps the most vulnerable because of rising seas and limited supplies of water. Africa may also be among the hardest hit. Latin America faces decreases of especially important crops. Comparatively, the threats to Europe, North America, Russia, and Japan are more limited. Those regions are not as climate sensitive, and they have greater capacities to adapt. And China may enjoy significant net benefits for a substantial period.

Quantifying the damages due to climate change in economic terms is difficult. In addition to sorting out uncertainties and making simplifying assumptions, quantitative estimates of the benefits of preventing climate change must often assign economic values to assets traditionally lacking market value, such as ecosystems. Several studies have tried to quantify the adverse economic effects within certain industries; few have examined aggregate damages.[12] A recent synthesis by Richard Tol of the literature on the effects of global climate change addressed several key endpoints: agriculture, forestry, water resources, energy consumption, sea level rise, ecosystems, and human health.[13] Tol found that some initial warming (1 degree Celsius) and carbon dioxide fertilization would likely help agriculture and human health in some areas (including Europe, North America, Japan, Australia, Russia, and China, which would enjoy an early gain of 1 to 3 percent of gross domestic product) but would have adverse effects in poorer areas (especially Africa and Southeast Asia, which would lose 1 to 4 percent of GDP). And he found that the impacts of greater than 1 degree Celsius warming would become adverse worldwide over time and would include losses of 1 to 2 percent in wealthy countries and 4 to 9 percent in Russia and developing countries (except for China, which exhibits persistent gains from climate change of about 2 percent of GDP).[14] Tol's synthesis did not account for a number of adverse effects, such as fisheries losses, extreme weather events, and the possibility of fundamental changes in polar ice systems, ocean currents, or other critical earth systems. His predictions for China have direct implications for the treaty negotiations: if China sees itself as gaining from global warming, it will be even more reluctant to join abatement efforts.

With specific respect to the United States, a comparison of studies suggests the total adverse impact on U.S. GDP to be about 1 to 2 percent, on the basis of a 2.5 to 4 degree Celsius change in temperature over the twenty-first century.[15] Regional effects within the United States would vary widely.

Some critics have argued that such numbers significantly understate the adverse impacts of warming because they do not adequately or properly value reductions in ecosystem services, many of which we do not know. Others have argued that estimates may be exaggerated because autonomous adaptation (for example, farmers changing their planting patterns) may offset much of the adverse effect of climate change and do so at low cost. In considering the policy significance of those risks, we must emphasize that adverse effects will most likely occur gradually, although at an increasing pace and over a long time period. Intensively managed ecosystems and ecosystems subject to market price signals (such as agriculture in developed countries) are more likely to adapt well than are unmanaged and unpriced ecosystems. Further, the possibility of highly disruptive shifts in critical earth systems (such as the Antarctic ice sheet and deep ocean circulation) at some point along the way cannot be entirely ruled out, but the likelihood of such effects occurring is not well understood.

The discount rate used when aggregating impacts over time is important; a lower discount rate implies greater weight given to future events, including the social costs of adverse impacts from climate change that occur decades hence. Different studies have used different discount rates, typically in the range of 1 to 5 percent, and different societies may implicitly adopt different discount rates. For example, more prosperous societies can better afford to take costly steps in the near term to reduce risks of future harms and thus may adopt lower discount rates. Poorer societies may of necessity care less about events beyond short-term survival and thus may adopt higher discount rates. By the same logic, the discount rate used by a society may decline as its wealth grows over time. Climate change models have been starting to employ discount rates that start at 3 or 5 percent and then decline over time.[16] A recent analysis suggested that incorporating uncertainty about discount rates—letting rates fluctuate randomly in an array of scenario runs—may be appropriate to reflect agnosticism about the ideal rate; such an approach tends to increase the estimated damages from future climate change compared with studies that choose a fixed rate at or near 3 percent.[17] The choice of an appropriate discount rate or of other methods or principles for evaluating climate policies that involve costs incurred decades in advance of the bulk of the benefits afforded is not a technical issue. It is an important normative question that deserves fuller consideration.[18]

The fact that different countries will be affected in different ways and to differing extents and that some may benefit in the short run significantly complicates the possibility of global agreement on measures to limit greenhouse gas emissions. A further complication is that developing countries, despite their greater physical vulnerability to climate change, may tend to value climate protection less than do industrialized countries. Luis Gomez-Echeverri has asserted:

> Many in developing countries will not, at least in the foreseeable future, pay any attention to [climate change, because it is] an issue that may cause a problem for the sustenance of life in the distant future when their principal concern is the preservation of life today.[19]

Populations under severe stress from poverty understandably focus their priorities on near-term necessities and steeply discount losses that would only occur long into the future.

The Costs of Limiting Emissions and the Role of Sound Regulatory Design

Significant uncertainties exist in estimating the costs of greenhouse gas limitations, depending on the methodology used and the assumptions made about matters such as technological innovation and discount rates.

Nevertheless, the transition from a high–greenhouse gas to a low–greenhouse gas economy will certainly not be a free lunch. For example, the cost of meeting the Kyoto Protocol targets through wholly domestic measures to reduce carbon dioxide emissions has been estimated to range from substantially less than 1 to more than 3 percent of GDP in the United States and a number of industrialized countries.[20] Yet sound regulatory design, including the use of a comprehensive approach, worldwide emissions trading, and other flexibility mechanisms can greatly reduce (up to 90 percent) the costs of achieving greenhouse gas limitations compared with a policy under which each country relies solely on domestic measures targeted at carbon dioxide emissions. Further, setting targets based on a balancing of relevant costs and benefits over time would avoid the high costs of steep near-term cuts in emissions by phasing in reduction over time, which would enable advantage to be taken of technological innovation and capital stock turnover.

Estimating the Costs of Greenhouse Gas Limitations. Estimating the costs of abating greenhouse gas emissions is an extremely complex undertaking. Models require that assumptions be made (in the face of considerable uncertainty) about business-as-usual emissions paths in the absence of regulation, the nature and performance of regulatory measures to limit emissions growth, the future trajectory of the economy, the development of technology, and the characteristics of markets. It is thus not surprising that estimates of the costs of achieving a given level of emissions limitation vary widely among different studies using different models and assumptions. The evaluation for current policy purposes of the future costs of emissions reductions (like their future benefits) can also be significantly influenced by the choice of the discount rate used to compute their net present value.[21] A recent study conducted by the Energy Modeling Forum used thirteen different models to estimate the costs of meeting the Kyoto Protocol targets for the United States. Each model used similar assumptions. The results offered a wide range of marginal costs for controlling a ton of carbon; they ranged from $70 to more than $400 in 1999 dollars—figures that translate to a 2010 GDP loss of .2 to 2 percent to meet the Kyoto Protocol targets.[22] A similarly wide range of costs is also found in other studies of the costs of meeting the Kyoto Protocol targets.[23]

Underlying the debate about the role of technology is a rift between engineers and economists in the methodologies used to estimate costs.[24] Economists tend to favor a macroeconomic top-down approach that extrapolates behavior in relation to changes in relative prices.[25] It assumes that consumers and firms operate efficiently under each set of incentives and that significant market and institutional barriers to the adoption of efficient responses are absent. Students of the engineering school, on the other hand, favor a bottom-up approach that identifies abatement opportunities available to specific consumers and firms.[26] Researchers using that methodology typically allege that information gaps, serious market imperfections, institutional obstacles, and perverse government policies (such as energy subsidies) prevent consumers and firms from adopting those new technologies. They insist that steps can be taken to address those problems and thereby facilitate market actors' adopting new technologies that will make huge contributions to reducing carbon emissions. Because researchers using a bottom-up approach tend to believe that significant untapped efficiencies currently exist that can be realized by realigning incentives and removing barriers, their analysis generally produces lower cost estimates than top-down approaches. One 1997 study using a bottom-up approach found that the United States alone could save $300 billion of energy costs annually through the increased use of energy-efficient technologies.[27] Other studies using that approach suggest that 20 to 25 percent of existing carbon emissions could be eliminated by switching to more efficient technologies.[28] Engineering methodologies frequently reject many of the factors used in economic models.[29] They also typically use a much lower market discount rate and are more optimistic in their predictions of technological advance.[30] Many economists, on the other hand, tend to believe that the assumptions used in bottom-up approaches are too sanguine and underestimate true costs, including information and transaction costs. Currently, researchers are trying to integrate the two approaches. Methodological advancements in that area could prove to be one of the keys to creating more consistent, reliable cost estimates.

In addition, retrospective regulatory analyses suggest that economists' initial estimates of the prospective costs of regulations tend to overstate the actual costs in many cases.[31] Such overstatements appear to be particularly likely where the regulatory program employs economic incentive instruments such as taxes or emissions trading, because those policy instruments provide powerful incentives for firms to innovate by finding and adopting less costly means of compliance over time. If that kind of error applies to studies that estimate the economywide costs of climate policies, especially studies involving climate policies using economic incentive instruments, then the cost figures cited above would need to be adjusted downward.

The Impact of Regulatory Design on the Costs of Greenhouse Gas Limitations. The costs of decreasing greenhouse gas emissions can be reduced dramatically by sound regulatory design, including use of regulatory instruments that allow flexibility to take full advantage of the opportunities for achieving reductions at least cost. Those design elements include the comprehensive approach, use of economic incentives such as emissions taxes or tradable emissions allowances, and flexibility in the timing of reductions. In addition, costs depend heavily on the ambition and shape of the emissions limitation pathway chosen in setting regulatory targets and timetables. We summarize these points here and develop them more fully in chapter 5.

A comprehensive rather than a piecemeal approach. Global warming is caused by increasing concentrations of a variety of different greenhouse gases, all of which trap solar energy. Greenhouse gases are both emitted by sources (such as fossil fuel combustion) and sequestered in sinks (such as forests). These circumstances invite use of a comprehensive approach to regulating greenhouse gas emissions[32] under which countries (and regulated firms) must meet total greenhouse gas limitations obligations but enjoy flexibility to focus their efforts on those greenhouse gases emission reduction or sink enhancement opportunities that, in their particular circumstances, cost the least. To provide that flexibility, a cross-gas index (such as the global warming potential index created by the

Intergovernmental Panel on Climate Change) is needed to translate each greenhouse gas emission or sink removal into a unit of carbon dioxide equivalent; emissions limitations obligations are then defined in terms of units of carbon dioxide equivalent based on the index.[33] Because of varied greenhouse gas abatement opportunities across gases and sectors, use of such a comprehensive approach could reduce the costs of global greenhouse gas abatement by up to 60 percent (and even more if enhancement of forests and other sinks that sequester greenhouse gases are counted), compared with regulating carbon dioxide emissions alone.[34] Although the practicality of the comprehensive approach has been challenged, as we discuss below, sound and workable means exist for addressing the uncertainties associated with measuring greenhouse gas emissions and sinks.

Economic incentives in place of command regulation. Furthermore, greenhouse gases are emitted throughout the world and mix globally. Accordingly, to limit the total atmospheric stock of greenhouses gases, it does not matter where on the earth limitations on net emissions are achieved. That feature invites the use of the geographic flexibility provided by economic incentive systems, such as emissions trading or emissions taxes, to ensure that emissions reductions are carried out wherever in the world they can be achieved at lowest cost, regardless of the initial assignment of abatement responsibilities. In addition, economic incentive systems allow countries and firms the flexibility to use whatever means they choose to reduce net greenhouse gas emissions. Command regulatory approaches, by contrast, impose fixed emissions limitations obligations on individual nations and firms. They also tend to limit, directly or indirectly, the means for achieving those requirements and thereby significantly limit flexibility and drive up costs. Economic incentive systems also provide firms with continuing incentives to develop and adopt innovations to reduce emissions so as to reduce tax payments or free up emissions allowances for sale at a profit. Domestic experience with emissions trading in the United States and elsewhere has confirmed its practicality and its cost savings and other advantages. While international emissions trading would involve additional complexities, it is, as we discuss below, nonetheless practicable, superior to an international emissions tax regime, and far superior to a command approach.

A number of studies have shown that, because of large variations in abatement costs across countries, international emissions trading (involving all major emitters, including China) would dramatically reduce costs compared with wholly domestic carbon dioxide emissions limitations—on the order of 50 to 70 percent.[35] Several studies have suggested that the costs of the Kyoto Protocol to the United States in 2010 would be on the order of 1 to 2 or even 3 percent of GDP without international emissions trading but only about half that with Annex B trading and 75 percent less (roughly .5 percent of GDP or below) with full international emissions trading.[36] Studies of the use of greenhouse gas emissions taxes have found similar cost reductions. Those estimates may overstate true savings because they assume smooth and universal adoption and implementation. Thus, it may not be feasible, at least initially, to implement tax or trading systems for some greenhouse gas–emitting sectors involving many small sources, and market imperfections and institutional barriers may prevent full realization of potential cost savings. On the other hand, retrospective analyses suggest that economic incentive instruments often reduce costs more than initially predicted by inducing innovation.[37]

Flexibility in timing of limitations. Further cost savings may be offered by allowing emitters flexibility in the timing of emissions limitations, including accelerating reductions to take advantage of low-cost, near-term abatement opportunities and postponing reductions to take advantage of capital stock turnover and technological advances.[38] Such flexibility includes the opportunity to "bank" allowances saved by early abatement for later use or to "borrow" future allowances for current use (ideally at an interest rate reflecting the environmental cost of earlier emissions). That flexible approach also allows setting targets in terms of cumulative emissions over multiyear periods. The Kyoto Protocol follows such an approach by framing emissions limitation obligations in terms of a multiyear average for the first commitment period, rather than in terms of a single specified year.

Combining cost-effective mechanisms for achieving reductions. Considered individually, the comprehensive approach, international emissions trading, and measures allowing flexibility in the timing of reductions can each produce large savings in the costs of achieving a given emissions limitation target. Using those instruments together can cumulate the savings and make them even larger. For example, as noted above, the costs of meeting the Kyoto Protocol targets through wholly domestic measures to reduce carbon dioxide emissions have been estimated at 1 to 3 percent of GDP in the United States. With the 60 percent savings from the comprehensive approach (plus more from sinks) and the 50 percent savings from Annex B trading, the combined cost savings would be about 80 percent (compared with an energy and carbon dioxide only policy with national caps and no trading). With the 60 percent savings from the comprehensive approach (plus more from sinks) and the 75 percent savings from full international emissions trading, the combined cost savings could be 90 percent (compared with an energy and carbon dioxide only policy with national caps and no trading). Indeed, the Massachusetts Institute of Technology model generated precisely that result: it predicted that comprehensiveness (all greenhouse gases), plus full international allowance trading, would reduce U.S. abatement costs under the Kyoto Protocol from $360 per ton of carbon-equivalent (with a carbon dioxide only, no-trading policy) to only $40—that is, by about 90 percent.[39] The cost savings projected by those and other modeling studies may be overstated by assumptions of perfectly efficient application of the flexibility mechanisms, but even where real-world implementation problems are taken into account, the cost savings would be quite large.

Apparently, when the Bush administration decided in March 2001 not to pursue the Kyoto Protocol,[40] it relied on a study by the U.S. Energy Information Administration that assumed no international trading and controls on carbon dioxide only and thus forecast high costs of U.S. compliance with the Kyoto Protocol. Full scope for cost-saving regulatory design would, however, imply a dramatically lower cost of the Kyoto Protocol (and other climate policies) and hence a more persuasive case for joining.

Sensible emissions limitations pathways. Of course, the fact that the costs of limiting greenhouse gas emissions can be greatly reduced by sound regulatory design does not necessarily mean that regulation is justified. Although reducing costs makes it more likely that regulation may be appropriate, regulation must be justified by balancing its costs against its benefits. Even if costs can be greatly reduced by the design features summarized above, they may still be greater than the benefits afforded, especially if the regulatory targets to be achieved are unsound. In the case of climate change, which involves long regulatory horizons extending over decades, the limitations pathway used to reach a long-term objective may be as important as the ultimate level of control.[41] Studies of greenhouse gas–emissions abatement that use integrated assessment models have shown that policies (including those reflected in the Kyoto Protocol targets and timetables) whose aim is sharp reductions in the near future involve costs that are far too high in relation to the benefits afforded. Regulatory targets should be based on long-term regulatory pathways that maximize the net benefits to society by balancing the costs and benefits of reductions at different times and taking appropriate account of the stock-flow relation between atmospheric concentrations of greenhouse gases and annual emissions. The studies conclude that the net benefits to society would be maximized by beginning with more modest reductions and increasing regulatory stringency gradually over time.[42]

Balancing Benefits and Costs in Designing a Global Regulatory Regime

While many uncertainties remain regarding the future rate of warming and its impacts, on the basis of what we know now, the risks of climate change are sufficiently serious to justify beginning some reasonable, prudent investment in regulatory insurance against such risks.

The risks of climate change are significant. They include not only the risks of the harms predicted to occur from average predicted warming and average ecological sensitivity, but the risks associated with higher warming levels (for example, 5 degrees Celsius over the twenty-first century) and higher ecological sensitivity, which together could produce much more serious harms, and also the risk of low-likelihood–extreme-impact events that might occur because of nonlinear changes in climate-related earth systems. Meanwhile, some impacts of climate change may be beneficial, especially those associated with modest and gradual warming and carbon fertilization in some regions. If we take all those effects together and account for the considerable uncertainties involved in such forecasts, we nonetheless find that the net expected value of damages from the portfolio of future climate scenarios is substantial and becomes significantly more adverse as climate change becomes more severe and more rapid.

Two basic means of reducing the harms associated with these risks exist. One is through adaptation measures to avoid adverse impacts by, for example, relocating human settlements away from low-lying coastal areas or developing drought-resistant crops. The other is through abatement measures to limit greenhouse gas emissions to reduce future warming. Both types of measures must play a role. The costs of greenhouse gas limitations on the scale required to reduce warming appreciably from that associated with business-as-usual emissions levels are not small. If, however, regulatory costs are reduced by broad global participation, with flexible incentive-based instruments, a comprehensive approach, and regulatory targets based on well-chosen emissions pathways aimed at maximizing net benefits, we believe that the costs of emissions limitations become sufficiently reasonable in relation to the benefits (reductions in risks of harm) to justify beginning some regulatory investments in climate insurance now.

The Framework Convention on Climate Change states in Article 2 that its "objective" is the stabilization of atmospheric greenhouse gas concentrations at a level that will avoid "dangerous anthropogenic interference" with the climate. But such a stabilization objective (which could be defined as maintaining the greenhouse gas concentration no higher than a certain level after a given year, such as 550 or 650 parts per million by 2100) can be achieved through many different time paths of abatement, some of which are much less costly than others. From that perspective, the Kyoto Protocol targets and timetables—which call for sharp reductions within a short time, requiring a 16 to 24 percent reduction in the business-as-usual emissions by Annex B countries by 2010—are excessively costly in relation to the benefits, even when disregarding that the protocol will in any event have only a small effect on warming trends because of its failure to include developing countries.[43] A strategy of requiring no abatement for some years (at least beyond 2010 and perhaps 2050 or later) and then reducing emissions sharply would greatly reduce the cost of stabilization (by 50 percent or more relative to the Kyoto Protocol) by taking advantage of capital turnover, new technologies, and discounting.[44]

Stabilization of concentrations, however, is an essentially arbitrary long-term objective and neglects the damages resulting from climate change in the interim. An alternative approach, which we favor, is to set emissions pathways and limitations targets by balancing the costs and benefits of emissions limitations so as to maximize the net benefits to society or, put another way, to minimize the sum of abatement costs and climate change costs. (Unlike the Framework Convention on Climate Change stabilization objective, this approach takes into account the adverse effects of near-term warming.) Under this approach, assuming "average" climate sensitivity and damages and assuming cost-effective strategies for global abatement, James Hammitt found that net social benefits would be maximized by reducing global emissions 3 percent below the business-as-usual level by 2010, 5 percent below the business-as-usual level by 2025, and 20 percent below the business-as-usual level by 2100.[45] That pathway calls for greater near-term abatement than implied by the least-cost path to stabilization but substantially less near-term abatement than required by the Kyoto Protocol.[46]

Because greenhouse gases are a stock pollutant, immediate measures to curb current emissions will have relatively little immediate impact on warming trends. This circumstance plus the potential for future development of new, cost-effective technologies for limiting net greenhouse gas emissions and the advantages of matching adoption of major new requirements with turnover of the capital stock seem to argue in favor of postponing regulatory action to limit greenhouse gas emissions to some indefinite point in the future, when the problem is more serious and controls are likely to be substantially less expensive. On closer examination, however, those factors and others argue for beginning some regulatory action now. The stock character of greenhouse gas pollutants means that if we wait until adverse effects are manifest, immediate drastic cuts in emissions will come too late. Also, substantial time will be needed to build the necessary international and domestic greenhouse gas regulatory institutions and to implement limitations measures. Furthermore, greenhouse gas–efficient technologies will not be developed unless a price signal encourages investment in such technologies; as long as the atmosphere is treated as an open-access resource, such a price signal is unlikely to arise. The incentive for greenhouse gas–efficient technologies will have to come in substantial part from a credible greenhouse gas regulatory program that limits emissions (either through price or quantity measures) and thereby creates market demand for application of such technologies and provides predictable guidance to firms making long-term investment decisions. A need also exists for extensive learning-by-doing to evolve successful policies and institutions to deal with a regulatory challenge of such daunting complexity. Those factors reinforce the lessons of the cost-benefit analysis summarized above: begin now with a comprehensive and flexible institutional framework that delivers moderate regulatory limitations on greenhouse gas emissions and builds them gradually over time in light of developing information on science, impacts, adaptation, abatement options, and progress in policy design.

In sum, a cost-benefit balancing approach indicates that, from a global perspective, well-designed greenhouse gas regulation is justified and regulatory initiatives should begin now. (We discuss the issue from the national perspective of the United States in chapter 4.) This cost-benefit analytical approach provides the appropriate framework for setting regulatory objectives generally and is the approach embraced by the Bush administration.[47]

Some proponents of the precautionary principle reject the use of cost-benefit balancing in environmental regulatory decisionmaking under conditions of substantial uncertainty. Preventive approaches to regulating uncertain environmental risks are often warranted. The absence of scientific certainty regarding the extent of warming and its effects should not preclude the adoption of greenhouse gas regulations. Those propositions, however, can be appropriately incorporated within the basic cost-benefit balancing framework that we propose. Preventive regulation should take into account social aversion to the risk of very large harms and our ability to make improved regulatory decisions in the future with additional information developed in the interim.[48] But beyond that, the precautionary principle provides little sound or beneficial guidance on setting regulatory objectives.[49] Thus, we do not ground our advocacy of climate protection policy on the precautionary principle. An approach that balances costs and benefits, broadly defined, in setting pathway goals for greenhouse gas emissions is the soundest and the one best calculated to win the broad assent needed to build an inclusive and effective global greenhouse gas regulatory policy.[50]

The key challenge is getting the institutional design right. Getting the institutional design wrong, out of haste or short-sightedness, would be far worse than delaying specific abatement measures by a few years. Once adopted, the institutional design may endure for decades and may be very difficult to revise. The high costs of undoing early mistakes will be high—as the outcry over even modest improvements to the Kyoto Protocol suggests. Thus, getting the institutional framework *wrong* now will have major costs—both economic and environmental.

3

Participation by All Major Greenhouse Gas–Emitting Nations in Climate Regulation

A sound global climate regime must engage all nations with significant greenhouse gas sources and sinks, including the United States and major developing countries, in measures to limit future emissions, to ensure that the climate is actually protected and that it is protected cost-effectively. If major emitters including the United States, China, and other significant developing countries (such as India, Brazil, and Indonesia) do not agree to join the global emissions limitations regime, the efforts of the Kyoto Protocol participants will be swamped by the unchecked emissions increases of the nonparticipants.

While the need for an inclusive global greenhouse gas regulatory regime is clear, significant obstacles to achieving it exist. Under the basic rules of international law, countries are bound by international agreements only if they consent to join. Each country generally decides whether to join on the basis of broad judgments about its overall national interest. In the climate change context, such judgments will, in the absence of specific inducements to join, turn to a large extent on the disadvantages and advantages—including economic costs and benefits, environmental benefits, reputational considerations, domestic political pressures, and other factors—to that country of participating or not participating in the Kyoto Protocol or a similar international agreement. Thus far, the United States and other countries have determined that it would not be in their respective overall national interests to join an international greenhouse gas regulatory regime such as the Kyoto Protocol.

Wide Participation to Make Regulation Effective and Affordable

It is obvious that any climate protection regime that does not include the United States—the world's largest greenhouse gas emitter—will be ineffective. But the participation of major developing countries is also essential. A number of developing countries, including China, India, Brazil, and Indonesia, are already major greenhouse gas emitters. China already accounts for over 13 percent of global carbon dioxide emissions, India about 5 percent, South Korea 1.8 percent, Mexico 1.7 percent, South Africa 1.5 percent, Iran 1.4 percent, Brazil 1.4 percent, and Indonesia 1 percent.[1] Developing countries as a group account for about 30 percent of global carbon dioxide emissions.[2] Their business-as-usual emissions levels are projected to increase sharply in the future with economic growth, so that somewhere around 2020, developing countries' emissions will equal and thereafter surpass the emissions of the industrialized countries.[3] Sixty-seven percent of the growth in carbon dioxide emissions between 1999 and 2020 is forecast to come from developing countries; China, the world's most populous country and the world's largest producer and user of coal, alone will produce 28 percent of the forecast increase in carbon emissions over the next twenty years.[4] China also currently produces 25 percent of the world's black carbon (dark soot), a substance that may play a key role in global warming.[5] China reported a decline in carbon dioxide emissions from 1997 to 2000, but that appears to be a temporary and overstated event.[6] Land use changes such as forest conversion in developing countries are likely to be a major source of carbon dioxide emissions and sink contraction and a major source of methane emissions as well.[7] Because of the fast-growing importance of developing country emissions, an international agreement that restricts emissions limitation obligations to the industrialized countries, as the Kyoto Protocol does, will have only a very modest impact on limiting global emissions.

Unchecked emissions by major nonparticipating nations (including the United States and major developing countries) will not only swamp the limitation efforts of the Kyoto Protocol participants but greatly discourage those Kyoto Protocol participants from maintaining or implementing their commitments. Because of the global character of the greenhouse gas problem, steps by some nations to limit their emissions benefit everyone, regardless of whether others join the control effort. That circumstance and the attendant risk of free-riding make nations and businesses reluctant to assume the burdens of limitations measures unless they are assured that others will do likewise and bear an appropriate share of the burdens of producing the global public good of reduced warming.

Inclusion of all major emitting countries is also necessary to prevent cross-border "leakage" of emissions. Leakage is the process that occurs when a subset of countries adopt regulations to limit their emissions: emissions-intensive activities, driven by global economic competition and changes in relative prices, tend to shift from regulated to unregulated countries to avoid regulatory costs.[8] As a result, the emissions of countries without limitations will grow even faster. Thus, under the Kyoto Protocol, developing country emissions will rise even faster and surpass industrialized country emissions even sooner than in the absence of the Kyoto Protocol. Leakage may be small when emissions limitations are modest, but as emissions limitations become more stringent (and as world trading markets become more integrated and economic competition intensifies), the prospects of leakage (and its competitiveness effects) become more significant. Recent studies suggest that the Kyoto Protocol–type emissions limitations adopted in industrialized countries would be offset by somewhere between 5 and 30 percent as a result of leakage of emitting activities to developing countries and a consequent increase in emissions in those countries above what they otherwise would be.[9] Such leakage has at least three negative consequences. First, it undercuts the effectiveness of the greenhouse gas limitations adopted by participating nations. Second, by making unregulated countries' economies even more emissions-intensive, it further raises the costs to them of joining an international greenhouse gas regulatory treaty as time goes on.[10] Third, it further undermines the willingness of the industrialized countries and their firms to adopt and implement emissions limitations.[11]

Another highly important consideration is that inclusion of all major emitting countries is necessary to ensure the widest scope for international emissions trading and thereby achieve the maximum cost savings in limiting greenhouse gas emissions. The cost savings from emissions trading will be greatly impaired if the low-cost abatement opportunities in

China and other developing countries are not available. Thus, emissions trading limited to the industrialized Annex B nations is estimated to reduce total costs of the Kyoto Protocol compliance by over 50 percent relative to a regime with no international trading at all, but full global trading including the developing countries is estimated to reduce total costs by over 75 percent relative to a regime with no trading at all.[12]

Finally, expanding participation is also important to constrain the market power that may be exercised in an allowance trading market. The omission of major developing countries from the Kyoto Protocol's emissions limitation obligations is likely to confer significant market power on Russia and Ukraine, the largest allowance sellers among industrialized countries.[13] Including China, India, and others would ensure a more competitive global market in allowance sales.

Obstacles to Expanding Participation in Global Climate Regulation

Despite the imperative need for a system of global participation by all major emitting nations and sources in an international greenhouse gas limitations regime,[14] important obstacles to achieving inclusive global participation exist. Even if prudent regulatory limitations on greenhouse gas emissions are justified from a global perspective, important individual countries may conclude that it is not in their overall national self-interest to agree to such limitations because the benefits to those nations of reduced warming are significantly less than the costs of greenhouse gas limitations, and the net costs are too great to be offset by other factors (such as reputation, favorable treatment by other major participants on other issues, and a nation's positive disposition to global cooperation). Because international agreements operate on the voting rule of consent by each nation, the national determination of interest is pivotal. In economic terms, international treaties, like contracts, must be Pareto-improving for all signatories; treaties must not only be collectively beneficial but also individually beneficial (compared with not joining).[15] Moreover, even countries that would benefit overall from joining an international greenhouse gas regulatory regime may avoid joining and seek to free-ride on other countries' efforts and thereby reap most of the benefits of participation while avoiding the costs of emissions limitations. Similarly, countries may not comply with their agreed treaty obligations; cheating and defection may occur.[16]

Even if the free-rider and compliance problems can be solved, some countries may still judge that it would not be to their overall national advantage to join in an effort to limit global emissions. The costs and benefits of greenhouse gas abatement vary widely across countries. Some countries see strong net environmental benefits from greenhouse gas abatement, while others may regard the net environmental impact of warming as neutral or unclear. Still other countries may believe that they will benefit from warming—for example, through enhanced agricultural yields from a warmer and more carbon-rich atmosphere.[17] If a country's perceived disadvantages of joining an emissions limitations regime exceed its perceived advantages, that country generally will not be interested in joining (absent other inducements).

The importance of national economic interests in this regard is reflected in the differing positions of industrialized countries with respect to the Kyoto Protocol. As discussed above, the European Union has already made substantial progress toward its Kyoto Protocol targets because of fortuitous post-1990 reductions in carbon dioxide emissions in the United Kingdom and Germany. Other industrialized countries, including the United States and Japan, would have to make much sharper reductions below the business-as-usual level to meet their Kyoto Protocol targets. The United States and Japan are also not expected to suffer significant net adverse effects from warming over the next few decades. Thus, it is not surprising that the European Union is a strong advocate of the Kyoto Protocol targets, while Japan and the United States have been much more reluctant or opposed.[18] The former Soviet Union countries have experienced significant declines in greenhouse gas–generating economic activity since 1990 (or other relevant historical baseline years) and have thus been happy to join the Kyoto Protocol with the prospect of being able to sell large amounts of surplus allowances.

Vast differences in circumstances also exist among developing countries. The Framework Convention on Climate Change and the Kyoto

Protocol effectively treat as "developing" all countries other than OECD members and countries with economies in transition. Some countries thus categorized as "developing" already have high per capita incomes, higher even than those of some of the "industrialized" countries that are subject to the Kyoto Protocol limitations on emissions,[19] while many other developing countries are indeed quite poor. As a group, the developing countries will likely suffer significant adverse environmental impacts as a result of substantial or rapid global warming. But some developing countries, such as the small island states and those located in dry tropical regions, will be much more significantly harmed than others. Other developing countries such as China may even perceive a benefit from warming over the next several decades because of longer growing seasons, carbon fertilization, and consequent enhanced agricultural productivity.[20] Meanwhile, most developing countries fear that limits on their greenhouse gas emissions would inhibit their economic growth. Even limits on industrialized country emissions are likely to affect, in differing ways, developing country economies.[21]

In general, many and probably most developing countries are likely to view the costs of greenhouse gas regulation as quite high and the benefits as relatively low. They typically have quite limited resources, and their more immediate and pressing social priorities—dealing with hunger, disease, illiteracy, and violence—are more important than seeking long-term climate protection.[22] Moreover, the developing countries have strong equity arguments against assuming emissions limitation obligations. The industrialized countries, they point out, got rich by burning massive amounts of fossil fuels, and the long atmospheric residence time of carbon dioxide and some other greenhouse gases means that many of the emissions generated in the past by the industrialized countries are still in the atmosphere and constitute the principal proportion of the current warming effect.[23] The developing countries argue, understandably, that they are entitled to the same freedom to develop as the industrialized countries have enjoyed. They oppose obligations to limit greenhouse gas emissions as a trap that will shackle them in poverty.[24] (Some developing countries that make such assertions, however, may actually enjoy net benefits from limitations but simply wish to free-ride on others' efforts or voice opposition as a negotiating tactic.)

Accordingly, for a variety of reasons, many major emitting countries, including China, India, Brazil, and perhaps the United States, may perceive greenhouse gas abatement as offering few or even negative national net benefits. We argue in chapter 4 that in fact it is in the overall national interest of the United States to join a well-designed global greenhouse gas regulatory program. Enlisting U.S. participation will nonetheless be a challenge. The challenges to enlisting developing country participation are even greater. The industrialized countries must, we believe, provide developing countries with side payments, such as financial inducements or extra "headroom" allowances, to help underwrite the costs of emissions limitations while simultaneously ensuring that the developing countries limit their emissions. That is, the developing countries must participate in limiting future emissions, but their abatement efforts should be financed by industrialized countries. Such an approach would render the climate treaty regime more effective than the Kyoto Protocol, while respecting the fairness concerns and differing priorities of developing countries. As explained more fully in chapter 5, the most efficient, effective, and credible method for providing such inducements to developing countries is not through official government assistance payments or a global greenhouse gas emissions tax system but through an international emissions trading system that assigns developing countries allowances above their existing emissions, providing "headroom" for future growth or profitable allowance sales or both, while also reducing the costs of emissions limitations to industrialized countries.

4

U.S. Interests and Global Climate Regulation

The United States cannot afford to ignore climate issues, do nothing about greenhouse gas emissions, and sit on the sidelines while other countries design and implement a global regime that the United States will later wish that it had helped shape. The United States has strong environmental, commercial, and strategic interests in the adoption of a responsible, well-designed global regime for greenhouse gas limitations that includes major developing country emitters, makes full use of international emissions trading and the comprehensive approach, and sets prudent emissions limitations pathways.

The advantages to the United States of joining the Kyoto Protocol as currently structured do not clearly outweigh the disadvantages. Even before the Bush administration withdrew from the Kyoto Protocol, the Clinton administration had decided not to submit the treaty to the Senate for ratification. But well-designed improvements to the current Kyoto Protocol arrangements, as we propose here, could offer the United States significant additional benefits and cost reductions and thereby attract U.S. participation. For that to occur, the participation of key developing countries such as China is especially important: it would improve the environmental effectiveness of the treaty, prevent leakage and the fear of competitive disadvantage, and reduce abatement costs by enlarging the scope for allowance trading.

Warming Effects and U.S. Welfare

The adverse environmental effects threatened by global warming are likely to harm the welfare of U.S. citizens through a variety of mechanisms. Some

44

of the environmental harms caused by rapid climate change would occur in the United States and would directly decrease the welfare of U.S. citizens. In the near term, those adverse effects will probably not be severe and may be counterbalanced by beneficial effects, such as increased agricultural productivity. But as the warming continues and accelerates, the adverse effects are expected to increase over time and eventually to dominate.[1] Those impacts include the impairment of major forests in the northern United States, the erosion of heavily settled coastlines, and the intrusion of tropical diseases such as malaria in the southern United States.[2] Warming may also trigger disruptions of basic climate-sensitive earth systems that would cause serious environmental harms in the United States. Further, many U.S. citizens are concerned about the adverse ecological and welfare impacts of climate change, whether they occur in the United States or elsewhere.

In addition, the environmental impacts of warming in other regions of the world could threaten political and economic destabilization and other consequences that would be contrary to U.S. interests. In an interconnected global economy, the U.S. economy could be harmed if other countries' incomes falter because of damage from climate change (or, for that matter, because of excessively costly climate policy). If the United States is perceived abroad as the lone outlaw causing global warming, then intense storms, coastal flooding, and crop losses in desperately poor countries—whether or not actually caused by global warming—may become flashpoints for anti-American backlashes. While the extent of those risks is highly uncertain, they cannot be ignored.

The studies on the impact of climate change reviewed in chapter 2 suggest that domestic environmental harms due to unchecked climate change could, as a best rough estimate, cost the United States from 1 to 2 percent of gross domestic product by the middle to the end of the twenty-first century and could cost the world as a whole even more (not counting the risks of high warming, high ecological sensitivity, and possible nonlinear disruptions). The Kyoto Protocol (with all Annex B countries participating, including the United States) is predicted to slow warming by 4 to 14 percent below the business-as-usual emission level, which translates into a reduction of .04 to .10 degree Celsius below a 1 degree warming forecast for 2050 and a reduction of .08 to .28 degree Celsius below a 2.5 degree warming forecast for 2100.[3] (One reason the Kyoto Protocol would make such a small dent in future warming is the omission of developing countries; another is the time lag between abatement actions and the effects on future warming.) Those benefits might be worth roughly .1 to .3 percent of global GDP and about .1 percent of U.S. GDP or perhaps up to .2 percent with nonmarket benefits included.[4] Marginal benefits, measured in economic terms, might be about $25 per ton of carbon emissions avoided.[5] In calculating benefits, we should add a risk premium to reflect the value to society of avoiding low-probability risks of very large harms, including the risks associated with high warming and ecosystem sensitivity and the risk of disruptive non-linear consequences.

Meanwhile, the studies on the costs of the Kyoto Protocol reviewed in chapter 2 suggest that the climate protection delivered by the protocol (without emissions trading, the comprehensive approach, or temporal flexibility) might cost the United States from 1 to 2 or even 3 percent of GDP. With Annex B (industrialized country) emissions trading, the cost to the United States of achieving the Kyoto Protocol limitations might fall about 50 percent, to roughly .5 to 1.5 percent of GDP. With Annex B emissions trading plus the comprehensive approach and temporal flexibility, the cost to the United States of achieving the Kyoto Protocol limitations might fall about 80 percent, to roughly .2 to .6 percent of GDP. With full global emissions trading (including developing countries) plus the comprehensive approach and temporal flexibility, the cost to the United States might fall by 90 percent or more, to roughly .1 to .3 percent of GDP or less.[6]

Thus, even if we optimistically assume maximally cost-effective means for compliance, the domestic environmental benefits to the United States of joining the Kyoto Protocol (roughly .1 to .2 percent of U.S. GDP) would not exceed the domestic costs to the United States of joining the Kyoto Protocol as currently written, authorizing Annex B trading but not full global trading (roughly .2 to .6 percent of GDP). This conclusion could well hold even if the negative economic and other consequences within the United States of the adverse impacts of climate change elsewhere were included in the analysis. It is therefore not surprising that presidents of both political parties have declined to seek ratification of the Kyoto Protocol. But our proposal to engage the participation of major developing countries would raise the benefits (because of the greater reduction in future warming as more of global emissions are covered) and would reduce the costs (because developing country participation in full global emissions trading would reduce U.S. costs to .1 to .3 percent of GDP or below and would reduce the fear of competitive harms due to leakage). Our proposals to ensure full scope for comprehensiveness (including sinks) and to remove unnecessary restrictions on emissions trading would also ease costs. And our proposal to set limitations targets based on emissions pathways that better balance benefits and costs would further increase net benefits. Hence, our proposals would substantially strengthen the case for U.S. participation.

Commercial Benefits of U.S. Participation in Global Climate Regulation

Moreover, an analysis that considers only the environmental benefits to the United States of participation in a global greenhouse gas cap-and-trade system in relation to the economic costs of compliance with caps is excessively narrow; it ignores important commercial benefits of U.S. participation that will be lost if the United States stays out.

At least in the short run, U.S. industry would escape regulatory burdens if the United States refuses to subscribe to greenhouse gas emissions limitations and could thereby enjoy a competitive advantage over firms in other industrialized countries that are subject to such burdens. (Some business leaders and scholars believe that the spur of greenhouse gas limitation measures would enhance U.S. firms' total efficiency and competitiveness. Our argument in favor of U.S. participation in global climate protection policy does not rely or depend upon that view.) But U.S. nonparticipation will also deprive U.S. businesses of many valuable commercial opportunities and impose significant business risks. Those harms may to a considerable extent offset the benefits to U.S. businesses of avoiding greenhouse gas regulation and must in any event be considered in assessing the total advantages and disadvantages to the United States of participation versus nonparticipation.

Many U.S. firms have the technology and know-how to achieve greenhouse gas limitations through products, processes, and techniques that improve energy efficiency, enhance sinks, and otherwise reduce net greenhouse gas intensity. A global greenhouse gas emissions trading system that includes major developing countries would provide those firms with enormous business opportunities. U.S. firms with the capital and the right technology and know-how would partner with ventures in foreign countries, including China and other developing countries, to achieve greenhouse gas limitations and to obtain valuable emission allowances as a part of the return on their investments. They would use those allowances to meet domestic regulatory obligations or sell them or both. Also, many U.S.–based services businesses, including those providing financial products, project finance, consulting, accounting, and legal services, and insurance and other forms of risk management have the technology and know-how to help run and use emissions trading markets and ventures effectively. For example, the Chicago Climate Exchange opened for trading in early 2003. Those opportunities for U.S. business are likely to be foreclosed or sharply restricted if the United States remains on the sidelines. London, not New York or Chicago, will become the center of global emissions trading.

Ironically, the United States has championed emissions trading and the comprehensive approach since 1990 but is now standing aside while others move first. Without U.S. participation, a danger exists that the international greenhouse gas trading system will be designed and implemented in ways that are adverse to U.S. interests, for example, by restricting full scope for emissions trading and the use of sinks. The United Kingdom, Denmark, Norway, and others are already launching their own domestic carbon dioxide emissions trading systems, and the European Union has adopted a Europe-wide emissions trading system, also limited to carbon dioxide emissions.[7] Without U.S. leadership, those European carbon dioxide emissions trading systems may become the models for the global trading system and disadvantage the United States if it decides to join later. Vested interests will arise in the initial system that will make it difficult to achieve future changes later. Such path dependence in the design of emissions trading will not only deprive U.S. businesses of market opportunities but may also restrict the full availability to the

United States of international trading and the comprehensive approach, including gases other than carbon dioxide, and sinks.

The lurking possibility of "carbon trade wars" also exists if the United States does nothing to regulate greenhouse gases while other countries move ahead. Competitiveness concerns may well lead the European Union or other industrialized countries with domestic emissions limitations systems to impose trade measures on the United States, such as countervailing duties or border tax adjustments on imports of American goods in proportion to the amount of greenhouse gas emissions assertedly involved in the production of those goods and the corresponding cost savings enjoyed by U.S. businesses; under the World Trade Organization shrimp-turtle precedent, such measures might be upheld against WTO challenge.[8]

Furthermore, firms based in Europe and other countries that are parties to the Kyoto Protocol may require their suppliers and others with whom they do business, including in particular businesses based in the United States, to adopt greenhouse gas limitations. In addition, U.S. firms are likely to be targeted for aggressive environmental group and consumer publicity and boycott efforts aimed at major multinational greenhouse gas emitters that are not subject to or do not otherwise adopt and implement limitation programs. That could hurt U.S.–based multinationals that will face pressure for limitations without any assurance that they will get credit for reductions against any future U.S. regulations. U.S. multinationals may also be subject to competition from other U.S. companies with fewer or no international operations that are not targeted for such measures.

U.S. accession to a global greenhouse gas regulatory regime and adoption of federal greenhouse gas regulation would also reduce the business risks currently faced by U.S. firms that must make major investment decisions in facilities and products that generate or use energy or that would otherwise be affected by greenhouse gas regulation. Uncertainty in greenhouse gas regulatory policies will create a bind for U.S. utilities and other businesses that are already subject to increasingly stringent U.S. environmental regulations aimed at air pollutants, including particulate matter, sulfur oxide, and nitrogen oxide, generated by sources that also create greenhouse gases as copollutants. Capital investments needed to comply with those regulations may be rendered obsolete by the subsequent adoption by the federal government or states of greenhouse gas regulatory controls that will require additional and different investments to limit carbon dioxide or other greenhouse gas emissions from the same facilities. Unless greenhouse gases are added to the regulatory mix sooner rather than later, those businesses will face a period of substantial uncertainty and regulatory risk. The Bush administration and members of Congress have made proposals for a new round of Clean Air Act legislation improving additional limitations on emissions of three major pollutants (covering sulfur oxide, nitrogen oxide, and mercury). States including North Carolina are initiating stricter regulation on utility emissions of some or all of those pollutants. It may well be more cost-effective over the longer run to adopt a strategy that includes carbon dioxide as well,[9] or even a strategy that covers five or more pollutants (including methane and other greenhouse gases), rather than to follow a piecemeal approach over time. That is the same logic on which the United States advocated the cost savings of the comprehensive (multigas) approach to global climate policy in the Framework Convention on Climate Change and the Kyoto Protocol. Many in industry might even prefer a single, integrated, multipollutant regime to a sequence of separate fragmented and potentially inconsistent partial regulations over time or across the states (or both), especially if a comprehensive regulatory program is provided for interpollutant emissions trading.[10] The U.S. auto industry is facing analogous risks as a result of California's imposition of restrictions on carbon dioxide emissions from new automobiles. (It is unclear whether such a measure will be held to be preempted by existing federal law.) At the same time, the absence of credit for early investments in greenhouse gas emissions abatement means that U.S. firms may be holding back on abatement investments, including investments that they would have made irrespective of climate policy, to be able to obtain credits in the future after regulatory controls on greenhouse gases are adopted. That drag on investment may adversely affect U.S. economic growth.[11]

For all those reasons, U.S. accession to a well-designed international greenhouse gas regulatory regime would provide significant commercial opportunities for U.S. firms and reduce a variety of business risks; those benefits must be weighed in the balance along with the disadvantages of accession in determining overall U.S. national interest.

Strategic Benefits of U.S. Participation in
Global Climate Regulation

In addition to the environmental and business rationales just noted, a third set of considerations relates to the strategic interests of the United States across a broader range of global issues. Especially after the terrorist attacks of September 11, 2001, the United States needs the cooperation of many other countries across the globe to help achieve its objectives in national security (including fighting terrorism and avoiding escalating regional conflicts) and global economic and political stability. (As mentioned above, adverse weather events could themselves become flashpoints for anti–U.S. behavior if the United States appears to be the lone cause of global climate change.) Many other countries upon whose cooperation the United States depends are deeply concerned about climate change; they will bridle at U.S. indifference or intransigence regarding climate issues. The United States cannot easily aspire to be an effective leader and persuade others to follow its views on other subjects while refusing any engagement on climate issues that are of major and legitimate environmental and economic concern to Europe, Japan, other industrialized countries, Russia, other members of the former Soviet Union, and developing countries. On the other hand, if the United States successfully engages China and other major developing countries and helps secure their participation in international greenhouse gas regulation, the United States will gain leadership on an important global issue and help strengthen multilateralism in ways that should benefit the United States in other areas of international policy.[12] Indeed, the United States may find benefit in pursuing a negotiating strategy of issue linkage that trades sensible U.S. cooperation on climate policy for others' cooperation on issues of greater interest to the United States. In effect, the United States could receive in-kind side payments on other strategic issues in return for agreeing to act on climate change.

Challenges to U.S. Participation in Global Climate Regulation

As discussed above, the advantages and disadvantages to the United States of joining the Kyoto Protocol "as is" appear to us to be fairly closely balanced. The changes in the global greenhouse gas regulatory regime that we propose, however, would tip the scales in favor of U.S. participation by greatly reducing the costs to the United States and expanding the benefits, including commercial and strategic as well as environmental benefits. The United States would, however, face significant international challenges in securing such changes if it sought to do so. There are also great domestic political challenges in getting the American government and people to support measures to address greenhouse gas emissions, especially given the long time horizon and international dimensions of the problem. In the near term the United States is expected to enjoy net agricultural benefits from warming and carbon fertilization, and the ecological effects of warming in the United States are expected to be less serious than in many other regions. A number of important and well-organized economic interests also exist, particularly firms and workers in the coal industry and certain other energy sectors as well as transportation, that would be adversely affected by greenhouse gas regulation and have strongly and successfully opposed it.[13]

Beyond public attitudes and perceived national net benefit, which are the primary factors in national choices to join a treaty or not, special features of the U.S. legal and political system may make ratification of international environmental treaties more difficult than in Europe or other countries. The United States has a long history of ambivalence toward and nonparticipation in multilateral treaties in many subject areas. The current U.S. posture reflects considerable hostility, suspicion, or indifference to many multilateral treaties and governance regimes, including environmental treaties and other regimes.[14] That broad pattern may reflect a long-standing U.S. tendency toward isolationism (although one wants to know the reasons that sustain any such tendency). It may reflect U.S. dominance as the lone superpower after the cold war, while Europe is geared toward building international institutions to redress the power imbalance.[15] It may reflect the perception in the United States that Europe is seeking costly international treaties to "raise its rivals' costs" in international trade competition.[16] It may also reflect important domestic institutional factors. The separation of powers between the president and Congress adds a hurdle to international treaty accession not found in parliamentary systems. Also, the United States is often regarded as having a more adversarial and rigid domestic legal system, one in which citizens can sue to enforce the law.[17] That circumstance tends to lead U.S. treaty negotiators to resist environmental regulatory treaties that they fear would be more rigorously applied in the United States than elsewhere.[18] Those and other features of the legal and political systems in the United States, Europe, and elsewhere may explain part of the story of the Kyoto Protocol, the Bonn and Marrakech accords, the talks at The Hague, and the challenge of leadership involved in securing U.S. engagement in global and domestic greenhouse gas regulation.[19]

Nonetheless, the United States has been an engaged, major participant in numerous multilateral regimes, including the creation of the United Nations, the Marshall Plan, the WTO, international peacekeeping, and many international environmental treaties such as the Convention on International Trade in Endangered Species and the Montreal Protocol—and the 1992 Framework Convention on Climate Change. The American public seems likely to support a responsible approach to climate change, as it has with respect to other international and environmental problems, if well informed by forward-thinking leaders of the national advantages of participation. The new Bush climate policy proposals, while eschewing any regulatory measures, recognize that climate change is a problem that requires a response and thereby open the way for more ambitious measures. Prominent voices in Congress are advocating further steps, provided that they meet concerns about competitiveness and net benefits. A number of states are initiating greenhouse gas regulation. Some major U.S. firms have formed voluntary programs to limit greenhouse gas emissions. The Chicago Climate Exchange will soon begin handling allowance trades among a group of volunteer businesses. A strategy such as we propose, to bring major developing countries into a global greenhouse gas regime at the same time as the United States, together with other needed modifications in global climate regulatory design, could provide a further significant and successful impetus to U.S. participation.

5

The Elements of Sound Regulatory
Design for Climate Policy

In this chapter we set forth the elements of a sound strategy for limiting greenhouse gas emissions at both the domestic and the international levels. Ideally, such a strategy should achieve emissions limitations at the lowest cost by providing maximum flexibility in the location, means, and timing of reducing net emissions. It should provide strong incentives for innovation in low greenhouse gas–emitting technologies. It should maximize net social benefits by setting emissions limitations pathways based on a balancing of the costs and benefits for both the level and timing of the limitations. At the international level the regulatory regime should be "participation efficient," designed to attract the widest possible participation of major greenhouse gas–emitting countries, including developing countries, subject to the cost of securing such participation. It should be politically, environmentally, and financially credible. It should be designed to be implemented and administered in a practical manner and include effective arrangements for monitoring and compliance assurance. In practice, real-world arrangements will inevitably fall short of fully realizing those various goals because of conflicts among the goals, transactions costs, political and administrative constraints, and other factors. Nevertheless, those goals should guide the design of greenhouse gas regulatory policy. They can best be realized by a design that makes maximum use of economic incentive instruments for achieving limitations, in particular, tradable permit systems.

Market Failures in Use of the Atmosphere
for Greenhouse Gas Disposal

An effective climate policy will involve government policies that gradually reduce the addition of greenhouse gases to the atmosphere. That will require legal rules and regulatory programs including monitoring, reporting, sanctions, liabilities, and other incentives for compliance. The Kyoto Protocol's critics have questioned whether legal measures to limit greenhouse gas emissions are necessary or appropriate, at least at the present time.[1] They maintain that we should rely on (unmodified) markets and on voluntary measures by firms. We disagree. Just as property rights and nuisance law are necessary to regulate conflicting land uses, similar rules, backed by the force of law, are needed to prevent wasteful overuse of the atmosphere. Legal rules backed by compliance assurances are needed internationally to cement cooperation and to police free-riding and defection among countries in addressing the global consequences of unrestricted use of the atmosphere to dispose of greenhouse gas emissions.

Today, the global atmosphere is being treated as an open-access resource and as a result is being overused in a classic "tragedy of the commons."[2] Those who generate greenhouse gases have little or no incentive for voluntary restraint because they bear only a fraction of the climate risks that they generate but would bear the full costs of abatement efforts. Accordingly, the atmosphere is overexploited, and climate risks are greater than they would be if the full social costs of emissions were appropriately reflected in the decisions of those using the atmosphere for greenhouse gas disposal. This is a classic market failure, one that ordinary market operations and voluntary firm behavior will not correct. Because government regulation is also costly, not all market failures necessarily justify a regulatory response.[3] In the case of climate change, however, the risks are sufficiently great and the costs of regulation can (through sound design) be made sufficiently low that some restrictions are warranted to prevent collective harm. Such restrictions could take the form of centralized commands on conduct, government purchases of reductions, emissions taxes designed to limit emissions, or quantity caps on emissions with transferable emissions rights. The latter approach—which amounts to globally agreed recognition and parceling of property (use) rights—is the foundation of current global climate policy.[4] In that light, the Bush administration and others should see the basic design of the Framework Convention on Climate Change and the Kyoto Protocol—a framework of marketable property rights—not as an intrusion on economic growth or sovereignty but rather as a kindred effort to the familiar parceling of property rights in land, oil, and other resources that enabled prosperity and stability to thrive in America. If properly designed and implemented, such systems are generally the most efficient and effective means of addressing the significant externalities that occur under open-access arrangements and of promoting social welfare. Such systems, like all property rights systems, depend on law—and on the compliance machinery that backs it up.

Legal regulation of emissions is, to be sure, only one tool among several in a sound climate policy. Investment in low greenhouse gas technological innovation needs to increase in both the public and private sectors. The scale for international cooperation in that effort is wide. The emphasis of government spending should be on basic science and transformative new technologies, in which private markets would not yet invest. Government must also identify and correct existing governmental policies and institutional failures that blunt the economic incentives that producers and consumers would otherwise have to conserve energy and economize on net greenhouse gas emissions. They include perverse government subsidies that exacerbate fossil-fuel extraction, consumption, and clearing of forests.[5] They also include current regulatory regimes, such as the New Source Review program under the Clean Air Act, that inhibit firms' flexibility to invest in greenhouse gas abatement options.[6] Information-based strategies, including mandatory public reporting by firms of net greenhouse gas emissions, may also be useful as a means of generating incentives, especially in the early years before a full-fledged regulatory system is implemented. Public visibility of such information would encourage firms to reduce net emissions, and the information would also be useful for developing the national greenhouse gas inventories and methods of measuring sources and sinks. Further, governments should invest in adaptation assistance, especially for vulnerable and poor regions that lack affordable insurance or access to adaptive technologies.

Such measures, however, will not be enough to secure reductions in the business-as-usual level of emissions on the scale required to moderate the climate risks resulting from the common pool character of the atmosphere. For example, although energy intensity has declined with economic development, carbon dioxide emissions have nonetheless increased significantly because of the increase in total economic activity.[7] Moreover, the appropriate new technologies will not be developed and adopted unless market actors, including both producers and consumers, have an incentive to demand and adopt them. For open-access collective goods, regulation is needed to provide such incentives at an adequate level. The essence of externalities is that they are not taken into account in market transactions. Although large insurance companies may adjust premiums (for example, on coastal real estate) to reflect increased risk of losses from adverse weather events, that move would influence the behavior of climate change victims rather than emissions sources. In general, the transaction costs of Coasean bargains between those adversely affected by climate change and greenhouse gas emission sources—which are separated by great distances and by uncertainties about specific causes and specific impacts—are far too high to expect much market-driven abatement. The same transaction costs inhibit the use of tort liability litigation and third-party liability insurance to internalize the costs of greenhouse gas emissions. Incorporating adequate climate protection into market-based decisions and transactions will therefore require new legal rules.

The Need for Maximum Flexibility of Means for Limiting Emissions

Climate policy must, as discussed below, set sensible greenhouse gas limitations objectives and pathways; it must also embrace the most cost-effective means for achieving emissions limitations goals. Because the costs of achieving significant limitations on rising greenhouse gas emissions are large, it is especially important to design greenhouse gas regulation to minimize those costs and to avoid wasting scarce social resources. Minimizing costs will also help to attract wider global participation in greenhouse gas regulation.

Cost-effectiveness requires flexibility in what, how, where, and when emissions are reduced. "What" flexibility involves the ability to achieve limitations benefits by limiting net emissions of any or all of the several greenhouse gases, weighted by their relative contribution to adverse climate change, rather than by confining abatement to one or a few gases and ignoring sinks. In other words, it requires a comprehensive approach. "How" flexibility relates to the choice of technical measures to reduce net emissions of the several greenhouse gases, such as fuel switching (for example, from coal to gas or nuclear or solar), energy conservation, process and materials changes in manufacturing, improved agricultural practices, sequestration in greenhouse gas sinks such as forests and soils, removal and storage of carbon from fuel inputs or emissions, and other options. "Where" flexibility denotes the ability to choose the locations where emissions reductions can be achieved at least cost. Because the cost of abatement varies significantly across locations both within a given nation and among nations, while the global climate impact of greenhouse gas emissions is essentially equivalent regardless of location, allowing where flexibility domestically or internationally can achieve the same climate protection at much less aggregate cost than a system of limitations targets without such flexibility.

"When" flexibility pertains to the timing of abatement. Because of technological change, capital turnover, and other variables, investments in a given unit of abatement may be more cost-effective at some points in time than at others. One form of "when" flexibility is provided by the right to bank extra emissions abatement credits achieved today for use to satisfy emissions limits in the future. A converse form, borrowing, involves the right to emit extra emissions in the present in return for assuming the obligation to achieve extra abatement in the future. Setting emissions targets for a nation or a firm as cumulative limits over multiyear periods (for example, summed emissions over ten years) rather than annually gives a nation or firm the flexibility to allocate limitations and thereby to bank or borrow within the more extended time period. The flexibility in the timing of limitations investments thus provided can create significant cost savings. On the other hand, the intertemporal flexibility to borrow heightens the need for effective compliance assurance measures to deter a nation or firm from doing little to reduce emissions in the early years and then failing to accelerate abatement in the later years to meet the aggregate limit.[8]

In the following two sections, we discuss more fully two key mechanisms for achieving cost-effective "what", "how", and "where" flexibility in greenhouse gas limitations: the comprehensive approach and economic incentive systems, especially emissions trading. Those mechanisms have been at the centerpiece of U.S. policy since 1990 and have spurred considerable international controversy and debate over climate regulatory design; they accordingly justify more extended consideration.

The Benefits of a Comprehensive Approach

On both environmental and economic grounds, it is imperative that a comprehensive approach that includes all gases, sources, and sinks be adopted in regulatory strategies to limit greenhouse gas emissions. The comprehensive approach has been advocated by the United States since 1989 and is embodied in both the Framework Convention on Climate Change and the Kyoto Protocol.[9] Under the comprehensive approach, emissions limitation targets are defined in terms of a common unit of measurement that includes all the greenhouse gases. That unit is typically expressed as a metric ton of carbon or the equivalent. The equivalencies among the various greenhouse gases are determined by their relative contribution to atmospheric warming on the basis of their heat-trapping power (radiative forcing) and residence time. Emissions of different greenhouse gases by different sources and the contributions of sinks in sequestering greenhouse gas can be estimated and compared.[10] Under the comprehensive approach, emissions limitation targets are expressed in metric tons of carbon equivalent. A nation or source may select whatever mix of limitations of different greenhouse gas emissions and sink enhancements it chooses to achieve its net greenhouse gas emissions limitation target.

Because there is so much variety in greenhouse gas limitation opportunities across gases and sectors, the comprehensive approach would yield large cost savings—up to 60 percent or more—relative to an approach that fixes limits for carbon dioxide alone.[11] The comprehensive approach is also environmentally necessary to prevent perverse shifts in emissions that would otherwise occur from regulated gases (such as carbon dioxide) and sectors to unregulated ones (such as methane), which could exacerbate climate change.[12] Further, the comprehensive approach yields valuable side benefits in reduction of other pollutants.[13] Criticisms of the comprehensive approach as too complex and difficult to implement are misplaced. Simplified default rules can be adopted to deal with cross-gas comparison indexes and the uncertainties presented in measuring greenhouse gases such as agricultural methane and carbon dioxide sinks; those rules can be revised as monitoring and measurement techniques improve.[14]

Environmental Benefits of the Comprehensive Approach. The comprehensive approach provides significant environmental benefits by avoiding the perverse shifts in emissions that would arise from piecemeal regulatory approaches. The essence of the environment is its interconnectedness. But the complexities of policymaking often push decision-makers toward narrow, piecemeal solutions that address one obvious symptom or cause of an environmental problem. Advocates of narrow solutions claim that limited incremental steps are easier to accomplish than broader comprehensive approaches.[15] While that point has merit, in many situations piecemeal regulatory strategies may, by ignoring the full scope of a problem, miss alternative, lower-cost options to achieve the same overall goal and produce unintended side effects that confound well-intentioned policies.[16] More comprehensive approaches strive to match the regulatory response to the full dimensions of the environmental problem, although informational, administrative, and political constraints often limit the extent to which such matching can be achieved in practice. Regulatory policy will always include a degree of episodic "muddling through" in establishing regulatory ends and means; full comprehensive rationality is unattainable. Nonetheless, policy measures should be guided by a comprehensive perspective and avoid being locked into short-run strategies that will be quite inferior over the longer run.[17]

The extent to which environmental regulatory policy should focus incrementally on discrete, tractable parts of a larger problem or should take a more comprehensive approach depends on the specific context. The circumstances of climate issues and greenhouse gas regulation argue powerfully in favor of a comprehensive approach. Discussions about global climate policy in the late 1980s centered on reducing the amount of fossil-fuel carbon dioxide emitted from the energy sector, because carbon dioxide was the most plentiful greenhouse gas, the energy sector was the largest source of carbon dioxide, and the administrative and monitoring costs of regulating fossil-fuel carbon dioxide emissions were significantly less than for other gases or for sinks. The initial negotiating positions of the European Union and a number of major countries proposed a treaty calling for cuts in energy-sector carbon dioxide. But scientists were at the same time demonstrating that carbon dioxide was only one of several important greenhouse gases. Although the volume of carbon dioxide emitted far exceeds that of other greenhouse gases and has a long atmospheric residence time, each carbon dioxide molecule is a relatively weak absorber of infrared radiation. Other greenhouse gases, such as methane and nitrous oxide, are important contributors to global warming potential because they are roughly 20 and 300 times more potent per unit of emissions, respectively, than carbon dioxide at retaining heat in the atmosphere over time, even though their emission volumes are far lower. In total, anthropogenic emissions of carbon dioxide make a greater contribution to atmospheric warming than the other greenhouse gases in the aggregate, but the role of greenhouse gases other than carbon dioxide is far too important to ignore.[18] Furthermore, the relative influence of methane and nitrous oxide is expected to increase in the future as the concentration of carbon dioxide in the atmosphere rises and more and more of the infrared radiation at the wavelength blocked by carbon dioxide molecules is being absorbed. Because of that "saturation effect," additional emissions of carbon dioxide, the most abundant greenhouse gas, will have decreasing marginal warming impacts relative to those of less abundant gases such as methane. Thus, narrowly targeting a greenhouse gas regulatory program solely at fossil-fuel carbon dioxide emissions and omitting the other salient greenhouse gases would seriously undermine regulation's effectiveness in averting climate change.

Experience with environmental problems that are analogous to greenhouse gas regulation underscores the risk that piecemeal strategies, adopted in the name of practicality, may prove self-defeating because efforts to solve one aspect of a problem often intensify other, neglected aspects.[19] Thus, during the 1970s the United States enacted piecemeal, separate environmental regulatory laws addressing discharges of residuals to the air, the water, and land. But restrictions targeted on one medium induced disposal into other media.[20] Like squeezing one end of a balloon, that approach shifted the problems elsewhere and delayed the attainment of the primary goal of a clean and safe environment.[21]

Similarly, focusing solely on energy sector carbon dioxide would induce perverse shifts in greenhouse gas emissions. For example, controlling energy sector carbon dioxide alone would invite fuel switching from coal to natural gas, because burning coal emits about twice as much carbon dioxide per unit of energy produced as does natural gas. But natural gas is almost pure methane, and methane is roughly twenty times more potent than carbon dioxide per mass at causing global warming. Hence, as little as a 6 percent rate of fugitive methane emissions from natural gas systems would be enough to offset fully the carbon dioxide–related benefits of that fuel switching.[22] In the United States, natural gas systems rarely release more than 2 percent of their methane, but in parts of Europe the methane leakage rate has been much higher, often exceeding 6 percent—especially in Russia, from which much of the natural gas to replace European coal would come. In such circumstances an exclusive focus on fossil-fuel carbon dioxide emissions could actually yield a net increase in the contribution to global warming.[23] Another example of the adverse environmental side effects of regulating only carbon dioxide is provided by replacement of fossil fuels with biomass fuels, such as ethanol made from corn.[24]

To prevent such perverse consequences, programs to limit greenhouse gas should aim to be comprehensive and to encompass all the major greenhouse gases (including methane and nitrous oxide as well as carbon dioxide) and all sectors (including agriculture and forests as well as energy). A comprehensive approach would give sources the incentive to find ways to reduce all those greenhouse gases across all sectors. It would also yield valuable reductions in other pollutants.[25] And firms would have incentives to invest in conserving and expanding sinks such as forests to sequester carbon and would thereby potentially aid biodiversity conservation as well as climate protection.[26]

Economic Benefits of the Comprehensive Approach. In addition to its important environmental benefits, a comprehensive approach provides significant economic advantages through the cost savings afforded by "what" flexibility. Because so much variety exists in opportunities to limit greenhouse gas across sectors and nations, the comprehensive approach would yield large cost savings as compared with a piecemeal approach that fixes limits for fossil carbon dioxide alone or for each gas separately or that ignores sinks.

For example, the U.S. Department of Energy estimated that meeting an emissions target for the United States of 20 percent below 1990 levels by the year 2010 by comprehensively addressing all greenhouse gases, instead of just controlling energy sector carbon dioxide alone, would reduce costs by 75 percent; adding the option of sink enhancement would reduce costs by 90 percent compared with the energy sector carbon dioxide emissions policy.[27] Similarly, a World Bank study found that India could reduce its costs by 80 percent by controlling all greenhouse gases instead of energy sector carbon dioxide alone.[28] The most recent and thorough study confirms the economic advantages of a comprehensive approach. Using an integrated assessment model of the world economy, a research team at the Massachusetts Institute of Technology found that a comprehensive approach to all greenhouse gases and sectors reduces the global costs of meeting the Kyoto Protocol targets by at least 60 percent.[29] The MIT study also noted that the multigas approach, in addition to sharply reducing costs, could actually be more effective at protecting the climate than the approach regulating only carbon dioxide. First, as explained above, because of the carbon dioxide saturation effect, the relative global warming impact of the non–carbon dioxide gases is expected to increase in the future. Second, carbon dioxide emissions fertilize plant growth and hence stimulate carbon storage, which reduces global warming.[30] Because emissions of other gases do not have this climate-beneficial feedback loop, it would, other things being equal, be preferable to target reductions on them. A study by National Aeronautics and Space Administration climate scientist James Hansen and his colleagues offers further support for the comprehensive approach. The study shows that control of non–carbon dioxide greenhouse gases would be cost-effective and would yield significant side benefits to human health from the reduction of local air pollutants.[31]

Practicality of the Comprehensive Approach. Some observers have worried about the administrative practicality of the comprehensive approach based on a greenhouse gas equivalence index, because of difficulties in measuring emissions of non–carbon dioxide greenhouse gases and in measuring sink uptake of carbon dioxide. They have proposed initially regulating only fossil-fuel carbon dioxide emissions, which are relatively easy to determine on the basis of fuel inputs to combustion processes. They argue that such regulation could be expanded into a more comprehensive program addressing additional greenhouse gases and sinks sometime later on.[32] The asserted uncertainties in measuring greenhouse gas sequestered by sinks were repeatedly invoked by EU representatives and other parties in the international negotiations on the Kyoto Protocol implementation rules to justify sharply limiting any recognition of carbon sequestration by land use change and forestry measures, at least until such uncertainties are resolved. Although the European Union grudgingly receded partway on that issue, the implementation rules of the Bonn and Marrakech accords retain limits on the use of land use change and forestry measures to reduce net greenhouse gas emissions.[33]

While the comprehensive approach involves substantial additional monitoring and administrative costs relative to an approach regulating only fossil-fuel carbon dioxide, those additional costs are far less than the enormous environmental and economic benefits of the comprehensive approach and are therefore amply justified.[34] Practicable default values that take appropriate account of monitoring uncertainties, with procedures that reward improved monitoring with greater abatement credit, can be developed for the major sources of all the greenhouse gases and for most sinks.[35] A piecemeal fossil-fuel carbon dioxide emissions strategy would forfeit the huge cost savings (60 percent or more, as discussed above) to be had from comprehensiveness and would fail to provide incentives for innovation in the monitoring and abatement methods for emissions of greenhouse gases other than fossil-fuel carbon dioxide and for sink enhancement. Without such incentives for improved monitoring and abatement, the promise of including the excluded activities in regulation at the point when such methods are developed could prove a mirage. The better route is to begin with comprehensive coverage by using appropriate default factors for emissions other than fossil-fuel carbon dioxide and for sink uptake while enabling nations or sources to secure more credit for their abatement efforts by developing and demonstrating improved measurement methods. The measurement of non–carbon dioxide gases and nonenergy sectors would improve in response to that incentive. Improvements can also be made in the greenhouse warming potential index.[36] On the other hand, ignoring the non–carbon dioxide gases and the role of sinks does not make them go away.[37] Furthermore, the politics of international economic competition would likely delay or thwart the promised subsequent evolution from piecemeal to comprehensive. The countries and interest groups enjoying a relative advantage by reason of the initial narrow design would become entrenched in their favored positions and would resist expansion to a more comprehensive approach later. The European Union has, for example, opposed credits for land use change and forestry measures in part because the European Union has fewer opportunities to use such measures than the United States and other global economic rivals.

Accordingly, in the specific context of climate policy, it is far better to begin with a comprehensive approach by using the best available methods for monitoring, estimating, and indexing with appropriate adjustments for uncertainties and to continue updating and improving over time, as incentives for improved methods bear fruit. Here as elsewhere, it is crucial to get the institutional design right at the outset.

Maximizing the Use of Economic Incentives—Emissions Trading

Sound climate policy also requires maximum use of economic incentive systems—in particular, emissions trading or taxes—rather than command-and-control regulatory instruments to limit greenhouse gas emissions.

In principle, both types of economic incentive systems can promote mitigation at least cost and promote essential low–greenhouse gas technology
development and investment. There are, however, important differences in
the operation, performance, and political and administrative implications
of emissions trading and taxes in the international greenhouse gas regulatory context. Some scholars have strongly advocated use of greenhouse gas
taxes to mitigate climate risks.[38] Whatever the case may be in domestic
contexts, greenhouse gas emissions trading has a number of decisive
advantages over taxes, including greater implementation credibility, greater
compatibility with national sovereignty concerns, and superior capacity to
enlist the participation of developing countries in a more inclusive global
greenhouse gas regulatory effort.

**Advantages of Economic Incentive Systems over Command Alter-
natives.** The choice among policy instruments depends on several factors
that influence their environmental effectiveness, administrative and political feasibility, and cost in the context of specific environmental problems
and institutional settings.[39] In the case of greenhouse gas abatement, tax
and emissions trading systems are much superior to command-and-
control regulatory approaches, whether at the domestic or international
level.

Incentive-based instruments such as taxes and tradable allowances
provide "how" flexibility because they are directed at greenhouse gas
emissions and allow individual sources to choose any means they please
to limit emissions, in contrast to command regulations, which impose
specific limitations requirements on each source and generally limit,
directly or indirectly, the means by which limitations can be achieved.[40]
Economic incentive systems, again in contrast to command regulations,
also allow "where" flexibility by allowing sources with high costs of control in one location to emit relatively more greenhouse gas while providing incentives for sources elsewhere with low control costs to control more
and thereby lower the total costs to society of abatement. (As previously
noted, because greenhouse gases mix globally, where emissions limitations
occur is environmentally irrelevant to global impacts.) Because of those features, economic incentive systems are significantly more cost-effective than

command-style technology standards or fixed command performance standards.[41] Experience at the domestic level with U.S. emissions trading programs, including most notably the Clean Air Act sulfur dioxide emissions trading program, shows that well-designed trading programs can cut costs by up to 20 to 50 percent compared with uniform emissions limits and even more compared with technology standards.[42] Because the range of greenhouse gas abatement costs across countries is so wide, the cost savings for international greenhouse gas emissions trading (compared with fixed national targets) are quite large. Several studies have found that emissions trading among the Annex B industrialized countries would reduce costs by about 50 percent, and full international emissions trading (involving all major emitters, including China and other developing countries) would reduce costs by 75 percent compared with wholly domestic greenhouse gas emissions limitations.[43] For example, one prominent model found that the costs of the Kyoto Protocol target to the United States in 2010 would be about $80 billion (just under 1 percent of forecast gross domestic product) without any international emissions trading and about $20 billion with full global emissions trading, for a cost savings of 75 percent.[44]

Incentive instruments such as emissions trading and taxes would also be more effective than command regulation in stimulating greenhouse gas–efficient technological and other innovation. Economic incentive systems give sources a continuous motivation to improve abatement methods. Sources can increase profits and gain competitive advantage by devising or adopting new abatement methods that are less costly than paying the tax or buying emissions permits. Under trading, firms that reduce emissions can sell surplus allowances at a profit, a result that provides a powerful incentive to innovate.[45] Technology-based command requirements, by contrast, generally provide no incentive for a firm to invest in improved abatement methods beyond what the regulator requires. While repeatedly ratcheted, tightly targeted command regulation may in some cases succeed in "forcing" technologies (for example, in upgrading equipment to control conventional pollutants from new automobiles), the innovations required in the climate context are far broader and cut across a very wide range of activities and sectors. The broad, deep, and continuous innovative incentives of emissions trading and taxes are far superior to command regulation in that context.

Incentive instruments do not entail undue administrative costs, especially considering the total cost savings that they provide. Technology standards require government officials to gather and analyze detailed engineering and economic information to devise hundreds of different commands for different types of sources. Tax and trading systems, relying on the price system, relegate those decisions to firms. The highly successful U.S. sulfur dioxide trading system, which has achieved a 50 percent reduction in U.S. sulfur dioxide emissions from 1990 through 1999 at a cost savings of several billion dollars per year,[46] is administered by a staff of twenty. Of course, economic incentive systems, like command regulatory systems, must monitor and enforce compliance. Because of the greater flexibility economic incentive systems afford sources, a greater need may exist to monitor actual emissions. Monitoring and verifying actual emissions can sometimes be costly, but doing so is worthwhile if it improves environmental effectiveness and is often needed under command controls as well.[47] Also, it will be substantially more complex and difficult to establish a successful operating emissions trading or emissions tax system at the international level—involving many different countries— than domestically within a single country. Yet developing a well-functioning international regime of command regulation presents similar challenges. And even if implementation of economic incentive systems did involve greater total administrative costs than technology standards[48] (a point we do not concede), the advantages in the climate context of economic incentive systems in cost-effectiveness and stimulus for innovation would far exceed such administrative costs. Moreover, technology standards would offer no incentive for developing countries—especially those that see abatement as very costly—to participate.

Emissions Trading versus Taxes. Policy analysts have engaged in significant debate as to which of the two major economic incentive instruments, tradable emissions allowances and emissions taxes, should be used to regulate greenhouse gas emissions at the international level.[49] In principle, those two instruments can yield identical environmental and economic results. Under conditions of uncertainty about actual abatement costs, however, taxes limit cost escalation but may allow emissions to rise, while tradable allowances (which generally involve a cap on aggregate emissions) limit emissions escalation but may allow costs to rise.[50] These characteristics imply that the choice between the instruments depends on which error (relative to the emissions goals initially selected and the costs initially envisaged for the regulatory program) one fears more: cost overruns or emissions exceedances. Some climate policy analyses have found that because greenhouse gases are a stock pollutant (annual emissions affect atmospheric concentrations only gradually), the marginal damages from increasing emissions rise more slowly than the marginal costs from progressively more stringent restrictions on emissions. Analysts argue that the risk of cost overruns is therefore more serious than the risk of emissions exceedances and that accordingly taxes should be preferred to emissions trading.[51]

But even if the marginal damage function is flatter than the marginal cost function (an issue of some uncertainty, particularly if emissions may trigger nonlinear earth system disruptions), that consideration alone would not be dispositive. A number of other important considerations exist in choosing between taxes and trading in the international greenhouse gas context. In those other respects, trading programs enjoy great and ultimately decisive advantages. Further, policymakers can build additional flexibility into trading systems to address the problem of cost overruns. The strong conclusion is that global greenhouse gas regulation should use emissions trading rather than taxes.

First, there are significant sovereignty-based political and institutional obstacles to international administration of greenhouse gas taxes. A system of taxes levied and collected by an international institution would cut sharply against traditional principles of national fiscal sovereignty and would not be accepted. Alternatively, national administration of greenhouse gas taxes might be harmonized to have nations impose the same, or at least mutually agreed, taxes on domestic emissions, in the context of widely differing tax systems and economic structures across countries. No precedent exists for such a system or for an international agreement that requires nations to impose new taxes on their citizens. Cap-and-trade systems, on the other hand, bear a much closer resemblance to established international environmental regulatory agreements.

Second, the credibility and effectiveness of an international system of greenhouse gas taxes would be severely compromised by "fiscal cushioning" games undertaken by participating nations. Countries would attempt to soften the impact of greenhouse gas taxes on domestic industries and consumers by adjusting other taxes and subsidies. Those strategies would reduce the effective greenhouse gas tax rate and increase actual emissions. The same cushioning games could be played under emissions trading to ease the burden on domestic industries, but those strategies could not affect actual emissions because of the quantity cap.[52] Hence, greenhouse gas taxes (whether administered internationally or by each national government) are likely to achieve much less in actual climate protection than are tradable allowances. Furthermore, tax-and-cushion games will distort fiscal policy in inefficient ways and thereby undermine the credibility of a global greenhouse gas tax program.

Third, and perhaps most important, greenhouse gas emissions trading has significant advantages over greenhouse gas taxes in attracting developing country participation by facilitating transfers of capital and technology to such countries to underwrite net greenhouse gas emissions limitations. The private sector would play a major role in effecting those transfers by identifying the most promising and cost-effective greenhouse gas reduction opportunities throughout the world and by mobilizing resources and know-how to achieve reductions with local partners. Those investments would further sustainable development in the host countries. To accomplish those objectives, emissions trading systems can be structured to assign developing countries "headroom" allowances in excess of their current emissions, perhaps up to or even above their forecasted business-as-usual emissions levels (sometimes called a "no harm" allocation).[53] Such an arrangement would enable poorer countries to grow economically through several means: undertaking new economic activities whose greenhouse gas emissions would be covered by headroom allowances; hosting greenhouse gas–reducing projects funded by investments and technologies from abroad in exchange (in part) for a portion of the allowances that become surplus as a result of the reductions achieved;

and obtaining revenues from selling allowances to others. At the same time, such an arrangement would address the problem of international leakage of emissions-intensive activities to developing countries by adopting a cap on emissions. That approach is far more effective and "participation-efficient"[54] than pure financial payments (which are subsidies for abatement and invite perverse increases in aggregate emissions),[55] or greenhouse gas taxes (which offer no incentive for nonbeneficiary countries to join), or taxes coupled with financial payments (which would undermine the incentive effect of the tax).[56]

An inclusive international greenhouse gas trading system would benefit poorer societies by giving them a revenue stream on the order of several billion dollars per year and enhanced foreign investments and technology transfers.[57] It would oblige richer countries to "take the lead" by financing emissions reductions worldwide (yet in a way that is also economically preferable to them compared with purely domestic abatement).[58] Moreover, the basic logic of voluntary exchange (that is, market trading) means that allowance sales would not occur unless both parties viewed the trade as desirable. (It will, therefore, be necessary to ensure that the developing countries participating in international greenhouse gas trading have the capacities to be informed and effective players.) On the other hand, insisting that industrialized countries must control their emissions primarily at home (as in proposals for "supplementarity" ceilings on use of trading, or allowance reserves) would increase global costs substantially and would deprive developing countries of the benefits of investments in greenhouse gas–reducing projects and allowance sale revenues. It would be like insisting that rich people must spend their money only in rich neighborhoods.

The extra allowances used to deliver side payments should be seen as headroom, not "hot air." They represent the necessary price to engage participation by major emitting countries that perceive no net benefit to participation and to meet developing countries' equity claims. Headroom allowances were used to engage participation by Russia and Ukraine in the Kyoto Protocol. Without that inducement, Russia and Ukraine would likely have stayed out of the agreement, which would have made their potential future emissions even higher.[59] Without the inducement of headroom allowances, China and many other major developing countries are most unlikely to agree to join any international greenhouse gas regulatory effort and thus will cripple its environmental effectiveness. Moreover, their nonparticipation would increase the abatement costs to the remaining signatories and could in turn induce them to neglect or relax their targets and further weaken the treaty.[60]

The use of headroom allowances to attract participation, whether of countries from the former Soviet Union or developing countries, runs the risk that such countries will abandon the international cap-and-trade agreement after selling their headroom allowances. That risk can perhaps be reduced by requiring that sales of headroom allowances be matched by sales of allowances generated by emissions reductions. More important, the current and future stream of allowance allocations should be structured so as to provide continuing incentives for participation by offering greater trading-based inflows of investment and technology to countries that participate honestly for longer periods of time. Those inflows will also help build political and economic constituencies within the country for continued participation. A country that withdraws will suffer reputational losses and risk unfavorable treatment from other nations on other issues of concern to it.

Because it involves significant transfers of resources to developing countries, emissions trading raises issues of domestic political feasibility for participating industrialized countries, including the United States. Those transfers, however, are simply a part of the costs that must be incurred in achieving greenhouse gas limitations; as discussed previously, in deciding whether to participate in a global greenhouse gas regulatory effort, countries must decide whether such costs are justified in relation to the benefits obtained. Emissions trading significantly reduces those costs relative to command alternatives. It also provides markets for the export by industrialized country businesses of greenhouse gas technologies and services to developing countries and thus creates domestic political constituencies in favor of participation. By promoting environmentally sustainable economic growth in developing countries, emissions trading could also serve the broader strategic interests of the United States and other industrialized nations.

Some have questioned the credibility of the financial flows associated with emissions trading and headroom allowances by comparing them with official overseas development assistance. For example, Mustafa Babiker and his colleagues have remarked:

> The flows [under the Kyoto Protocol with U.S. participation] are very large, with an annual transfer from the United States to Russia and Ukraine of near $20 billion. The fact that total U.S. overseas development assistance to all countries in 1999 was only $9 billion, and had declined at a rate of some 4 percent per year through the 1990s . . . , raises serious questions about the realism of the Kyoto Protocol, even if the United States would have been willing to go along on other grounds. . . . [T]hese flows were not likely to prove politically sustainable, particularly when a substantial portion of the funds would be paying for hot air. The idea that governments will allocate permits in such a way that their citizens must first send abroad large amounts of money to get them back as permits is most generously viewed as unrealistic.[61]

But the comparison with overseas development assistance is inapposite. The financial flows under emissions trading would be via multiple small transactions by private firms, not large centralized government outlays. They would be trade and investment, not aid. They would involve, in return, imports of a new, commercially valuable global property right (greenhouse gas allowances). And they would be far less expensive than obtaining the equivalent abatement services domestically. Hence, the better comparison is with all U.S. imports, purchases of services abroad, or foreign direct investment outlays. Those sums would utterly dwarf $20 billion in U.S. allowance purchases. Of course, $20 billion for greenhouse gas allowances may still be too high; that figure is an artifact of the abrupt Kyoto Protocol targets, which would require a 30 percent or more reduction in U.S. emissions below the business-as-usual level in 2010 (and the assumptions of the economic model used to make this estimate).[62] A reconstructed climate regime, with better balanced targets and with participation by China as well as the United States and India, would likely exhibit financial flows from the United States to China, Russia, and other nations of less than $20 billion (and, in any case, would amount to a small fraction of total U.S. foreign direct investments or imports), while still adequate to secure their participation.

Emissions taxes are far inferior to emissions trading in attracting the participation of developing countries. Developing nations would never agree to adopt greenhouse gas tax rates at the same level as those adopted by the developed countries; at best, they might agree to adopt taxes at sharply lower rates. Significantly lower tax rates in developing countries would, however, result in significant leakage of emissions-intensive activities to those countries and consequent increases in their emissions and would undermine the global regulatory regime. A theoretical alternative is to adopt uniform rates and channel the major share of aggregate proceeds to developing countries. But no prospect exists that the industrialized nations would agree to taxation by an international authority that would dispose of a large share of the proceeds through payments to developing countries. National systems of taxation and international redistribution would encounter the problem of fiscal cushioning games and, potentially, official aid displacement games.[63] Also, trying to couple side payments to major developing countries (such as China) with taxes will undermine the incentive effect of the taxes on emissions, because the side payment must compensate the country for both its net cost of abatement and its net incremental cost of paying the tax (otherwise the country would probably not participate in the regime).[64]

Another option for inducing participation by relevant developing countries is the use of pure financial subsidies for abatement in the form of a cash side payment for reduction of the business-as-usual levels emissions.[65] The Kyoto Protocol "clean development mechanism" resembles that approach. It provides credits that can be sold for cash, with no limit on total national emissions in selling countries. Unfortunately, subsidies for abatement, even assuming that they would be politically feasible at the levels required, can generate perverse incentives for countries to increase aggregate emissions.[66] Emissions trading surmounts that problem by coupling side transfers with a quantity constraint on aggregate emissions.[67]

A conceptually elegant approach has been suggested by David Bradford: countries interested in preventing climate change would contribute sums of money to a central fund, and that fund would then purchase abatement reductions from the business-as-usual emissions level worldwide on the economically most advantageous terms.[68] Countries would not adopt quantity limits on emissions; all the abatement would be accomplished through the central fund's purchases of abatement efforts. Hence, the total quantity of abatement would depend on the total amount of money contributed to the fund and the price of abatement. Bradford's approach nicely illustrates how a "beneficiaries pay" model could work.[69] And it shows how the total amount of abatement (resource allocation) and its location can be distinguished from each country's degree of contribution (distributional equity). But Bradford's approach has important difficulties. Although international negotiations on national targets (allowance allocations) would be unnecessary, there would have to be international agreement on the business-as-usual emissions for each country over a number of years (the baseline for purchases of reductions by the central authority), which may be almost as difficult. The administration of a huge central fund would raise strong concerns about national sovereignty, international organizational power, and corruption. Also, reliance on a central purchasing agency rather than on a decentralized trading market could undermine cost-effectiveness; political pressures could force the fund to spread abatement purchases "equitably" among countries and sectors rather than target the lowest-cost abatement opportunities. In addition, the central fund would act as a monopsonist; with no competition in the market to purchase abatement efforts, it might fail to find the most cost-effective abatement opportunities or might seek to depress purchase prices or both. Finally, the central fund would act as a pure subsidy for abatement, with no quantity cap on aggregate emissions. As discussed above, subsidies for abatement can have the perverse effect of increasing aggregate emissions.

Issues in Implementing Emissions Trading. Despite its superiority to emission taxes and other alternatives, international greenhouse gas emissions trading faces several potential implementation difficulties. They include the risks (previously noted) that quantity limits on emissions could result in unexpectedly high compliance costs or that countries could sell allowances and withdraw; potential problems of market power and transaction costs; and the compatibility of international emissions trading with domestic regulatory systems that rely on other instruments. While those issues need attention, reasonable means for addressing them are available.

Cap-and-trade allowance trading systems, like all quantity-based regulatory systems, create the risk of excessive costs when compliance with the quantity limit proves more expensive than was expected at the time that the quantity limit was set.[70] Policymakers can address that problem in several ways. Most obviously, keeping the targets modest in the near term will keep costs down while allowing the development of more information useful for setting future targets so as to avoid costly surprises. Second, ensuring wide participation by developing countries in a global greenhouse gas trading system will help ensure a large supply of allowances at low costs.[71] Third, "when" flexibility through banking and borrowing can ease risks of cost overruns.[72]

A fourth means of avoiding excessive costs with emissions trading is use of the flexibility afforded by a hybrid system, dubbed a "safety valve," in which governments supplement an emissions trading system with a promise to sell unlimited additional allowances at a predetermined trigger price.[73] In effect, the safety valve converts a cap-and-trade allowance system into a trading system that becomes a tax once the price of allowances rises to the trigger price. Alternatively, the safety valve price can be viewed as the penalty (a fine per ton of emissions) for noncompliance with the allowance limits. It can also be seen as a version of borrowing (emitting more now while promising to emit less in the future), but at a fixed trigger price rather than at an interest rate reflecting the time value of abatement. Critics of the safety valve concept fear that it would open the climate policy to unlimited increases in emissions. A more accurate characterization is that the policy would act as a tax and discourage emissions by imposing a price (but without the firm quantitative assurance provided by a cap), while avoiding the risk of cost escalation presented in a pure cap-and-trade allowance system.[74] One question about the safety valve is whether it would be administered by national governments or by an international institution.[75] If the former, revenue-seeking governments might compete to sell the extra allowances by setting lower trigger prices (or competing on nonprice variables), which would contribute to emissions escalation. If the latter, the problems associated with international taxation and international handling of revenues would arise anew. Alternatively, the trigger price might be set by international agreement. The notion of a safety valve is intriguing and deserves further consideration. Such an approach might be especially attractive in enlisting developing countries; by eliminating a cap on emissions, the approach should ease the fear that greenhouse gas limitations will impose a ceiling on economic growth that will subject developing countries to perpetual underdevelopment.[76]

A fifth way to moderate the risk of unduly high costs under quantity caps is to set targets in terms of "emissions intensity," or emissions per unit of economic output (GDP), rather than in terms of emissions. For example, all countries could be required to reduce their emissions per GDP by a designated percentage by a designated year or suite of years. The Bush administration's economic advisers advocated such an approach,[77] and President Bush proposed it in February 2002, along with a set of tax credits and voluntary measures intended to reduce U.S. greenhouse gas emissions by 500 million metric tons of carbon-equivalent by 2012.[78] Such an approach provides flexibility by allowing increased emissions when the economy grows rapidly (and hence contains costs). But the approach also has difficulties. By allowing emissions to grow as the economy grows, this approach could result in less climate protection than would be justified on the basis of a consideration of the relevant costs and benefits. In addition, this approach could provide incentives to countries to exaggerate their GDP to satisfy their emissions intensity target; monitoring compliance would thus be more complicated than under a quantity limit where one need measure only emissions. Further, it is conceivable that an emissions intensity target could encourage countries to overheat their economies to increase GDP faster than emissions are growing and thereby reduce their intensity ratio; in domestic regulatory programs, an analogous incentive can lead firms to overproduce output when constrained by an emissions-per-unit-of-output standard.[79] Those problems, however, are not necessarily fatal. Eliminating the risks of high costs posed by emission caps and helping to dispel the specter of a ceiling on development through targets based on emissions intensity could help attract the participation of developing countries and might even lead countries to adopt targets that are in general more stringent than comparable targets based on emissions.

While a variety of problems exist with the specific measures proposed by the Bush administration to implement the emissions intensity concept,[80] there seems no reason in principle why such an approach could not be made compatible with the principles of sound greenhouse gas regulation that we advocate here: the approach could be comprehensive (covering net emissions of all greenhouse gases), it could be implemented through legally binding allocations of emissions intensity allowances to nations and sources, and there could be a system of domestic and international emissions intensity allowance trading.

In addition to concerns about cost escalation, a system of tradable allowances, like any market in commodities, faces the potential problem of market power.[81] For example, a country could try to amass enough allowances to corner the market on emissions allowances, create an artificial shortage, and exact monopolistic rents. Or a small group of countries might function as an oligopoly. That is a particularly knotty potential problem in greenhouse gas emissions trading at the international scale, where there is no antitrust law and where large emitters like Russia or China might enjoy substantial market power. Indeed, under the Kyoto Protocol, Russia and Ukraine might be the only major sellers of allowances; one estimate suggests that such a situation would raise costs to the United States by 25 percent compared with full global trading with competition among several sellers.[82] Enlisting the major developing countries in participation is the most obvious solution to that problem.

Another potential problem for a greenhouse gas allowance market, like any market, is transaction costs.[83] The costs of finding trading partners, negotiating deals, monitoring and enforcing contract performance, and insuring against nonperformance can hinder efficient transactions. Formal allowance trading seeks to reduce transaction costs by making allowances fungible and enforcing aggregate performance through comprehensive emissions monitoring and reporting and enforcement against noncomplying sellers (possibly supplemented by buyer liability) rather than through regulatory review of each individual trade. The U.S. experience with sulfur dioxide allowance trading shows that the transaction costs of a system of formal allowance trading can be quite low. But case-by-case emissions credit trading systems, such as those contemplated by the Kyoto Protocol provisions for joint implementation and the clean development mechanism, may face high transaction costs.[84]

Some critics have asserted that negotiating the assignment of greenhouse gas emissions allowances (and the corresponding allocation of abatement burdens) among countries would be so difficult that the system would never get off the ground.[85] But that concern applies to any regulatory instrument: all forms of regulation, including command requirements and greenhouse gas taxes, allocate burdens among those regulated; and all forms of international regulation require a burden-sharing negotiation under the consent voting rule for international treaties. While climate agreements involve difficult negotiations over burden sharing or asset distribution, so do many other successful negotiations, such as corporate mergers, arms control talks, and international monetary policy accords. If the joint gains are large enough, the distributional issues can generally be worked out. The real question for climate policy is the relative difficulty of negotiating the initial assignment using the alternative policy instruments, given the consent framework for international treaties.[86] In the global greenhouse gas regulatory context, use of tradable allowances should ease rather than impede the problem of negotiating the allocation of regulatory burdens. As Ronald Coase taught, the lower the impediments to subsequent contractual reallocations of entitlements among the parties, the less the risk that an initial assignment will lock the parties into an inefficient situation that reduces the welfare of one or more parties relative to the status quo and undermine the potential for agreement; that risk is much greater if the initial assignment is binding.[87] Technology standards and fixed taxes provide no flexibility for subsequent reallocations of burdens among nations. On the other hand, allowance trading both permits and facilitates postagreement reallocations and thus reduces the risk of excessively costly or otherwise inefficient lock-ins and thus eases initial negotiations.[88]

A further potential obstacle to international greenhouse gas regulatory agreements is that developing countries may fear that agreeing to any quantitative limitation on emissions will constrain their long-term ability to develop economically. That concern is best addressed by structuring the emissions trading system, as described above, so that developing countries receive extra headroom allowances, perhaps up to or above their business-as-usual forecast. In addition, limitations might, as discussed above, be expressed in terms of the greenhouse gas intensity of GDP rather than emissions, which would further ease concerns that limitations would unduly crimp economic growth. Such arrangements would presumptively leave developing countries no worse off than the status quo ante and make them better off because the tradable allowances are a new asset that they can trade or sell at a profit (though still at prices attractive to industrialized countries). Put another way, future economic growth on a lower–greenhouse gas path can be financed by allowance trades or sales, so that an emissions trading system can enhance rather than limit developing countries' growth prospects. Concerns may still exist with long-term lock-in. The practical answer is that allowance allocations will be renegotiated from time to time; the pace of renegotiations must balance investment and other interests in stable expectations with the need to respond to new information and changed circumstances.[89]

A final issue is the compatibility of international emissions trading with the domestic policy instruments adopted in each country. If countries adopt technology standards, fixed performance standards, or taxes rather than emissions trading to achieve domestic abatement, the cost savings expected under full global trading could be curtailed.[90] The beneficial role of the private sector in trading would be reduced. One solution is for the international treaty to provide that signatories must employ emissions trading domestically, at least in the sectors likely to be involved in international greenhouse gas–related transactions. An alternative is to rely on the economic and administrative gains from compatibility with international emissions trading to motivate countries to adopt emissions trading domestically. Countries with domestic emissions trading systems would stand to benefit more from international emissions trading—the gains both from selling and from buying—than those with alternative domestic policies.[91]

Balancing Costs and Benefits in Setting Regulatory Targets

Wise greenhouse gas regulatory policies must not only use the most cost-effective means for achieving greenhouse gas emissions limitations, but must also set sensible limitations objectives that balance relevant costs and benefits. They must strike a balance between prevention measures and adaptation measures.[92] They must appropriately time investments in greenhouse gas emissions limitations by taking into account the relations among the stringency and timing of emissions limitations, the atmospheric greenhouse gas stock, the damages associated with changing atmospheric temperatures, the differences in the costs of achieving different levels of emissions reductions at different time periods (incorporating an appropriate discount rate to translate into net present value costs incurred and benefits afforded in future years), and capital stock turnover and technological innovation.

As previously noted, several efforts have been made to quantify the path of emissions reductions over time implied by such a climate policy. Those efforts, of course, involve very large uncertainties, but they provide a sound framework for setting informed and wise regulatory targets. Studies have identified two basic approaches: the least-cost path to stabilize atmospheric greenhouse gas concentrations at designated levels (as suggested by the objective in Article 2 of the Framework Convention on Climate Change),[93] and the net benefits maximizing path. As already noted, Hammitt has found that the net benefits maximizing path involves more stringent near-term emissions reductions below the business-as-usual emissions forecast (roughly 3 percent below the business-as-usual level by 2010, 5 percent below that level by 2025, and 20 percent below that level by 2100) than does the least-cost path to stabilize atmospheric greenhouse gas concentrations at 750, 650, or even 550 parts per million by the period 2100 to 2150. (Current atmospheric carbon dioxide concentrations are at about 375 parts per million.) Both paths call for substantially less stringent near-term emissions reductions than required under the Kyoto Protocol.[94]

We believe that the approach of maximizing net benefits is conceptually preferable to the stabilization strategy, which is based on an arbitrarily chosen stabilization target and timetable. With expert advice, countries would negotiate a schedule of future aggregate global emissions targets (with targets set for, say, every ten years over the next three or four decades) on the basis of the principle of maximizing net benefits. That would require judgments about the expected value of damages from emissions and the costs of abatement. Targets would be set on assumptions of workably cost-effective implementation with comprehensiveness, global trading, and temporal flexibility. Setting such pathways confronts significant uncertainties about both future costs and future benefits of alternative pathways. Sensitivity analysis (as performed, for example, by Hammitt in his studies) can help inform judgments about how to address such uncertainties. Our limited ability to assign economic values to many types of impacts also complicates the task of setting pathways based on maximizing net social benefits. The degree of social risk aversion to adopt with respect to risks of catastrophic harms and the discount rate or rates to use with respect to costs and to benefits accruing at different times present additional issues. Thus, the setting of pathways will necessarily involve substantial social and political elements and judgments. Nonetheless, the judgments involved would be disciplined and made more transparent by the social benefit-cost framework for the decision and the facts and analysis generated in implementing it. And the pathways would be revised on a periodic basis in light of experience and new information. Thus, the pathways could be used to set targets for successive periods (say, ten years). The targets would then be divided into national allowance allocations for each period. Such allowances could then be subassigned by national governments to private firms and other emitting entities and traded internationally. Such an approach would be similar in concept to the schedule (with allowance trading and banking) successfully employed in the U.S. lead phasedown in the 1980s.

6

Assessing and Correcting the Kyoto Protocol's Flaws

How well does the design of the Kyoto Protocol accord with the principles, outlined in chapter 5, for the design of a sound greenhouse gas regulatory system? Here we address this question and conclude that the protocol's basic regulatory design is sound but that the protocol suffers from three basic flaws. They include the adoption of limitations obligations without deciding the means for achieving and ensuring compliance (including in particular the role of sinks, the scope for emissions trading, and remedies or sanctions for noncompliance); the total omission of obligations for any developing country to limit emissions, now or in the future; and the selection of arbitrary, excessively stringent emissions limitation targets. The Bonn and Marrakech accords have remedied to a considerable extent though not entirely the first of those flaws, but unjustified restrictions on the use of the comprehensive approach and emissions trading remain, and many issues related to compliance assurance are still unresolved. Further, the delay and acrimony that have occurred in the process of addressing those gaps have been quite costly. The second flaw, the omission of developing country obligations, and the third, arbitrary targets, persist and must be remedied.

Sound Basic Regulatory Design

The Kyoto Protocol's basic regulatory design is sound. It embraces the comprehensive approach and provides for international trading in greenhouse gas emissions allowances (limited to Annex B countries) as well as two project-based credit trading systems (joint implementation among

Annex B countries, and the clean development mechanism in which developing countries may participate).[1] As discussed below, however, the implementation measures adopted at Bonn and Marrakech impose some unjustified limitations on the use of the comprehensive approach and the trading mechanisms. Another beneficial feature of the basic Kyoto Protocol design is providing for intertemporal flexibility in limiting emissions by defining limitations obligations for the initial compliance period in terms of the average of a country's emissions over a five-year period; that feature allows countries the flexibility to balance higher emissions in some years with lower emissions in others.

Those basic design elements—a comprehensive approach to gases and sinks and international emissions trading—have been espoused consistently by the United States across administrations of both parties. They were initially advanced in the first Bush administration by the authors and others.[2] They are nonpartisan ideas for good policy. As discussed above, those design features dramatically reduce the costs of achieving greenhouse gas limitations relative to approaches that use command regulation and focus on fossil-fuel carbon dioxide emissions. The Kyoto Protocol's use of cost-effective means for achieving limitations does not, however, mean that its regulatory targets are justified. But their use is an essential first step in devising a sound climate strategy.

The comprehensive approach and emissions trading have been attacked as too complex and difficult to implement and enforce. As discussed above, that criticism is misplaced. As the U.S. sulfur dioxide trading experience shows, emissions trading can work very well if regulators adopt simple, straightforward, transparent rules. While it is substantially more difficult to establish the institutional arrangements for successful emissions trading at the international than at the domestic level, that would be true for any regulatory strategy. It should be feasible to build, with appropriate participation from the business and nongovernmental organization sectors, the basic arrangements to implement the international emissions trading program authorized under Article 17 of the Kyoto Protocol.[3] Simplified default rules can be adopted to deal with difficult-to-measure greenhouse gases such as agricultural methane and carbon dioxide sinks. Monitoring, implementation, and enforcement problems are significant at the international level, but that would be true of any regulatory strategy that might be adopted.

Failure to Set Ground Rules for Implementation and Compliance Simultaneously with Regulatory Targets

Although the Kyoto Protocol's basic regulatory design is sound, the protocol as negotiated and signed in 1997 was seriously flawed because it set quantitative emissions limitations obligations without agreement on the ground rules for determining reductions of greenhouse gas emissions, enhancement of greenhouse gas sinks, emissions trading and joint implementation–clean development mechanism projects, and arrangements to ensure compliance. The failure to resolve those important issues made many countries, including the United States, unwilling to ratify the protocol, because the ultimate costs of compliance remained highly uncertain, and that hampered assessment and development of the requisite measures for national implementation.[4] Achieving even partial resolution of those open issues required several further rounds of acrimonious negotiation that left the United States on the sidelines. That approach was a serious mistake that should not be repeated in future agreements. Ends (emissions targets) and means (regulatory design, flexibility options, and methods of ensuring compliance) for achieving them should be negotiated simultaneously, at least in cases such as greenhouse gas regulation, where the costs of achieving the ends are very large and depend critically on the means allowed.

Setting targets without agreement on the means for compliance gave free rein to those nations that opposed full scope for international emissions trading and the use of sinks to obstruct their negotiation and then claim that the demands of the United States and others in favor of such measures amounted to a weakening of the initial targets, notwithstanding the general authorization of such flexibility in the Kyoto Protocol. In the post–Kyoto Protocol negotiations, the European Union sought to restrict emissions trading at the international level (such as by insisting that trading could be only a minor "supplement" to domestic abatement) while simultaneously proceeding with plans for unrestricted emissions trading within Europe. And at The Hague in December 2000, the European Union balked at minor increases in sink credits. It blocked agreement, claiming that it could not accept the risk of increased emissions while refusing to take any steps to bring major emitting developing countries into the treaty. Later, at Bonn and Marrakech, the European Union agreed to allow trading unrestrained by "supplementarity" and agreed to large increases in allowed credit for sinks. Those paradoxes demonstrate that the European Union's objections to the comprehensive approach and to global emissions trading were in large measure political and strategic in character, rather than opposition on the merits. They appear to have been aimed at least in part at placating domestic "Green" constituencies by shaming the United States and at the same time securing relative competitive advantage over the United States and other international economic rivals.[5]

The United States must bear a share of the blame for creating that situation by not insisting that the means for achieving compliance be resolved simultaneously with the adoption of the quantitative emissions targets and by signing the Kyoto Protocol notwithstanding the gaps in the protocol. Furthermore, the absence of any U.S. policies to manage domestic emissions during the Clinton administration—the result in part of differences between the president and Congress—contributed along with strong economic growth to rapid increases in U.S. emissions, a trend that the Bush-Cheney administration has not acted to curb. U.S. reservations about the Kyoto Protocol (in both the Clinton-Gore and Bush-Cheney administrations) reflect factors previously discussed: the disproportionate emissions reductions burdens faced by the United States, the failure to include developing countries, and uncertainties regarding the availability of lower-cost abatement options through international emissions trading and the comprehensive approach. It also reflects U.S. fear that international greenhouse gas limitations obligations will be more effectively implemented and enforced in the United States than in other countries that are its trade rivals, a fear exacerbated by the failure of the Kyoto Protocol to specify compliance arrangements.[6]

After years of contentious negotiation, agreement on some of the important issues left open in the Kyoto Protocol was eventually reached through the Bonn and Marrakech accords, which establish some basic ground rules for emissions trading and the use of sinks and some (but far from all) compliance arrangements. Those arrangements, however, impose a number of unjustified limitations on the use of emissions trading and the comprehensive approach that should be removed. The Kyoto Protocol does not give credit for conservation of existing forests. Also, Appendix Z to the Bonn accord lists specific quantitative limits on the use of sinks by each Annex B country to meet its targets under Article 3, although at Marrakech Russia negotiated an increase in its Appendix Z limit from 17 million to 33 million tons of sink enhancement. Further, the Marrakech accord prohibits the banking of sink enhancement credits (emission removal units).[7] It also limits to 1 percent of its base year emissions the amount of clean development mechanism credits that a selling country can derive from sink activities.[8] In addition, the Bonn accord limits trading by imposing a sellers' reserve requirement that restricts the amount of emissions allowances that a country can sell (which we discuss further in chapter 7). Moreover, compliance arrangements are incomplete and inadequate. The current authorized penalty for a country that exceeds its first commitment period emissions limitation targets is a reduction in its second commitment period allowances in an amount 1.3 times the first commitment period exceedance (the second commitment period allowances, however, are not yet negotiated and could be adjusted to vitiate the effect of that sanction) and loss of eligibility to participate in the flexibility mechanisms.[9] Further, application of those sanctions is in the "facilitative" branch of the Compliance Committee. The "enforcement" branch of the Compliance Committee as yet has no powers; they are to be discussed in future negotiating sessions.

The delays and controversies involved in the process of filling in the gaps in the Kyoto Protocol have been costly in several ways. Protracted rearguard opposition by the European Union and others to full scope for emissions trading and the comprehensive approach was undoubtedly one factor in the eventual U.S. refusal to continue engagement in the Kyoto Protocol process. The delay in filling the Kyoto Protocol gaps has also delayed the process of implementing the protocol and actually beginning serious efforts to limit emissions. For example, the protocol envisaged that the clean development mechanism, which allows voluntary participation by developing countries in project-based greenhouse gas credit trading, would be open for business by 2000.[10] But the year 2000 has come and gone as the design and ground rules of the clean development mechanism have been mired in bickering. While opponents of full scope for emissions trading and the comprehensive approach justify their positions by the need to ensure that emissions are actually reduced, their actions have only succeeded in postponing the achievement of that goal.

Ducking the Vital Issue of Developing Country Participation

The Kyoto Protocol's failure to face more squarely the issue of limiting developing countries' emissions was a second major flaw. The Kyoto Protocol does not just omit the developing countries from initial emissions limitations. It absolves them of any meaningful substantive responsibilities, even in principle, now or in the future. In that respect the Kyoto Protocol is contrary to all prior global environmental treaties, including the Convention on International Trade in Endangered Species, the Ramsar Convention, the Basel Convention, the Montreal Protocol, the Biodiversity Convention, and most notably the UN Framework Convention on Climate Change itself, to which the Kyoto Protocol must ostensibly conform. The Framework Convention on Climate Change obligates all parties to "common but differentiated responsibility," which envisages that all parties will assume some obligations, even if the specifics of magnitude and timing differ.

As discussed in chapter 3, omitting developing countries from any emissions limitation commitment drastically undermines the Kyoto Protocol in several ways. First, given the significant forecasted growth in developing country greenhouse gas emissions, their omission means that the treaty will hardly affect global emissions at all.[11] Second, omitting developing countries means forfeiting the opportunities that they offer for low-cost abatement. Third, omitting developing countries while constraining industrialized country emissions will give rise to cross-border leakage of greenhouse gas emissions. Such leakage will increase the amount of unregulated developing country emissions[12] and raise concerns about competitiveness within industrialized countries.[13] Fourth, the absence of developing countries from the emissions trading system raises the risk that the remaining allowance sellers (chiefly Russia and Ukraine) will exercise significant market power and raise allowance prices and global costs. In short, the omission of developing countries makes the treaty much less (if at all) environmentally effective and much more costly.

On the other hand, as also discussed above, developing countries have strong equity arguments, reinforced by practical economic and political considerations, that the industrialized countries should take the lead and the principal burden of limitations. Accordingly, the industrialized countries must, to a large extent, finance emissions limitations efforts in developing countries to enlist their cooperation. The richer industrialized countries' incentive to do so lies in their desire to insure against climate change risks and in the cost savings that can be achieved by securing emissions reductions in developing countries rather than at home. The developing countries' principal incentives are the economic benefits from selling allowances and attracting new sources of capital and technology; they will also benefit environmentally from reduced global warming and from cleaner production and consumption technologies that will reduce local pollution.

In such circumstances international law can develop techniques for fostering mutually advantageous agreements between industrialized and developing countries. The Montreal Protocol, for example, has used "carrots," in the form of side payments and technical assistance, as well as "sticks," in the form of potential trade sanctions, to enlist the participation of developing countries in the global regulatory effort to phase out or limit ozone-depleting substances. Those provisions have invested the Montreal Protocol with significant credibility and contributed importantly to its ability to attract developing country participation and to its effectiveness. The Biodiversity Convention also provides for assistance grants by industrialized countries to developing countries to enlist their participation. Under both treaties, the developing countries' discharge of their treaty obligations is contingent on the provision by the industrialized countries of assistance. A similar quid pro quo contractual approach, backed up by monitoring and compliance assurances, can be used to build an inclusive and credible global climate regime. For reasons explained previously, the best way to implement such a strategy for enlisting developing country participation in the global greenhouse gas regulatory effort is to arrange for transfers of capital and technology from the industrialized to the developing countries through an international greenhouse gas emissions trading program in which the private sector would play a major role and in which developing countries would be given headroom allowances over and above their existing emissions.

Currently, the only Kyoto Protocol mechanism for developing country participation in international greenhouse gas emissions trading is the clean development mechanism established in Article 12 of the Kyoto Protocol. Article 12 provides for certification of emissions reduction credits for investments in projects in developing countries that reduce emissions below what they otherwise would be. Article 12 provides explicitly for private sector participation in those arrangements. Industrialized countries can use clean development mechanism project credits to help meet their Kyoto Protocol limitations obligations, and, pursuant to domestic legislation, private firms could use those credits to meet domestic regulatory obligations. Participation by developing countries is voluntary, and no caps are imposed on such countries' emissions. Examples of clean development mechanism credit projects include investments in energy efficiency, fuel switching (for example, conversion of urban buses from diesel fuel to natural gas), and afforestation measures.[14] The clean development mechanism is a potentially constructive arrangement for involving developing countries in the global greenhouse gas limitations effort by helping them make investments in technologies and practices that will enable them to shift to an economic growth path that involves lower greenhouse gas emissions. Yet the clean development mechanism, like any project-based credit system, suffers from a number of inherent limitations and other drawbacks and should be regarded as a transitional measure toward full developing country involvement in an international greenhouse gas cap-and-trade system.

As previously noted, although the clean development mechanism was supposed to be up and running by 2000, it has been hindered by squabbling over ground rules, by opposition from those objecting to emissions trading and the comprehensive approach, and by some developing countries that view it as the opening wedge of greenhouse gas limitation obligations. In addition, the clean development mechanism could be overly centralized and politicized in its administration in contrast to a decentralized market in greenhouse gas allowances. The clean development mechanism is to be governed by an executive board, accountable to the Conference of the Parties to the Kyoto Protocol, which will set policies for determining which clean development mechanism credits can count and, perhaps, which investments and individual projects may go forward. Those arrangements could bog down the clean development mechanism in political battles over the allocation of projects and undermine the economic advantages of trading. Further, the clean development mechanism is likely to involve high transaction costs because of the need for project-by-project administrative determinations of project eligibility, baselines, and certification of credits. Transaction costs would be much lower in a global cap-and-trade allowance program that does not require such determinations for each individual transaction.

Another fundamental problem with the clean development mechanism is that it accords regulatory credit for local abatement projects in countries without total emissions caps, a structure that leads to unintended but predictable and counterproductive side effects from cross-project leakage. Greenhouse gas emissions abatement in one location—such as growing a new forest on what was previously farmland—may be offset by increases in emissions at other locations within the same country—such as the clearing of forests at other locations, spurred by the market demand for farmland, the supply of which has been contracted at the clean development mechanism project. And the clean development mechanism also risks the fate of subsidies for abatement: reducing marginal emissions at specific firms or locations but also reducing the average cost of operating in the emitting sector and thereby inducing an increase in the total size of the emitting sector in the recipient country.[15]

A further drawback of the clean development mechanism is that it may undermine the incentives for developing countries to join an international cap-and-trade system. If developing countries can sell clean development mechanism credits at a price close to the price they would receive for selling formal allowances under a cap-and-trade system, then there is little added gain to joining the cap-and-trade regime. To address that problem and the problems of cross-project leakage and growth of emitting activities, the value of clean development mechanism credits ought to be significantly discounted compared with the price for formal allowances to reflect the difference in real environmental value of the two commodities; a clean development mechanism ton is not equal to a cap-and-trade allowance ton. Perhaps the higher transaction costs of the project-based, centrally supervised clean development mechanism (and the adaptation fund surcharge on clean development mechanism credits imposed pursuant to Article 12) will achieve that price differential anyway. In the absence of such a differential, proposals to make the clean development mechanism competitive and fully compatible with Annex B emissions trading run the risk of undermining the ability to attract developing countries to the cap-and-trade system in the future.

Accordingly, while the clean development mechanism can play a useful transitional role in introducing developing countries to a limited form of emissions trading, it is a distinctly second-best approach relative to a cap-and-trade system with headroom allowances and is not a viable long-term means for enlisting developing country participation in an effective global climate regulatory effort. Priority should be given to enlisting major developing countries in some form of international greenhouse gas trading program.

Unjustified Short-Term Targets

Even with enhanced flexibility in the means of achieving compliance, the Kyoto Protocol targets would still demand too much in the way of emissions reductions too soon to be justified or even feasible. As noted previously, the Kyoto Protocol requires the Annex B industrialized countries to reduce their emissions by an average of between 16 and 24 percent below projected 2010 business-as-usual emissions. The United States, if it joined, would be required to make around a 31 percent reduction. A number of other major Annex B countries, including Japan, face the need to make similar large reductions, and even the European Union faces a substantial challenge despite the fortuitous greenhouse gas reductions that it has enjoyed since 1990. Compliance by all Annex B countries would require major purchases of headroom allowances from Russia and Ukraine by the other Annex B industrialized countries. The emissions trading systems to make those transfers, as well as the monitoring and other machinery to determine and ensure compliance (including compliance by Russia and Ukraine), have yet to be set up, which raises important questions regarding the Kyoto Protocol's credibility. If such systems are established, they would enable Russia and Ukraine to exercise the significant market power that they would enjoy under such circumstances and provoke potentially serious conflicts.

Even if the Kyoto Protocol targets could be achieved with the benefit of a well-functioning international trading system, the costs involved would exceed the benefits. As discussed above, the Kyoto Protocol requires that participating countries achieve much sharper (and more costly) near-term emissions reductions than those required by a net-benefits-maximizing path. The Kyoto Protocol targets for industrialized countries, combined with unrestricted emissions in developing countries, translate to a global emissions reduction of roughly 15 to 20 percent below the business-as-usual level in 2010. Assuming "average" sensitivity and damages, Hammitt's net-benefits-maximizing path, by contrast, requires global emissions to be 3 percent below the business-as-usual level by 2010, 5 percent below that level by 2025, and 20 percent below that level by 2100.[16] Although the net-benefits-maximizing paths that result from conservative assumptions of high climate sensitivity or high damages would require greater near-term reductions than "average" assumptions, the Kyoto Protocol requires substantially more aggressive and costly near-term reductions than even those pathways.[17]

The most fundamental flaw in the Kyoto Protocol's emissions reduction targets, however, is that they were arbitrary. They were insensitive to costs (including the costs associated with high emissions growth due to high economic growth and other changes in the interim between establishing targets in 1997 and implementing them a decade and more later) and the relation between costs and benefits. They were established without reference to any articulated, sustainable climate policy. They do not correspond to the "objective" of stabilizing atmospheric concentrations at a level that is not "dangerous," advanced in the Framework Convention on Climate Change, which is itself vague and lacking an articulated basis. They were set for only one initial compliance period without any guidelines or principles for establishing subsequent limitations objectives. We believe that the soundest approach in principle for establishing international emissions limitations obligations, and the one most likely to win wide and lasting adherence by different countries, is by reference to a longer-term pathway that seeks to maximize net global benefits; the international distributional and equity issues involved should be addressed through the allocation of allowances. By maximizing total net benefits, that approach has the best promise of being able to generate and then distribute substantial gains widely enough to attract broad participation and also absorb the transaction costs involved in such an arrangement. The Kyoto Protocol fails to measure up to that principle; it requires reductions that are too steep too soon and therefore too costly to be justified in relation to the benefits afforded. The proper alternative to the Kyoto Protocol is not, however, to postpone regulatory action to the distant future. The net-benefits-maximizing approach, which we favor, calls for beginning some emissions reductions in the near future. As Hammitt notes, we need to start building the international and domestic institutional structures for climate policy now, to send credible policy signals that will in turn stimulate the needed shifts in private and public sector investments, practices, and technologies.

Accordingly, the principle of net benefits maximization should be used to set, as goals, long-term emissions pathways that would provide the framework for setting emissions targets for successive specific time periods and that would in turn form the basis for aggregate and national emissions caps. As discussed previously, setting pathways would confront significant uncertainties and other difficulties in estimating the relevant costs and benefits, and social and political elements would play a substantial role in the ultimate judgments made in setting pathways. Nonetheless, the net-benefits-maximizing principle, supplemented by sensitivity analysis and other established decision analytical methods, is normatively sound and would provide salutary direction and discipline to the decision process. The pathways would, of course, have to be revised and updated periodically in light of new information and circumstances, and targets adjusted accordingly. There would also have to be arrangements to provide flexibility to deal with shorter-term changes in circumstances, including fluctuations in economic growth, at both the global and national levels. Setting emissions targets and obligations as an average over a multiyear period to provide flexibility in timing should be adopted to address that need. Setting national obligations in terms of emissions intensity, as discussed above, is an additional possibility that merits careful consideration. The safety valve concept is another.

Of course, specific emissions limitations obligations will inevitably be the product of difficult, contingent political negotiations. But those negotiations should take place in the context of a clearly acknowledged, basic long-term principle—emissions pathways based on net benefits maximization. The circumstances that national emissions allocations would be negotiated to deal with distributional issues, and that allowances would subsequently be transferable, should further improve the attractiveness of the net-benefits-maximization principle for establishing total limitations obligations. As we state in chapter 7, the Kyoto Protocol should be modified to incorporate that principle as the fundamental lodestar, and its initial targets should be modified accordingly.

7

U.S. Leadership in Reconstruction

In light of the shortcomings as well as successes of the Kyoto Protocol and the Bonn and Marrakech accords, the global interest in effective, efficient, and fair climate policy, and the strong U.S. national interest in a sound international climate regime, the United States should lead a reconstruction effort to build and join an improved international climate regime. The role of the United States is pivotal because of its large share of global emissions and of global economic activity (about 25 percent of each). Its efforts should proceed simultaneously at the international and national levels.

As noted in chapter 1, attention has focused on two paths from the Bonn and Marrakech accords. The United States could stay out of the Kyoto Protocol regime and international climate agreements altogether and thereby thwart any effective global climate policy. Or the United States could join the Kyoto Protocol and the Bonn and Marrakech accords essentially as currently drafted and then work within the treaty group to promote the comprehensive approach and trading, developing country participation, and optimal target setting. The first option is unrealistic and contrary to the interests of the United States as well as those of the world. The second option would require an unlikely about-face by the Bush administration (but might be pursued by its successor) and is unlikely to result in developing country participation or other fundamental improvements anytime soon.

We urge consideration of a third option that would involve U.S. accession together with China (and additional developing countries) to an international greenhouse gas cap-and-trade system within a number of years. The United States would take serious domestic actions to prepare to join such a regime, while insisting that it will join only if major developing countries join as well (though on differentiated terms); if emissions targets are set on a sound, longer-term basis; and if full scope is provided for use of the comprehensive approach and emissions trading to achieve targets under arrangements providing compliance assurance. Under one possible scenario for implementing that approach, the United States, China, and perhaps other developing countries, such as India, Brazil, and Mexico, would initially establish one or more separate cap-and-trade systems independent of the Kyoto Protocol (in which some industrialized countries other than the United States, such as Canada and Australia, might participate), which would eventually be merged with a modified Kyoto Protocol regime. Such an approach would have the benefit of providing experience with different versions of an international greenhouse gas trading program. Alternatively, the United States, China, and other developing countries might work together to join a suitably modified version of the Kyoto Protocol without the interim stage of creating a separate trading system or systems. Under either scenario (or other variations on them), the United States and China and other major emitting developing countries would eventually join a reconstructed global cap-and-trade regime with the Kyoto Protocol parties, a regime that would yield a much greater collective contribution to climate protection at far less cost than would the Kyoto Protocol and the Bonn and Marrakech accords without the United States or even with the United States.

Our suggested approach is likely to be of interest to the industrialized Kyoto Protocol parties—the European Union, Japan, Russia, and others. They will have important environmental and economic interests, based on the price of tradable allowances, to prefer accession to the Kyoto Protocol by the United States and China together (rather than either joining alone). Without emissions limits on the United States and China—the world's two largest emitters—the Kyoto Protocol will amount to little. Accession by both countries together will maintain price stability, balancing allowance supply and demand by matching a major allowance buyer (the United States) and a major seller (China).

We recognize that for the United States to join the global regime down the road, special terms will be needed to enable accession without meeting the requirements just agreed to in Marrakech for the first commitment period. But better late than never. Moreover, better "later with substantive improvements" than either never or now without such improvements. Further, the United States and China (and perhaps others) would, together, represent such an overwhelming share of global emissions and global economic activity that they would likely have sufficient influence to persuade the European Union, Japan, Russia, and others to revise the treaty regime as a condition of full participation.

The hardest part in that third path will not be persuading the United States (although that may prove difficult, at least in the near term, even if the basic elements of a sound global climate regime were satisfied), but attracting participation by the major emitting developing countries through arrangements that are environmentally, economically, and politically credible. As explained above, the best way to attract China and others to join the abatement regime will be through assignments of headroom allowances, just as was done in the Kyoto Protocol and the Bonn and Marrakech accords to engage Russia. We emphasize that we are *not* suggesting that the United States demand that China limit its economic growth. We recognize that such a demand would fail to engage China's participation.[1] Rather, we are suggesting a plan for mutual benefit. Under our proposal, the United States and other industrialized countries would, through the assignment of headroom tradable allowances to China, finance China's greenhouse gas abatement and its transition toward a lower-emitting growth path. China would thereby reap significant net benefits from joining the cap-and-trade system. A similar approach would be taken with other major developing country emitters.

By taking such a path, the United States can exercise real leadership in global environmental affairs: leadership viewed not just as aggressiveness or "first-mover" prominence, but as wisdom, judgment, and resolve. The United States and China could lead the world toward a more effective, efficient treaty framework. Such a strategic collaboration with China could also be helpful in improving U.S.–China relations.

International Components of U.S. Climate Strategy

As detailed in chapter 3, participation of all major emitter nations in a cap-and-trade system is crucial to ensuring the environmental effectiveness of the global climate policy regime, preventing leakage, and reaping the full cost savings available from international trading. Other critical features of international greenhouse gas regulatory design are unrestricted international trading, comprehensive coverage of all greenhouse gases and sinks, and regulatory targets based on emissions pathways aimed at maximizing net social benefits.

We do not propose abandoning the Kyoto Protocol to obtain those objectives. The strategy should be evolution from the current Kyoto Protocol and the Bonn and Marrakech arrangements. That evolution could occur through the interim development of a separate cap-and-trade system or systems involving the United States (and possibly other industrialized countries) and China (and possibly other developing countries) that is eventually merged with a revised version of the Kyoto Protocol or through the direct joint accession of such countries to a reconstructed Kyoto Protocol. There are already indicia that evolution from the Kyoto Protocol is possible. For example, at Marrakech in November 2001 Kazakhstan proposed to join Annex B and hence to join the cap-and-trade system. Korea, which is treated as a developing country under the Kyoto Protocol, has recently announced that it will set targets and take steps to reduce its greenhouse gas emissions. And at Marrakech the conference agreed to consider a process at the eighth Conference of the Parties to the UN Framework Convention on Climate Change (November 2002) to evaluate commitments by developing countries—a preliminary move but in the direction of expanded global participation in the cap-and-trade system.

A rich literature addresses the evolution of law and institutions.[2] But that literature is largely retrospective and descriptive and shows how legal systems did evolve. Our current challenge is prospective and prescriptive: to design institutions so that they will evolve in the future in a sound manner. The Montreal Protocol provides an example of successful evolution in global environmental regulation; it added several ozone-depleting substances, progressively tightened its targets, and attracted follow-up participation by China and India and other developing countries in regulatory limitations (through a phased approach and various inducements for their participation, including an assistance fund).[3] Given the character of the greenhouse gas problem, where any annual change in greenhouse gas emissions has a quite small effect on the global stock and sharp near-term emissions reductions are not the appropriate goal, an evolutionary approach is especially appropriate for climate policy.

If, as seems likely as of this writing, the Kyoto Protocol is ratified by a sufficient set of countries (though not the United States) and enters into force in 2003, what then? New entrants must consent to join, which means that they must perceive net gains to joining; they will assess the advantages and disadvantages of joining or staying out of the Kyoto Protocol as the Kyoto Protocol parties attempt to implement it.[4] The current Kyoto Protocol parties may block new entrants by withholding the votes required to amend the treaty or to add countries to Annex B. If the United States, China, and other developing countries sooner or later form a single global cap-and-trade regime with the current Kyoto Protocol parties, the Kyoto Protocol will have to be significantly modified or a new successor agreement adopted to provide for a larger number of participants and to establish new emissions limitations targets and obligations and other changes in existing Kyoto Protocol arrangements. The new arrangements will require the negotiation of a structure that will provide sufficient net benefits to the new participants to attract them and at the same time also offer sufficient net benefits to the current Kyoto Protocol parties to persuade them to agree to needed modifications and not to defect and free-ride on the contribution of the expanded group of participants.[5] An individual country's accession may not satisfy both of those criteria, but joint accession by appropriately matched sets of countries—in particular, the United States and China—might.

Participation by the United States. First, we start from the premise that the United States will not join an international cap-and-trade regime (or adopt serious domestic controls) until at least China, and perhaps other major emitting developing countries, do so also (though on differentiated terms). That is clearly the position of the current Bush administration, but it was also the position of a unanimous U.S. Senate that in 1997 voted ninety-five to zero to announce that it would not ratify a treaty omitting meaningful participation by major developing countries.[6] Further, that view was buttressed by the stance of the Clinton-Gore administration, which stated the day after the Kyoto Protocol talks ended that it would not even submit the treaty to the Senate until the participation of developing countries was obtained. (Clinton never did send the treaty to the Senate.)[7]

The reason for that consistent position is often professed to be fairness—that it would be unfair to impose costs on Americans if Chinese and Indian citizens did not also shoulder similar burdens. We find that claim unpersuasive. Americans are far better off economically than the citizens of China or India. If fairness means the Rawlsian version, then the climate regime ought to help elevate the least-well-off and not add to their burdens.[8] If fairness corresponds to causal responsibility, the United States and Europe have, through past emissions, contributed an even greater share of the buildup of current atmospheric greenhouse gas concentrations than they contribute to annual emissions today, which implies a correspondingly greater abatement responsibility for the rich industrialized nations. Accordingly, the notion of fairness based on causal responsibility would imply much greater abatement action by the United States and Europe than by China and India. Reflecting perhaps the Rawlsian approach and perhaps the notion of fairness as causal responsibility, the Framework Convention on Climate Change (which the United States has fully ratified) calls on the wealthier countries to take the lead in preventing future climate change.

Whatever the moral or political potency of those fairness claims,[9] we doubt that they or other principles of fairness explain the real basis of the American stance. The deeper reasons for U.S. reluctance to join the Kyoto Protocol relate to environmental benefits and economic costs. As detailed in chapter 4, without China and other major developing countries participating, the Kyoto Protocol is likely to yield minor environmental benefits at significant costs; the participation of China and other major emitting developing countries would substantially increase the benefits and decrease the costs of the Kyoto Protocol as a whole and of U.S. participation in particular. The U.S. reluctance to join the Kyoto Protocol also clearly reflects fear of leakage and the resulting threat of excessive costs and competitiveness impacts, both nationally and in the electoral districts of key members of Congress, if the United States joins a cap-and-trade system but major developing economies (which offer low-cost abatement options if they participate) do not.[10] The 1997 Senate resolution expressly noted cost and competitiveness as the basis for its position.[11] If that analysis is correct, then it has been a strategic error for the European Union to try to cajole U.S. participation and limit use of the comprehensive approach and emissions trading, while neglecting China (whose inclusion would ease U.S. compliance costs and competitiveness concerns). The result has been to push the United States away from rather than toward ratification of the Kyoto Protocol.[12] Merely browbeating the United States seems futile. The European Union should accordingly support our proposal, which would significantly enhance the environmental and economic benefits to the United States of participation.

Attracting Participation by China and Other Major Developing Countries. As long as the United States is out of the Kyoto Protocol, major developing countries will almost certainly not join. The flip side of the fairness concerns voiced by U.S. politicians is that China, India, and other developing countries will surely perceive great unfairness in being asked to limit their emissions if the United States does not. Moreover, if China's or India's costs of participation exceed that country's environmental benefits (both global and local cobenefits) and other possible benefits of participation, then that country will need to receive side payments to attract its participation. That may well be the case, because the costs of abatement to China or India, albeit low in monetary terms compared with marginal abatement costs in the industrialized countries, may represent a high social opportunity cost to those countries in terms of the forgone investments in other more pressing priorities such as poverty alleviation, education, nutrition, and health care. Moreover, at least in China, higher greenhouse gas concentrations and global warming could yield benefits (extended growing seasons and carbon fertilization) to agriculture, so that global environmental benefits of greenhouse gas abatement to China could be perceived to be negative.[13]

For those reasons, we believe that major emitting developing countries (such as China, India, and Brazil) will require side payments or other incentives to secure their participation. That was the experience with Russia and Ukraine under the Kyoto Protocol and with China and India under the Montreal Protocol regarding chlorofluorocarbons. The amount of side payments necessary to attract developing country participation would need to cover at least their net costs of participation. Those net costs would consist of the costs of abatement, plus any forgone benefits of warming, plus the costs of forgone leakage to the country, minus the benefits of participation including the benefits of reduced warming and the local environmental cobenefits of abatement (such as reducing other pollutants and their associated adverse health effects). The use of headroom allowance allocations to make those side payments would provide additional benefits in the form of profits from allowance sales and transfers, enhanced inflows of investment and technology, and the gain in export sales of ordinary goods to industrialized countries as wider emissions trading reduces abatement costs and raises import demand in industrialized countries. The amount of those additional benefits would have to at least exceed a developing country's net costs to attract its participation.

The corresponding willingness of the rich industrialized countries to make such side payments will depend on the net benefits of attracting developing country participation, including the environmental benefits of a more effective global greenhouse gas regulatory regime, the economic benefits of an expanded supply of allowances at lower cost, reduced leakage, reduced market power by Annex B allowance sellers, and expanded markets for technologies and services relating to net greenhouse gas abatement and global emissions trading.

Will the aggregate environmental and economic benefits of an expanded greenhouse gas trading regime that includes major developing countries and the United States be sufficient to support the level of side payments by the industrialized nations that will be needed to attract developing country participation (as well as to cover the transaction costs involved)? While further studies are needed on that vital question, the very large abatement cost savings to be gained through an expanded trading system along with the environmental and other economic benefits to the rich industrialized countries of a more inclusive global cap-and-trade system strongly suggest an affirmative conclusion. Indirect support for such a conclusion is provided by the successful Kyoto Protocol negotiation of "headroom" arrangements for Russia and Ukraine; the European

Union's adoption of a burden-sharing agreement among its wealthier and less-developed member states; and the successful U.S. experience with headroom allowance assignments to electric utilities in reluctant states in the 1990 Clean Air Act amendments adopting a sulfur dioxide trading system.

Economic models developed at the Massachusetts Institute of Technology suggest that under a system of international emissions trading limited to Annex B countries, the major net beneficiary is Russia and other former Soviet Union countries, while under global emissions trading China would profit even more than Russia. Under the Kyoto Protocol with trading limited to Annex B countries (including the United States), in 2010 the former Soviet Union sells allowances for 345 million metric tons of carbon at $127 per ton for revenues of $43.77 billion and enjoys a net gain from trade, after domestic abatement costs are subtracted, of $33.2 billion; the only other seller, Eastern Europe, sells only 6 million metric tons of carbon. Hence, the former Soviet Union controls essentially the entire supply of allowances available for sale. By contrast, under the Kyoto Protocol with full global trading, in 2010 China would sell 437 million metric tons of carbon at an allowance sale price of $24 per ton, for revenues of $10.4 billion and a net gain from trade of $6.17 billion; India would sell 102 million metric tons of carbon for revenues of $2.44 billion and net gains from trade of $1.49 billion; the former Soviet Union would sell 211 million metric tons of carbon for revenues of $5.03 billion and a net gain of $4.22 billion.[14] Hence, global trading markedly reduces the market power of Russia and Ukraine and spreads sales and gains across China and India and other countries.

Under Annex B trading, the industrialized countries would spend about $43 billion on allowance purchases but save $32 billion compared with achieving their targets domestically; the United States would buy $13.44 billion in allowances and save $3 billion in costs; Japan would buy $12 billion and save $19.49 billion; the European Union would buy $13.5 billion and save $7.27 billion. Under full global trading, the industrialized countries would spend about $22 billion on allowances and save $94 billion compared with achieving their targets domestically. The United States would buy $9.27 billion and save $26.69 billion; Japan would buy $3.15 billion and save $31.08 billion; the European Union would buy $5.57 billion and save $24 billion.[15] After the Kyoto Protocol first commitment period, the net profits to China, India, and the former Soviet Union (and the percentage savings to the richer industrialized countries) could expand as the global emissions trading system operates under tightening limits on emissions.[16] If necessary to attract their participation, China and other developing countries could be assigned allowances up to their business-as-usual level emissions (as assumed in the MIT model) or perhaps even extra headroom above the business-as-usual level (as Russia received in its Kyoto Protocol assignment), depending on the net surplus generated by expanded trading.

Steps to expand the global cap-and-trade system to include China and other major developing countries would generate conflicts of interest between Russia and Ukraine and the new entrants, whose entry will undercut the market power of the former Soviet Union countries and reduce allowance prices; the extent of that impact will depend on the extent of headroom allowances allocated to the new entrants. Conflicts among potential new entrants in the allocation of headroom allowances will also exist, as the industrialized countries will want to minimize the total amount of such allowances granted. Thus, there will be hard bargaining over the terms under which major developing countries will join a global cap-and-trade system. The potential gains to all parties from expansion of the system should, however, permit ultimate resolution of those issues.

With those considerations in mind, why have China and India, which would be two of the primary beneficiaries of a global emissions trading system, and other developing countries, which could similarly benefit economically by participating, consistently refused in international negotiations even to discuss participation in a global cap-and-trade system? Several hypotheses are plausible. Those countries may feel as a matter of fairness that "industrialized countries should take the lead"—but under our scenario they would do so, by financing abatement through allowance purchases and investments in developing countries. For a variety of reasons, developing countries may also doubt that emissions trading will work in practice to their advantage. Because of their relative inexperience with trading, they may face higher costs of learning how to operate successfully in such a system, if it does work. They may fear being outnegotiated by savvy emissions traders from the industrialized nations (a fear that may be linked in the historical experience of developing countries with exploitation of their natural resources by colonial powers). Those fears suggest that transparency and competition (antitrust) rules should be applied to global emissions trading and that the industrialized countries and multilateral financial institutions should assist developing countries with capacity-building efforts to help assure the developing countries that they will be able to participate effectively and confidently in a global emissions trading system.

China and India may also fear that adopting any cap on greenhouse gas emissions will inhibit their economic growth. One way that could happen is that, even if the cap is at the business-as-usual level, that level can be difficult to forecast, and actual growth might turn out to be higher.[17] Especially when regulatory targets are set long in advance of the period for implementation, and future emissions and abatement costs are highly uncertain, developing countries may demand allowance allocations based on worst-case assumptions. That fear could be allayed by several means, including allowance assignments even above their business-as-usual level, adopting a cap in terms of greenhouse gas intensity of output, use of a safety valve mechanism, and providing for interim revisions of targets based on specified criteria or triggers or both. It should also be emphasized that economic growth can occur with less than proportionate growth in greenhouse gas emissions, especially through inputs of greenhouse gas–efficient investments and technologies under the trading system.[18]

China and India may also fear selling low-cost abatement options now and then needing them later to comply with future emissions limitations. If so, sellers should charge a price that reflects the net present value of the allowance, including its future option value. That evaluation, of course, would be up to the selling country and its business firms and other entities involved in emissions trading and related transactions; if they think that the allowance price is too low, they need not sell. One might expect poorer countries, with higher discount rates because of more immediate priorities, to prefer cash now rather than distant options. Some developing

countries may face the added risk that corrupt or short-sighted government officials will sell off a nation's emissions allowances in such a way as
to cripple its economic future. One response to such risks is to issue
allowances for relatively short periods or make them leasable only, or
both.[19]

In addition, China and India may decline to entertain a cap-and-trade
system because they believe that the clean development mechanism will
provide them with similar revenues without a cap. But clean development
mechanism sales are unlikely to yield revenues nearly as high as would
formal allowance sales in a cap-and-trade regime, because of the higher
transaction costs of clean development mechanism deals and the surcharge for adaptation funds to be imposed on clean development mechanism credits. Also, as noted in chapter 6, the Kyoto Protocol parties or
authorities should consider adopting a discount on clean development
mechanism credits to reflect their lower environmental value relative to
cap-and-trade allowances. The clean development mechanism should be
viewed as a transitional measure, to be phased out as developing countries
graduate to national caps and emissions trading.

Finally, the emphatic public opposition of China, India, and other
developing countries to emissions trading may also be part of a negotiating tactic of holding out for a better deal. If so, the U.S. decision to stay
out of the Kyoto Protocol opens the door for direct negotiations between
the United States and India and China on what such a deal would involve.

Certain recent developments may affect China's willingness to participate in a greenhouse gas cap-and-trade system. The apparent decrease in
China's carbon dioxide emissions over the 1997–2000 period[20] may indi-
cate a new willingness by the Chinese government to restrain emissions,
although more likely that decline was not for emissions reduction purposes and instead reflects the effects of other economic changes unrelated
to climate or other environmental policies, such as a slowdown in economic growth, a restructuring of the economy, a reduction of coal subsidies, and other changes. Given the limited reliability of Chinese economic
data and the continued heavy role of the state in the energy sector, it is difficult to know just what has happened to China's carbon dioxide emissions and the reasons for and significance of any departures from earlier

trends. If there was a substantial decline because of significant decreases in greenhouse gas intensity, that experience may foster confidence by Chinese leaders that decreases in emissions below the business-as-usual level can be accomplished without hindering economic growth as much as might have been feared and that allowance sales could accordingly be quite profitable and not hinder economic development. On the other hand, the emissions decline may be temporary; China's marginal abatement cost curve may be rising, as the lower-cost abatement options such as reductions in coal subsidies are being used up and only more costly abatement options remain; if so, such a circumstance may discourage Chinese accession to a cap or imply that a greater side payment is needed to secure Chinese participation.

China's move to embrace markets, both domestically and through its entry into the World Trade Organization, may make it more receptive to market-based environmental policies. China has begun to experiment with domestic emissions trading markets.[21] And WTO membership may bring greater confidence that international economic arrangements will help shield China from industrialized countries' market power or sharp dealing in a greenhouse gas allowance market. Further, the Chinese government's assessment of the impacts of climate change on China may be changing; instead of perceiving gains from warming, China may now be worrying more about harms.[22] Finally, the experience of the 1997–1998 Asian financial crisis suggests that China might undertake some possible economic sacrifice to build its role as a world leader and a player in international economic regimes.[23]

Our expectation is that China and India (and other major developing countries) will come to appreciate the benefits to them of joining a cap-and-trade regime in which they can sell allowances and enjoy other economic and environmental benefits at a profit. But such a view depends on U.S. participation as well, not only for reasons of fairness but also because the profits from allowance trades and sales will be much diminished if the United States does not add its demand for allowances to the global market. In addition, the international greenhouse gas cap and trading market must be credible, politically, economically, and environmentally. That will require good monitoring and reporting of emissions and adequate compliance assurance arrangements. Meeting those requirements will be a challenge in the case of many developing countries, but also in some industrialized countries such as the former Soviet Union nations. There will need to be an effective international system of quality assurance for emissions monitoring and reporting (which should probably include a major role for nongovermental organization and private certifying bodies). Developing countries and other allowance seller countries that failed to meet quality assurance requirements could be prohibited from selling allowances, or the value of their allowances could be discounted by an international supervisory authority. A system of buyer liability with serialized allowances would provide additional market-based incentives for quality assurance (although at higher transaction costs).

One of the advantages of a multiple track approach under which China and other developing countries would first participate in one or more emissions trading agreements with the United States (and possibly other industrialized countries), before merger with a reconstructed Kyoto Protocol in a single global cap-and-trade system, is that the distinctive issues and problems presented by developing country participation could be addressed for a period through regimes that involve far fewer parties and can be more readily modified to adapt to the lessons learned by experience before negotiating and undertaking a global regime that includes participation by all of the Kyoto Protocol parties. Targets based on emissions intensity and the safety-valve approach are examples of new approaches that might be tested in a separate regime, parallel to the Kyoto Protocol.

Interests of the Initial Kyoto Protocol Parties. The arguments just offered for joint accession by the United States and China, India, and other countries could have been made in 1997 as well as today, but they would probably have been less persuasive to the European Union and other Annex B parties then than they would be today. After the U.S. withdrawal in 2001 and in light of the likely ratification of the Kyoto Protocol by sufficient other Annex B countries to enable the protocol to enter into force in 2003, the situation has changed. We believe that now the Kyoto Protocol parties—the European Union, Japan, Russia, Ukraine, Canada, and others—will, as a group, strongly prefer the United States and China (and India and other major developing countries) to join the Kyoto Protocol regime together rather than separately.

The Kyoto Protocol parties are implementing an international emissions trading system without the United States or China but with headroom allowances assigned to Russia and Ukraine. Without U.S. participation, the price of allowances within the Annex B trading system will most likely be lower than had the United States joined the Kyoto Protocol. In the MIT model of emissions trading among Annex B countries (including the United States and with no clean development mechanism), Russia and Ukraine sell 345 million tons of allowances, and Eastern Europe sells a total of 6 million tons, for a total of 351 million tons. The other Annex B countries buy 350 million tons of allowances, of which 106 million tons are bought by the United States, 106 million tons by the European Union, 95 million tons by Japan, and 43 million tons by other OECD nations. The price of an allowance is $127 per ton.[24]

With U.S. demand for 106 million tons of allowances removed from the market, allowances would presumably sell at a lower price. New model runs are necessary to gauge the effects of such a change on the supply, demand, and price of allowances, but interpolating from the MIT study, a fall in demand of 106 million tons (from 351 to 245 million tons sold) would intersect the supply curve somewhere near $60 per ton.[25] Thus, without U.S. participation, the former Soviet Union stands to sell fewer allowances at a much lower price than $127, and the European Union, Japan, and others stand to pay less for allowances.[26] It is accordingly conceivable that the European Union and Japan decided to go ahead with the Kyoto Protocol because they realized that their costs would be much lower under the Kyoto Protocol regime with former Soviet Union allowances available but without the United States in as a buyer.[27]

Recent analyses support the conclusion that U.S. nonparticipation in the Kyoto Protocol will result in large reductions in allowance prices. For example, William D. Nordhaus estimates that under the Kyoto Protocol with U.S. participation, the price of an allowance in 2010 would be about $55 per ton of carbon, but under the Kyoto Protocol without U.S. participation the price would fall to about $15.[28] Other recent model runs suggest that the allowance price under the Kyoto Protocol without the United

States would be somewhere between $0 (zero) and $35 or even $65, depending on the former Soviet Union's market power, choices to bank allowances, and other factors.[29] Alan S. Manne and Richard G. Richels project that allowance prices under the Kyoto Protocol with full Annex B participation (including the United States) would be about $140 in 2010 but that without U.S. participation the price in 2010 would drop drastically.[30]

Assuming that U.S. nonparticipation would substantially lower the price of allowances (to, say, $65 or less) relative to the price with U.S. participation, then subsequent U.S. accession to the Kyoto Protocol would raise the allowance price significantly, perhaps back to $127 or even higher. That would clearly harm the European Union, Japan, and other Annex B nations that were buying allowances for much less before U.S. accession. Alternatively, if China joined alone (or with India, Brazil, and other nations), it would flood the market with low-cost allowances (as low as $24 per ton in the MIT model or lower without U.S. demand). That would harm Russia and Ukraine, which had been selling allowances for much more. The precise impact of accession by the United States, China, and others on allowance prices would depend on several factors, including the targets assigned to new participants.

Accordingly, taken together, the Annex B parties to the Kyoto Protocol will have strong incentives to avoid accession by the United States alone or by China and other major developing countries alone. They will be highly likely to prefer joint accession by the United States, China, and such other countries to keep allowance prices stable, so that neither the Annex B sellers (former Soviet Union nations) nor the Annex B purchasers (Europe, Japan, and other wealthy industrialized country parties) are seriously harmed by changes in allowance prices.[31]

As noted above, conflicts of interest will exist between the former Soviet Union countries and potential developing country entrants to a global cap-and-trade system over their entry and the amount of allowances they will receive; conflicts between potential new entrants as a group and the industrialized countries regarding the total amount of allowances the latter will agree to provide the former; and conflicts among the potential new developing country participants regarding the allocation of allowances. The implications of accession by the United States, China, and other major developing countries need to be assessed through new model runs that take account of U.S. withdrawal, banking, clean development mechanism sales, China's apparent emissions decline from 1997 through 2000, and various scenarios for individual or combined accession by the United States, China, India, and other countries, with different targets and at different points in time. Such scenarios should be modeled and compared in terms of their effects on emissions, temperature change, cost, resource flows, and other outcomes. In addition, the analysis should examine the net economic and (to the extent feasible) environmental gains owing to participation by the various groups of countries under the alternative scenarios to help design arrangements that will maximize aggregate net benefits while also providing substantial net benefits for each participant to enhance the possibility of negotiating a broadly inclusive global cap-and-trade regime.

Despite the incentives for the Kyoto Protocol parties to favor combined accession by the United States and major developing countries, they might have reasons to resist such a step if it meant allowing the United States to sign on to targets less stringent than those accepted by the initial parties or making other significant changes to the provisions of the Kyoto Protocol and the Bonn and Marrakech accords. Also, other developing countries, less well equipped to participate in international trading than China or India, might resist their accession and the precedent that it would set for developing country caps. But with the United States, China, India, and other developing countries accounting together for 50 percent of global emissions and growing, their leverage to obtain joint accession and changes in the current agreement would be high.

International Components of a U.S. Strategy for the Evolution of Global Climate Policy. The need to correct the Kyoto Protocol's omission of developing countries is compelling. But any approach to engaging developing countries must be sensitive to their legitimate economic, political, and equity concerns and to the positions of other industrialized countries. We cannot say here exactly how much in the way of commitments from developing countries would be appropriate or realistic to expect in the near future and what in the way of headroom allowances or other inducements might be necessary to secure their participation. We do, however, believe that principles could be devised to attract sufficient developing country participation over time, provided that the industrialized countries also make credible international commitments to emissions limitations and begin to implement them.

In addition to taking initiatives to enlist participation by major developing countries, the United States should seek to ensure that any more inclusive global greenhouse gas cap-and-trade system eliminates the current Kyoto Protocol restrictions on the comprehensive approach and emissions trading, has adequate compliance assurances, and sets targets in the context of long-run emissions pathways based on maximizing net social benefits. To accomplish those objectives, U.S. policy at the international level (matched by domestic initiatives discussed below) should seek to promote reconstruction of global climate policy, either through one or more independent cap-and-trade systems with China and other developing countries (possibly including other industrialized nations as well) that would later be merged with a revised version of the Kyoto Protocol, or by directly joining, along with major developing countries, a reconstructed Kyoto Protocol. In doing so, the United States should aim eventually to secure a global cap-and-trade system with the elements that follow.

Individual country accession. The new arrangements should explicitly adopt a principle of voluntary accession to international commitments and participation in a cap-and-trade system by any interested country, including developing countries. Such action would remove the implicit obstacle to such accession created by the omission of any such provision in the Kyoto Protocol and by the politics of the G-77 plus China negotiating bloc. The agreement could go further, by adopting quantitative emissions limitation criteria for accession, but that should probably be avoided as too contentious a matter to resolve in advance of individualized negotiations over actual quantitative emissions limits and associated headroom allowance assignments for individual developing countries. The agreement could also allow for a country's participation in emissions trading on a sector-based approach that would permit participation at scale without the full adoption of total national caps, although that would create a potential for leakage from capped to uncapped sectors.

Developing country graduation. The new global regime would also adopt the principle that developing countries will automatically but incrementally join the cap-and-trade system once their per capita income passes certain agreed levels. Such a principle of "graduation" will help bring developing countries into the regime on a fair basis, while addressing their concern that poorer countries not be subject to obligations to correct a problem originally caused by and of primary concern to wealthier countries. The specific emissions limitations taken on by developing countries through that graduation process could include headroom to grow further.

Joint accession by the United States and major developing country emitters. The United States and China (and perhaps India, Brazil, Australia, and others) would join an expanded and improved global cap-and-trade regime together, by one or a combination of the scenarios previously sketched. Most likely they would join on a time frame to meet emissions limitations in a second commitment period (perhaps around 2016–2020). Those new parties would begin to participate in emissions trading before the time when they must achieve limitations under the agreement. For China, India, Brazil, and other countries, caps would be at or near their business-as-usual level (perhaps with some headroom above their business-as-usual level as a side payment); for the United States the cap would be below its business-as-usual level (though not necessarily with reference to 1990 levels).

Capacity-building in developing countries. Although developing countries and their firms participate effectively in many international financial and commodity markets, it would be appropriate to establish arrangements to help, as needed and appropriate, developing countries (especially the less developed countries) participate in emissions trading without fear of being disadvantaged by more knowledgeable market participants from industrialized countries. That could involve the creation of a new fund or additions to the capacity-building funds established under the

Kyoto Protocol and the Marrakech accord or adaptations of other existing assistance mechanisms for that specific purpose. The World Bank,
regional development banks, and agencies of the United Nations could
play a role in implementing those efforts.

Emissions pathways and regulatory targets. The agreement should set a
time path of emissions reductions based on net-benefits-maximizing criteria, not on an arbitrary basis such as reductions from a given base year,
nor the most cost-effective path for achieving an arbitrary atmospheric
greenhouse gas stabilization target and timetable. For example, a net-
benefits-maximizing path based on "average" warming and climate sensitivity might call for global emissions reductions of roughly 3 percent
below the business-as-usual level by 2010, 5 percent below that level by
2025, and 20 percent below that level by 2100. A path based on a more
conservative assumption of high climate sensitivity might call for global
emissions reductions of 8 percent below the business-as-usual level in
2010 but still remain 40 percent above 1990 levels through 2100 before
declining.[32] The pathway would be revised from time to time in light of
new information. The emissions pathway would provide the basis for setting (and revising) a schedule of stepwise emissions limits over time,
rather than (as in the Kyoto Protocol) one target with no future path indi-
cated. The initial targets would have to strike a balance; they would have
to call for reductions that are large enough to make the new regime credible, stimulate business innovation and investment, and create sufficient
demand to jump-start international emissions trading, while at the same
time avoiding unrealistically stringent and excessively costly short-term
cuts.[33] Pathways and future targets would be revised from time to time in
light of new information and changed circumstances. They would form
the basis for determining individual country allowance allocations.

Simultaneous agreement on targets and implementation. Regulatory targets and obligations should not be adopted without simultaneous agreement on implementation and compliance methods (including flexibility
mechanisms) so that implementation costs and assurances of mutual commitment to recognize flexibility mechanisms would be known at the time

that emissions limitations are agreed to. The circumstance that no limitations commitments could be made until the basic elements of implementation and compliance-assurance arrangements were resolved would provide a strong impetus for prompt resolution of those matters. There are, to be sure, limits to how far such arrangements can be specified in advance. Some details of implementation rules may not be resolvable until the trading system comes into operation. Compliance arrangements in particular present many difficulties in the context of a global cap-and-trade system involving many diverse nations and private sector actors.

Eliminating unjustified restrictions on use of sinks. Existing restrictions on the use of sinks to meet the Kyoto Protocol emissions limitations obligations should be removed. Those include the Bonn accord Appendix Z country-by-country limits on credit for sinks; the denial of credits for conservation of existing forests (at least until such time as emissions from forest removal or alteration are included in emissions inventories and reporting); and the Marrakech accord prohibition on banking of sink credits. Consideration should also be given to removing the Marrakech accord restriction on the sale of sink credits under the clean development mechanism (no more than 1 percent of the selling country's base year emissions).[34] Appropriate default sequestration factors and accounting rules should be adopted to address special uncertainties in determining the effects of such activities on net emissions.

Improving the comprehensive approach. To include all emissions that affect global warming, international arrangements should build on the multigas approach adopted in the Framework Convention on Climate Change and in the Kyoto Protocol by including black carbon, sulfur dioxide, particulate matter, and other relevant emissions, at least in reporting and possibly in abatement-credit provisions. The Intergovernmental Panel on Climate Change should be asked to initiate a sustained, continuing process to revise or replace the global warming potential index (specifing the equivalency for regulatory purposes of the various greenhouse gases and sinks) to account for factors such as the following: changing marginal impacts under future atmospheric concentrations (saturation and intergas effects), discounting, damages rather than just physical effects, the damages associated with the rate of warming as contrasted with the level of warming, and nonwarming impacts (such as local health effects and carbon dioxide fertilization of plant growth). Uncertainty-weighted abatement credits (for both domestic abatement and international trading) should be adopted by employing appropriate default factors that take due account of relevant uncertainties for measuring source reductions and sink enhancements for different greenhouse gases, with an opportunity for countries (and, domestically, for sources) to justify claims for greater net emissions reductions by developing and demonstrating more accurate measurement methods.

Relaxing the Kyoto Protocol emissions trading "commitment period reserve" requirement. The Marrakech accord adopted an emissions trading reserve requirement that prohibits an Annex B country from selling emissions allowances or credits if by doing so it would retain less than 90 percent of its assigned amount for the five-year commitment period, or 100 percent of five times its most recently reviewed emissions inventory, whichever is lower.[35] That commitment period reserve requirement will limit abatement by countries with low marginal abatement costs and tend to inhibit aggressive investment in abatement technology innovation. It will also raise the transaction costs of allowance sales, which will all need to be checked against the treaty system's transaction log to ensure that the reserve requirement is not violated. The reserve requirement is clearly intended to prevent selling of "hot air" allowances in excess of current emissions, but that goal is dubious; it limits the value of headroom allowance assignments and in effect prevents the delivery of the side payments necessary to attract participation and thereby curtails the evolution toward global participation. Further, if Russia and Ukraine do not sell their "hot air," they will use it domestically, perhaps by increasing coal combustion to replace natural gas that they export to Europe, in which case limiting sales of hot air will not reduce global emissions; the reduction in emissions in Europe will assist the European Union in meeting its international obligations, but emissions in Russia and Ukraine will increase. The prospect of that parochial benefit for Europe may help explain the adoption of the reserve requirement. The effort to limit Russian and Ukrainian "hot air" may also be a move by non–Annex B countries to gain a greater share of sales revenue for the clean development mechanism. If the concern motivating the reserve requirement is that governments will be excessively optimistic about their ability to make up current sales of emissions allowances with future reductions or that unscrupulous government officials might oversell allowances and pocket the revenues (in official or underground bank accounts) while the country fails to curtail emissions in the future and as a result fails to comply, the better solution is to devise effective compliance-assurance arrangements (which are needed in any event), including buyer as well as seller liability, rather than to set an arbitrary limit on allowance transfers.

Reforming the clean development mechanism. A number of modifications to the clean development mechanism should be adopted. It should allow host country designation of sectorwide programs as clean development mechanism projects, such as a program to reduce emissions from the electric power sector in a country. Such an approach would improve the basis for certifying emission reduction credits under the clean development mechanism, reduce the potential for delays due to case-by-case clean development mechanism project reviews, reduce transaction costs, reduce the risks of project failure by diversifying risk across a broader portfolio of abatement investments, reduce the problem of emissions leakage, and reduce the potential for the clean development mechanism to function as a perverse subsidy for abatement that increases aggregate emissions. A sectorwide approach could also set the stage for large-scale bilateral or multilateral assistance agreements between a developing country and one or more industrialized countries and their firms, which would provide capital and technology to reduce greenhouse gas emissions on a sector or subsector level in exchange for credits. The clean development mechanism should be structured around a decentralized, market-based approach to investment decisions; its executive board should accredit monitoring and certification entities (including commercial firms and not-for-profit nongovernmental organizations) but resist allocating or managing investments. Clean development mechanism credits would be expected to sell at a lower profit than other tradable greenhouse gas emissions units because of the 2 percent adaptation fund charge and the higher transaction costs of the clean development mechanism. In addition, a discount should be imposed on the certified abatement value of clean development mechanism credits to reflect the lower environmental effectiveness (due to in-country leakage) of project-based reductions in a country without caps. The consequent lower profit of clean development mechanism credits would help remove the disincentive for developing countries to join a formal cap-and-trade regime.

Simplifying and strengthening the international trading system. The Kyoto trading system creates four different types of tradable units: assigned amount units for emissions trading under Articles 3 and 17; emission reduction units, which are project-based emissions credits recognized under the joint implementation provisions in Article 6; certified emission reduction credits, which are project-based emissions credits recognized under the clean development mechanism provisions in Article 12; and emission removal units for sink activities. The Marrakech accord treats those as fully fungible, so it is unclear why they should be denominated separately. Certainly, assigned amount units and emission reduction units should be merged. Certified emission reduction credits could remain distinct commodities (although traded in markets with assigned amount units and emission reduction units) to recognize the differential value of such credits. Further, joint implementation and the clean development mechanism would be phased out as the formal cap-and-trade system expands. To reduce transaction costs, the global emissions trading system would employ formal allowances traded on accredited organized exchanges.[36] Parties would agree not to interfere with international trade in allowances. Allowance trading would also be governed by WTO rules, perhaps as goods, as services, as investments, or as a new type of asset.[37] Parties would agree not to exercise market power in the allowance trading market and to be subject to remedies for market power, either under a special competition-antitrust agreement for the green-house gas cap-and-trade regime or under emerging cooperative multilateral approaches to applying and enforcing competition-antitrust policies generally.[38]

Improving the compliance-assurance regime. Compliance measures in the context of a global greenhouse gas regime include centralized strategies based on seller liability, under which nations or firms that sell allowances in excess of their actual abatement are subject to multilateral sanctions or other liabilities to induce compliance and to correct non-compliance. They also include more decentralized strategies such as buyer liability, under which allowances sold in excess of actual abatement are rendered invalid or discounted in value. That approach encourages buyers to police compliance and provides incentives for sellers to provide credible compliance commitments to boost the salability and value of their allowances. Buyer liability, however, would raise transaction costs. It could also discourage participation by developing countries whose political risk would be rated as high in trading markets. It is also possible to combine seller liability and buyer liability arrangements.[39] Some of the details of compliance-assurance arrangements may also have to be developed only as the trading system comes into operation, but the basic arrangements must be sufficiently established to make the trading system credible both for nations and for private actors.

The current Kyoto Protocol compliance arrangements should be strengthened by giving authority to the "enforcement" branch of the Compliance Committee to impose financial penalties and adverse publicity (shaming sanctions) for emissions exceeding allowances. Those could include a fine per ton of exceedance set at a rate higher than the expected market price for allowance purchases. Consideration should be given to requiring advance posting of assurance bonds to secure penalty payments. In addition, measures for buyer liability or a combination of seller and buyer liability arrangements should be seriously considered. Given the inevitable weaknesses of most treaty-based sanctioning and compliance regimes, a strong argument exists for also enlisting market-based incentives for compliance through a system of buyer liability. Financial penalties for exceedances could be dedicated, in whole or in part, to abatement investments, in the form of allowance purchases; that could be one means of implementing the "safety valve" concept.[40] Those and other measures, which are essential to ensure the environmental and economic integrity of tradable allowance rights, should be designed to ensure a comparable degree of compliance among parties to overcome U.S. fear of differential commitment. Private sector firms, investors, and other entities that will be important players in global trading are an important constituency that should support credible and consistent monitoring, reporting, and compliance arrangements.

Adaptation assistance. The industrialized countries should provide for assistance for poorer countries to take adaptive measures against adverse weather events and climate effects, whether due to anthropogenic global warming or to "natural" variability, with no need to determine causal responsibility. Such assistance would benefit poorer countries in the near term, rather than make them wait for decades for the long-term benefits of reduced global warming. Greater adaptive resilience would also help shield poorer countries against a wide range of adverse conditions (such as storms, floods, droughts, and disease) that are of immediate concern, regardless of whether they are caused by global warming.[41]

Mechanisms to foster evolution and updating of the global climate regulatory system. The participants in the global climate regime should continue investment in the Intergovernmental Panel on Climate Change and link its findings to treaty talks through periodic updating of emissions pathways and regulatory targets, global warming potential indexes, and monitoring and accounting procedures and rules, as discussed above. Adaptive management—learning and updating—is particularly valuable in cases such as climate change regulation that involve fundamental uncertainty about how the relevant ecological and social systems work.[42] Climate policy should be based on an evaluation of multiple scenarios regarding business-as-usual emissions levels, the warming effects of predicted emissions, climate sensitivity, the impacts of climate change on the environment and human welfare, and the cost of abatement and mitigation measures, rather than on a single "best" scenario. One approach is to use a collage of several conceptually different models, with predictions weighted by experts' relative confidence in the different models. In the face of uncertainty, policy measures should begin by instituting those that would be desirable under all the scenarios, either for reasons of climate protection or otherwise. Such measures could include reducing subsidies for energy use, reforming incentives for forest clearing, supporting basic research into low–greenhouse gas energy systems, improving the capacity for technology diffusion and application in developing countries, reducing emissions of air pollutants in ways that both protect human health from local and regional air pollutants and help prevent climate change, and making social and environmental systems more resilient against the effects of climate change.

To carry out that agenda, support should be sought from the market sector and its political allies within developing countries and from international development, poverty relief, and forest conservation organizations that may not worry primarily about climate change but that could see major benefits from greenhouse gas abatement investment flows to developing countries.

Domestic Components of U.S. Climate Strategy

We propose a two-step process for the adoption of domestic U.S. measures in tandem with the U.S. approach at the international level. The domestic first step would not impose binding greenhouse gas limitations but would lay the groundwork for adopting such measures in the near future, encourage voluntary emissions limitations and trading, and launch some of the nonregulatory elements of a serious U.S. climate policy. The February 2002 Bush administration climate policy proposals, including a national greenhouse gas intensity goal, strengthened mechanisms for registration of voluntary greenhouse gas reductions, potential development of credits against future regulation for early voluntary reductions, and tax and other incentives, can be regarded as making a beginning on that first step, but much more needs to be done. In conjunction with that first step, the United States would begin exploratory discussions with China (which might subsequently include other developing counties) about joint cap-and-trade arrangements. As the second step, the United States would adopt domestic greenhouse gas limitations using the comprehensive approach and domestic and international trading to the maximum feasible extent. Those limitations would be adopted only in conjunction with U.S. accession to an international climate agreement or agreements (either independent of the Kyoto Protocol or a substantially modified version of the Kyoto Protocol) with binding limitations, adequate compliance assurances, maximum scope for flexibility, developing country participation, and a sensible incremental time path to net greenhouse gas emissions reductions.

A U.S. commitment to adopt domestic limitations is essential for its international credibility and ability to promote a sound global climate regime. Emissions trading requires emissions caps at some level. The United States cannot persuasively advocate such flexibility mechanisms unless it eventually adopts caps itself. Nor, for similar reasons, can it persuade developing countries to join the emissions limitation effort unless it does so itself. On the other hand, the United States would not want to adopt a domestic regulatory program requiring significant emissions limitations except in conjunction with an international regime that includes the essential elements that we have identified. Thus, the timing and sequence of developments at the domestic and international levels will have to be carefully orchestrated. That will be a challenging task, given the need of a U.S. administration to persuade Congress and the number of other nations that must also be involved as participants or otherwise.

Domestic Step One: Goals, Monitoring, and Early Action Incentives. The first step in the domestic components of a U.S. climate policy would undertake measures to jump-start voluntary emissions reductions and emissions trading by using the power of information and the prospect of second-stage regulation to provide incentives for early limitations efforts. First-step measures would include eight elements.

Organization and planning. Policymakers should establish a government-wide Climate Policy Office, headquartered in the White House, that would lead an intensive program of information gathering and analysis on policies to limit net greenhouse gas emissions. That office would also study needed changes or consolidations in existing federal agencies' authorities and programs and the potential creation of new agencies, authorities, and programs. Such an office has already existed for several years (in both the Clinton-Gore and senior Bush administrations) under the rubric of a task force or working group.

In addition, policymakers should adopt a national plan for limiting U.S. net greenhouse gas emissions with quantitative goals and timetables (expressed in terms of greenhouse gas intensity of output as well as emissions), set, for example, over a ten-year period (as in the Bush proposal) but with interim milestones. Such a plan would form the basis for the U.S. proposals on its international emissions limitations commitments.

Policymakers should restructure the administration's National Energy Strategy to address greenhouse gas limitations goals and means. The country may need to expand the supply of energy, especially cleaner energy, by freeing up regulatory bottlenecks and other steps, but at the same time it needs to redirect energy supply and demand toward lower greenhouse gas intensity, at least or especially where private markets lack the long-term planning horizon and collective action to invest in such long-term collective goals. Greater greenhouse gas efficiency will require both more energy efficiency and greater use of cleaner energy.

Government fiscal initiatives. Policymakers should develop a program of low–greenhouse gas technology R&D, with an emphasis on basic science. The focus should be on research projects that provide long-run benefits, surmount coordination hurdles, and would not otherwise be undertaken by the private sector. Elements of such an initiative would include publicly funded research programs, tax and other incentives for private sector undertakings, and private-public partnerships.

Federal and state governments should also invest in programs to reduce net greenhouse gas emissions by the government sector.

Removing barriers. Policymakers should identify and correct market barriers and nonmarket barriers (including existing government programs and policies) to the adoption of measures to reduce energy use and otherwise reduce greenhouse gas emissions, including barriers that blunt market incentives that would otherwise operate to promote adoption of such measures. Examples could include reducing government programs that subsidize excess energy consumption; easing Clean Air Act New

Source Review restrictions on modifications of facilities that would reduce greenhouse gas emissions; and devising a "pay at the pump" method for collecting automobile insurance premiums.[43]

Informational measures. Policymakers should create a national climate protection scorecard. Once a national plan with goals for limiting U.S. net greenhouse gas emissions had been established, a year-to-year national scorecard would be created by the White House Climate Policy Office and publicized by the president. The scorecard would rate progress in meeting the national plan goals in light of fluctuations in the level of economic activity and other major variables.

Policymakers should also establish comprehensive greenhouse gas emissions monitoring, record keeping, and reporting procedures for domestic sources and sinks. That information would be used to establish a Climate Release Inventory, akin to the Toxics Release Inventory, to record and publicize net emissions of greenhouse gases by U.S. entities. It would also be used to construct the national climate protection scorecard. That information system should include default values for hard-to-measure gases, sources, and sinks that take into account measurement uncertainties and a procedure for private entities to demonstrate more accurate measurement methods. Policymakers should phase in mandatory monitoring and reporting for domestic sources and sinks.

Voluntary limitations programs for the private sector. Policymakers should establish subsidiary goals for net greenhouse gas limitations by industry sectors.

The president would be authorized to contract (perhaps through a federal agency such as the Environmental Protection Agency or the Department of Energy) with business and other private entities to achieve reductions in net greenhouse gas emissions relative to specified baselines, in return for certified reduction credits that could be applied against future emissions limitation regulations.[44] Credits would be accorded to actions taken outside as well as within the United States and would be recorded in a central registry, on terms comparable to the Kyoto Protocol emissions trading systems. A major challenge in such a system of credit for early action is how to establish the baseline for credits and prevent gaming of the baseline. The credit system should award credit only to early abatement actions that meet exacting criteria for additional, verified, actually achieved reductions below baseline net emissions.[45] Such a system could also accord favorable government publicity and recognition for those who make and meet voluntary limitations commitments. Clearly, firms already interested in reducing emissions would favor such a program; the challenge is to engage firms to do more than they would have done otherwise and engage additional firms. One step in that direction is to accord cost-saving regulatory flexibility to voluntary actions that go "beyond compliance" by reducing air pollutants (including greenhouse gases as copollutants) more than required by existing law (similar to the EPA's Project XL). If such regulatory flexibility is or could be restricted by law (as it has often been under Project XL), new statutory authority for according such flexibility could be provided.

Multipollutant regulatory legislation. Policymakers should adopt multipollutant legislation that would regulate carbon dioxide and possibly other greenhouse gases, as well as a number of air pollutants already regulated, through an integrated cap-and-trade system for selected sectors, such as utilities and industrial sources, that emit those gases in large quantities, or for the entire economy. Current bills in Congress would enact a new air pollution regulatory law with a three pollutant strategy (sulfur oxides, nitrogen oxides, and mercury) or a four pollutant strategy (those three plus carbon dioxide) for electric power plants. The administration's "Clean Skies" proposal calls for legislation on the three pollutants; it would provide for major reductions in sulfur oxides, nitrogen oxides, and mercury. If, however, such legislation were enacted, a separate law for carbon dioxide and possibly other greenhouse gases might be adopted only a few years later. A "three pollutant plus carbon dioxide later" approach threatens to be inefficient; it requires investments in plants and equipment to reduce sulfur oxides, nitrogen oxides, and mercury that may later need to be scrapped or retrofitted to reduce carbon dioxide. Also, some efforts to reduce sulfur oxides and nitrogen oxides may increase carbon dioxide emissions; for example, stack gas scrubbers may require more fuel combustion per energy output to yield equal energy output (a risk-risk tradeoff). Thus, legislation that includes carbon dioxide and perhaps other greenhouse gases may be more efficient by giving industry a consistent, single set of regulatory requirements to guide investment in measures that reduce all four pollutants in concert.[46] Indeed, legislation should probably include at least five pollutants (including methane and possibly other greenhouse gases as well) or include at least the option to offset carbon dioxide emissions with methane and other greenhouse gas reductions as well as sink enhancements. But limits on greenhouse gases may be premature in this domestic first step, pending international agreement and the domestic second step (described below). Another option might be a "three and a half" bill that sets limits on sulfur oxides, nitrogen oxides, and mercury and imposes informational requirements on carbon dioxide and credits against future regulations. Any legislation addressing carbon dioxide and other greenhouse gases domestically should provide maximum scope for sink enhancement and allowance trading, both domestically and internationally. Such legislation would make a start on greenhouse gas regulation, limited to one or a few sectors, with the expectation that regulation of greenhouse gases could be extended to other sectors subsequently.

Initiatives to promote domestic and international emissions trading. To help establish a sound infrastructure for international emissions trading, the United States should encourage international emissions trading by U.S. firms and support the development of international monitoring protocols, accounting rules, and registries to support international trading by and with participants in domestic trading. In the first-step phase, the United States could allow certified early reduction credits to be traded domestically and internationally (subject, as discussed above, to the challenge of defining and enforcing credible baselines). In addition, the United States could establish a registry for all net greenhouse gas emissions and reductions, including reductions achieved abroad as well as domestically. The United States could establish comprehensive greenhouse gas monitoring, record keeping, and reporting procedures for projects financed outside the United States (by building on experience with transnational project-level initiatives to reduce greenhouse gas emissions and clean development mechanism discussions in cooperation with evolving international arrangements). The United States could also extend credit recognition (good against future U.S. greenhouse gas emissions limitation regulation) to allowances or credits generated by the domestic regulatory systems of other countries, including developing countries, on a principle of mutual recognition (that is, if other countries commit to recognizing U.S. credits or allowances). The United States could coordinate the U.S. registry to record credits, trades, and holdings with registries maintained by other governments and international organizations in a move to establish a single international registry. The United States could actively support the development of such an international registry for emissions credits and allowances.

Designing a U.S. greenhouse gas regulatory program. Policymakers should design a domestic U.S. cap-and-trade system, including consideration of sectoral design (for example, electricity and transportation); point of application (upstream, downstream, mixed designs); and other regulatory or incentive measures for sectors and activities where trading may not be feasible. In addition, policymakers should study the design and feasibility of a hybrid trading and fee system, in which target exceedances trigger a noncompliance penalty that is equivalent to a price at which the government will sell extra allowances (a "safety valve") and possibly use the revenue to invest in abatement efforts both domestically and internationally. Policymakers should also study trading in emissions intensity allowances, options for incorporating sink enhancement credits in an allowance trading system, and the design, equity, and efficiency characteristics of programs (such as allowance allocations) to ease impacts on sectors and localities that will be hard hit by greenhouse gas regulation.

Domestic Step Two: U.S. Greenhouse Gas Cap-and-Trade Program. Building on the groundwork established in the first step of domestic greenhouse gas policy, and in conjunction with accession to an international greenhouse gas emissions limitation and trading system that incorporates the basic elements previously discussed, the United States would take five measures.

First, it would adopt domestic regulatory net emissions limitations, with primary reliance on a cap-and-trade regime using a comprehensive approach to all greenhouse gases, plus supplemental regulatory measures. Ideally, that regime would be part of an integrated multipollutant strategy also addressing sulfur oxides, nitrogen oxides, mercury, and related emissions, as described above. Caps would be set as cumulative limits for a substantial period (for example, five or ten years, or with banking and borrowing), on the basis of national and sectoral emissions limitation targets expressed in terms of emissions amounts and emissions intensity. Maximum opportunities for international as well as domestic trading should be incorporated into the system. Allocation of allowances could be by auction or government issuance without charge or a combination of the two; issuance by the government without charge has potential efficiency drawbacks but can contribute significantly to securing legislative adoption of greenhouse gas regulation.

Second, greenhouse gas regulation could be phased in by sector—for example, utilities and transportation might be first. But other sources should have opportunities to opt in (as in the U.S. sulfur dioxide trading program).

Third, maximum opportunities for international trading should be built into the system by designing and operating it to allow ready import and export of allowances (or other tradable units) with full fungibility of domestic and foreign allowances and appropriate recording and regulatory credit and debit arrangements. The United States should have much to gain and can set a useful precedent for the world by establishing a domestic trading system that is as open and integrated with international trading and the domestic trading system of other countries as possible.[47]

Fourth, penalties for noncompliance with net emissions reductions targets set by the federal government could include financial penalties, debiting of future allowance allocations, tightening of caps, raising the safety valve (excess allowance purchase) price, and other measures. The potential domestic U.S. policy implications of an international regime of buyer liability should be carefully considered.

Fifth, the United States could possibly adopt programs (beyond issuance of allowances without charge) to ease the impact of greenhouse gas emissions limitations on the most adversely affected sectors (including especially workers) and localities; funds might be provided by recycling revenues from sales of excess permits. A better way of addressing this distributional issue may be to assign extra allowances to sectors and locales likely to be more heavily burdened by the cap-and-trade regime. Such an approach was used in the sulfur dioxide allowance trading system created in 1990 to reduce acid rain. Initial research indicates that only modest allowance allocations would be needed to shield the hardest-hit industries (and thereby overcome their opposition to the program).[48]

8

Conclusion

With the Kyoto Protocol likely to enter into force in early 2003, the major climate policy issues remaining are the potential participation of the United States, China, and other major emitting developing countries, as well as further improvements in the Kyoto Protocol's regulatory design and the development of a rational target-setting process. Unexpectedly, the gaps in the Kyoto Protocol and the Bonn and Marrakech accords and the failure of the United States to join have set the stage for an even better result: the simultaneous accession of the United States and China (and other major developing country emitters) to a global cap-and-trade regime, along with improvements in the existing international climate regulatory regime.

Those changes will not be easily accomplished. The U.S. government and public must take an appropriately broad view of the national interest. They must take account of the substantial cost savings from the comprehensive approach and global emissions trading as well as the multiple benefits of securing participation by China, India, and other developing countries. The European Union and other current participants in the Kyoto Protocol regime must give priority to ensuring that the planet's health and well-being are protected at reasonable cost instead of imposing blame and rehashing past differences; they must accordingly recognize the necessity of engaging participation by the United States, China, and other major developing countries, with sensible targets and cost-effective implementation mechanisms.

Meanwhile, participation in an international greenhouse gas regulatory regime by China, India, and other major developing countries will occur only if participation appears to them to be in their interest. The climate regime must be structured to engage such participation. The most efficient way to do so, we have argued, is through assignment of headroom tradable greenhouse gas emissions allowances in the context of a global cap-and-trade system.

We recognize that our proposed strategy might, at least for a number of years, yield two or more parallel international climate regimes: the Kyoto Protocol regime and one or more regimes involving the United States and the major developing countries (as well, possibly, as some Annex B industrialized countries). If such a multiple track system operated for a while, it would provide valuable experience for the design of a single global regime that might eventually emerge,[1] perhaps after those regimes became functionally connected through interregime trading of allowances. Such an approach would likely be far superior, on both economic and environmental grounds, to the present prospect of a limited Kyoto Protocol regime that omits half or more of global greenhouse gas emissions. If a multiple track system persisted indefinitely, however, it would inhibit allowance trading across the regimes. Precisely the economic interests in promoting such trading are likely to lead the separate regimes to interconnect and ultimately to merge into a global trading system—via private trading and arbitrage if not via formal negotiations. And the interest of the Kyoto Protocol parties in allowance price stability is likely to lead those parties to prefer joint accession by the United States, China, and other major emitters into the Kyoto Protocol regime—that is, a full merger of the Kyoto Protocol regime and the parallel regime we have proposed here—over piecemeal accession by the United States, China, or others individually.

The present situation poses a moment of truth for those advocating global climate protection. The easy route is to lambaste the United States for its current stance but do nothing to bring the United States on board. In our view, jawboning the United States (or developing countries) will have very limited impact. The more serious route is to design a strategy that will engage the United States and major developing countries in an effective and efficient global regime. We believe that engaging the United States also depends on engaging China and other major developing countries in a cap-and-trade regime, for without them, the United States will not join. And, eventually, it means fashioning a modified version of the Kyoto Protocol, with developing country participation in a cap-and-trade system, full comprehensiveness (in gases, sources, and sinks), full scope for flexibility mechanisms such as emissions trading, better compliance assurances, and more sensible target pathways. It is in the national interest of the United States to take the necessary initiatives to build such a regime and to join it.

Notes

Chapter 1: Introduction and Summary

1. The European Union ratified the Kyoto Protocol on May 31, 2002, Japan ratified on June 4, 2002, Poland on December 13, 2002, and Canada on December 17, 2002. By December 20, 2002, the total was one hundred countries representing 43.7 percent of Annex I carbon dioxide emissions in 1990. See the UN Framework Convention on Climate Change Web site, www.unfccc.int. But the United States, Russia, Australia, Kazakhstan, and Ukraine have not ratified. See Natsource, "Japan Ratifies Kyoto and Plans for Implementation" and "Australian PM Clarifies His Position on Kyoto Protocol," *Airtrends* 5 (7) (July 3, 2002): 5; "Australia, U.S. Reach Alternative Climate Change Agreement," *Australian Broadcasting Corporation News Online* (July 11, 2002); Natsource, "Canada Floats Climate Options Paper, EU Ratifies Kyoto Protocol," *Airtrends* 5 (6) (May 31, 2002): 1.

2. Under Article 25 of the Kyoto Protocol, the treaty will enter into force after ratification by fifty-five countries representing at least 55 percent of the 1990 carbon dioxide emissions of Annex I (industrialized) countries.

3. The Carbon Dioxide Information Analysis Center reports country shares of global fossil-fuel carbon dioxide emissions: United States 23.7 percent, China 13.5 percent, Russia 6 percent, Japan 4.9 percent, India 4.6 percent, Brazil 1.3 percent, Indonesia 1 percent. See Carbon Dioxide Information Analysis Center at Oak Ridge National Laboratory, "National Fossil-Fuel CO_2 Emissions," available at www.cdiac.esd.ornl.gov/trends/emis/tre_coun.htm (visited February 8, 2002) (showing data for 1998). Country shares of total greenhouse gas emissions may be somewhat different but are not available with precision because most developing countries do not yet report their emissions of greenhouse gases other than carbon dioxide. The United States reports that carbon dioxide emissions account for 82 percent of its total greenhouse gas emissions. U.S. Department of State, *U.S. Climate Action Report 2002* (Third National Communication to the United Nations Framework Convention on Climate Change) (Washington, D.C.: Government Printing Office, May 2002): 5, available at www.epa.gov/global warming/publications/car/index.html (visited June 4, 2002). Total greenhouse

gas emissions data for industrialized countries are available in UN Framework Convention on Climate Change COP-4, "Review of the Implementation of Commitments and of Other Provisions of the Convention: Summary Compilation of Annual Greenhouse Gas Emissions Inventory Data from Annex I Parties," FCCC/CP/1998/INF.9, October 31, 1998, available at www.unfccc.int/resource/docs/cop4/inf09.pdf (visited May 14, 2002).

4. See Andrew C. Revkin, "Bush Offers Plan for Voluntary Measures to Limit Gas Emissions," New York Times, February 15, 2002; Office of the White House Press Secretary, "President Announces Clear Skies and Global Climate Change Initiatives," February 14, 2002, available at www.whitehouse.gov/news/releases/2002/02/20020214-5.html (visited February 14, 2002); Andrew C. Revkin, "U.S. Is Pressuring Industries to Cut Greenhouse Gases," New York Times, January 20, 2003 (reporting Bush administration efforts to enlist voluntary reductions).

5. See Carbon Dioxide Information Analysis Center at Oak Ridge National Laboratory, "National Fossil-Fuel CO_2 Emissions."

6. Absent the United States (and assuming no exercise of monopoly power by allowance sellers), several economic models predict that the Kyoto treaty's environmental effectiveness and greenhouse gas emissions allowance prices would drop essentially to zero. See Mustafa H. Babiker, Henry D. Jacoby, John M. Reilly, and David M. Reiner, "The Evolution of a Climate Regime: Kyoto to Marrakech," Report 82, MIT Joint Program on the Science and Policy of Global Change, February 2002, 12–13, available at web.mit.edu/globalchange/www/abstracts.html#a82 (finding no net effect on emissions); Andreas Löschel and ZhongXiang Zhang, "The Economic and Environmental Implications of the U.S. Repudiation of the Kyoto Protocol and the Subsequent Deals in Bonn and Marrakech," FEEM Working Paper 23.2002, April 2002, available at www.papers.ssrn.com/abstract=299463 (finding allowance prices drop to zero); Carlo Carraro, Barbara Buchner, and Igor Cersosimo, "On the Consequences of the U.S. Withdrawal from the Kyoto/Bonn Protocol," FEEM Working Paper 102.2001, December 2001, 9 and table 1, available at www.papers.ssrn.com/abstract=296930 (summarizing studies finding that U.S. withdrawal will reduce allowance prices in 2010 by 13 to 100 percent). Still, other factors could keep allowance prices above zero and yield some net reduction in emissions by participating countries, such as Russian exercise of monopoly power see Babiker et al., "The Evolution of a Climate Regime," and Löschel and Zhang, "The Economic and Environmental Implications of the U.S. Repudiation of the Kyoto Protocol." For Russian withdrawal from the treaty, see Carraro, Buchner, and Cersosimo, "On the Consequences of the U.S. Withdrawal from the Kyoto/Bonn Protocol." For reduced investment in energy-saving R&D, see Carraro, Buchner, and Cersosimo, "On the Consequences of the U.S. Withdrawal from the Kyoto/Bonn Protocol." For Russian banking of allowances to sell in later trading periods and anticipatory abatement by U.S. sources, see Alan S. Manne and Richard G. Richels, "U.S. Rejection of the Kyoto Protocol: The Impact on Compliance Costs and CO_2

Emissions," Working Paper 01-12, AEI–Brookings Joint Center for Regulatory Studies, October 2001, available at www.aei.brookings.org/publications/work ing/working_01_12.pdf.

7. A useful survey and comparison of alternatives to the Kyoto Protocol is provided by Scott Barrett and Robert Stavins, "Increasing Participation and Compliance in International Climate Change Agreements," draft, May 2002 (on file with authors). Examples include: (1) carbon taxes, see Richard Cooper, "Toward a Real Global Warming Treaty," *Foreign Affairs* 77 (2) (1998): 66–79; William D. Nordhaus, "After Kyoto: Alternative Mechanisms to Control Global Warming," paper prepared for a joint session of the American Economic Association and the Association of Environmental and Resource Economics, January 4, 2002, available at www.econ.yale.edu/~nordhaus/homepage/ PostKyoto_v4.pdf; (2) allowance trading with a "safety valve" trigger price at which unlimited additional allowances could be purchased, see Raymond Kopp, Richard Morgenstern, and William Pizer, "Something for Everyone: A Climate Policy That Both Environmentalists and Industry Can Live With," *Weathervane* (Washington, D.C.: Resources for the Future, September 1997); Joseph E. Aldy, Peter R. Orszag, and Joseph E. Stiglitz, "Climate Change: An Agenda for Global Collective Action," Pew Center on Global Climate Change, October 2001, available at www.pewclimate.org/media/stiglitz.pdf; David Victor, *The Collapse of the Kyoto Protocol and the Struggle to Slow Global Warming* (Princeton: Princeton University Press, 2001); (3) assignment of allowances at business-as-usual forecast levels and purchase by a central international body funded by interested national governments, see David F. Bradford, "Improving on Kyoto: Greenhouse Gas Control as the Purchase of a Global Public Good," Global Public Good Model Version 01, Princeton University and New York University, April 30, 2002 (copy on file with authors); (4) technological R & D and technology standards, see Scott Barrett, "Towards a Better Climate Treaty," *Policy Matters* 01-29, AEI–Brookings Joint Center for Regulatory Studies, November 2001; (5) a climate "Marshall Plan" with development assistance to poorer countries and agreed abatement actions by industrialized countries, see Thomas C. Schelling, *Costs and Benefits of Greenhouse Gas Reduction* (Washington, D.C.: AEI Press, 1998); (6) domestic trading with no international trading, see Warwick J. McKibbin, "Moving Beyond Kyoto," *Policy Brief* no. 66, Brookings Institution, October 2000; and (7) a series of diverse policy experiments, see Robert W. Hahn, *The Economics and Politics of Climate Change* (Washington, D.C.: AEI Press, 1998).

8. Byrd-Hagel Resolution, S. Res. 98, *Congressional Record* 143 (July 25, 1997): S8113–39; "Climate Change: Senate Approves Resolution to Require Binding Controls on Developing Nations," *Environment Reporter* 28 (BNA) (August 1, 1997): 621.

9. See John M. Broder, "Clinton Adamant on Third World Role in Climate Accord," *New York Times,* December 12, 1997. Opined the *New York Times* a year later: "[T]he giant developing countries like India and China have yet to be

brought on board. Until that happens, Senate ratification is out of the question." "Remember Global Warming?" editorial, *New York Times,* November 11, 1998.

10. See, for example, Victor, *Collapse of the Kyoto Protocol;* John K. Setear, "Learning to Live with Losing: International Environmental Law in the New Millennium," *Virginia Environmental Law Journal* 20 (2001): 139.

11. For a summary of the decisions made at Bonn and Marrakech, see Babiker et al., "The Evolution of a Climate Regime." The official documents are available at the UN Framework Convention on Climate Change Web site, www.unfccc.int.

12. See Revkin, "Bush Offers Plan for Voluntary Measures to Limit Gas Emissions"; Office of the White House Press Secretary, "President Announces Clear Skies and Global Climate Change Initiatives."

13. See Richard B. Stewart and Jonathan B. Wiener, "A Comprehensive Approach to Climate Change," *American Enterprise* 1 (6) (November–December 1990): 75; U.S. Department of Justice, *A Comprehensive Approach to Global Climate Change* (Washington, D.C.: Government Printing Office, 1991); Richard B. Stewart and Jonathan B. Wiener, "A Comprehensive Approach to Climate Change Policy: Issues of Design and Practicality," *Arizona Journal of International and Comparative Law* 9 (1992): 83, 85.

14. The history is detailed in Jonathan B. Wiener, "Something Borrowed for Something Blue: Legal Transplants and the Evolution of Global Environmental Law," *Ecology Law Quarterly* 27 (2001): 1295.

15. See S. 556 (Clean Power Act of 2001), introduced by Senator Jim Jeffords, March 15, 2002, and reported out of the Committee on Environment and Public Works, June 27, 2001; Jim Jeffords, "Unhealthy Air," *New York Times,* June 30, 2002; Natsource, "Jeffords Multi-Emissions Bill S. 556 Passes Committee Vote," *Airtrends* 5 (7) (July 3, 2002): 1 (reporting 10–9 vote on June 27 in favor of S. 556 to regulate emissions of sulfur oxide, nitrogen oxide, mercury, and carbon dioxide). In early 2003, a bipartisan bill was introduced to create an economywide cap-and-trade program covering all greenhouse gases from all major sectors. See Katharine Q. Seelye, "McCain and Lieberman Offer Bill to Require Cuts in Gases," *New York Times,* January 9, 2003.

16. For details on the National Academy of Sciences report, the Environmental Protection Agency's report to the Framework Convention on Climate Change, and the Bush proposal, see chapters 2 and 5. On the states' initiatives, see James Sterngold, "State Officials Ask Bush to Act on Global Warming," *New York Times,* July 17, 2002; Eileen Claussen, "The Global Warming Dropout," *New York Times,* June 7, 2002.

17. See C. Boyden Gray, "Energy and Environmental Policy after September 2001," *ABA National Resources and Environment* 16 (Winter 2002): 153; Thomas L. Friedman, "Drilling for Freedom," op-ed, *New York Times,* October 20, 2002.

18. See A. Denny Ellerman, Henry D. Jacoby, and Annelene Decaux, "The Effects on Developing Countries of the Kyoto Protocol and CO_2 Emissions Trading," Report 41, MIT Joint Program on the Science and Policy of Global Change, December 1, 1998, table 1 (indicating that the Kyoto Protocol would require a

24 percent reduction below the business-as-usual level in 2010 for all Annex B countries); Richard Richels, personal communication, January 27, 2002 (using Manne and Richels MERGE model to estimate that the Kyoto Protocol would require a 17 percent reduction below the business-as-usual level in 2010 for all Annex B countries). A key difference between the Ellerman, Jacoby, and Decaux estimates and the Manne and Richels estimates is that Manne and Richels forecast lower business-as-usual levels in 2010 for Russia (and Eastern Europe) and therefore a greater quantity of allowances available to Russia to sell (294 million tons compared with Ellerman and colleagues' 111 million tons), which diminishes somewhat the aggregate emissions reduction required of all Annex B countries.

19. Richard G. Richels, personal communication, January 27, 2002. See Ellerman, Jacoby, and Decaux, "The Effects on Developing Countries of the Kyoto Protocol and CO_2 Emissions Trading," 4 and table 1. Ellerman and colleagues' forecast of the U.S. share of total Annex B reductions below the business-as-usual level in 2010 is lower (just under 50 percent) than the Manne and Richels forecast (81 percent) because of the latter study's lower business-as-usual emissions forecast for countries in transition and the resulting reduction in Annex B requirements, which in turn raises the percentage of that aggregate reduction represented by the United States. See also William D. Nordhaus, "Global Warming Economics," *Science* 294 (November 9, 2001): 1283, figure 3 (finding that almost 100 percent of the net costs of the Kyoto Protocol and about 70 percent of the costs to OECD countries would be borne by the United States).

20. Some endorsement of the view that human activities are likely to cause adverse climate change is reflected in the latest U.S. report to the United Nations. See U.S. Department of State, *U.S. Climate Action Report 2002*. The report emphasizes "considerable uncertainties," chap. 6, "Introduction," 1, but also states that "[s]ince preindustrial time (i.e., since about 1750), concentrations of these greenhouse gases [carbon dioxide, methane, and nitrous oxide] have increased by 31, 151, and 17 percent, respectively. This increase has altered the chemical composition of the Earth's atmosphere and has likely affected the global climate system." Ibid., chap. 1, 5. The report details the adverse effects of climate change on the United States. On the political reaction, see Andrew C. Revkin, "U.S. Sees Problems in Climate Change," *New York Times,* June 3, 2002; Katherine Q. Seelye, "President Distances Himself from Global Warming Report," *New York Times,* June 5, 2002.

21. See Carbon Dioxide Information Analysis Center at Oak Ridge National Laboratory, "National Fossil-Fuel CO_2 Emissions."

22. See the proposals cited in note 7 of this chapter and evaluated in chapter 5.

23. For a more detailed discussion of the design of cost-effective side payments to engage participation in an effective multilateral climate change treaty, including "headroom" allowances and alternatives, see Jonathan Baert Wiener, "Global Environmental Regulation: Instrument Choice in Legal Context," *Yale Law Journal* 108 (1999): 677.

Chapter 2: Prudent Investment in Regulation to Mitigate Climate Change

1. See Intergovernmental Panel on Climate Change, Working Group I, "Climate Change 2001: The Scientific Basis—Summary for Policymakers and Technical Summary," 2001, 8, 36–47.

2. For example, relative to one kilogram of carbon dioxide = 1, the global warming potential over a 100-year time horizon for one kilogram of methane is 23, for nitrous oxide is 296, for carbon tetrafluoride is 5,700, for trifluoromethane is 12,000, and for sulfurhexafluoride is 22,200. Ibid., 47 and table 3. For further discussion of the global warming potential index and its revision, see chap. 2, n. 33, and chap. 5, n. 35.

3. Some actions being taken for other reasons may have the effect of reducing the growth of greenhouse gas emissions. For example, market-driven incentives for resource efficiency, in both industrialized and developing countries, are causing some reduction in greenhouse gas to GDP intensity. And existing and future regulatory measures aimed at environmental problems other than global climate change, including performance-based regulation of sulfur dioxide and nitrogen oxide emissions from fossil-fuel combustion, may have the side effect of reducing carbon dioxide and other greenhouse gas emissions by inducing fuel conservation and fuel switching (although they may at the same time contribute to warming by limiting air pollutants such as sulfur dioxide that exert a reflective cooling effect). Anticipation of post-2012 emissions limits may also affect present investment decisions enough to reduce U.S. emissions in 2012 below the business-as-usual forecast even without U.S. ratification of the Kyoto Protocol, although the extent of such anticipatory abatement depends in part on the likely availability of allowances from other countries to meet the post-2012 target. Alan S. Manne and Richard G. Richels, "U.S. Rejection of the Kyoto Protocol: The Impact on Compliance Costs and CO_2 Emissions," Working Paper 01-12, AEI–Brookings Joint Center for Regulatory Studies, October 2001, available at www.aei.brookings.org/publications/working/working_01_12.pdf.

4. Intergovernmental Panel on Climate Change, Working Group I, "Climate Change 2001"; Committee on the Science of Climate Change, *Climate Change Science: An Analysis of Some Key Questions* (Washington, D.C.: National Academy Press, 2001).

5. See Kirk A. Smith, "The Basics of Greenhouse Gas Indices," chap. 2 in Peter Hayes and Kirk Smith, eds., *The Global Greenhouse Regime: Who Pays? Science, Economics, and North-South Politics in the Climate Change Convention* (New York: United Nations University Press, 1993), available at www.unu.edu/unupress/unupbooks/80836e/80836E00.htm. Each year's net emissions of carbon dioxide have been increasing global concentrations by about one to two parts per million, or about .3 to .5 percent per year. See the atmospheric carbon dioxide records from Mauna Loa Observatory kept by C. D. Keeling and T. P. Whorf et al. at www.cdiac.ornl.gov/ftp/ndp001/maunaloa.co2.

6. See U.S. Department of State, *U.S. Climate Action Report 2002* (Third National Communication to the United Nations Framework Convention on Climate Change) (Washington, D.C.: Government Printing Office, May 2002), available at www.epa.gov/globalwarming/publications/car/index.html.

7. National Assessment Synthesis Team, U.S. Global Change Research Program, *Climate Change Impacts on the United States: The Potential Consequences of Climate Variability and Change* (Washington, D.C.: U.S. Global Change Research Program, 2001), available at www.usgcrp.gov/usgcrp/nacc/default.htm.

8. The National Assessment Synthesis Team relied on two models. One supposed a 2.7 degree Celsius change while the second model considered a 4.4 degree Celsius change. See Committee on the Science of Climate Change, *Climate Change Science,* 19.

9. See Jonathan Baert Wiener, "Protecting the Global Environment," in John D. Graham and Jonathan Baert Wiener, eds., *Risk vs. Risk: Tradeoffs in Protecting Health and the Environment* (Cambridge: Harvard University Press, 1995), chap. 10; Robert Mendelsohn, *The Greening of Global Warming* (Washington, D.C.: AEI Press, 1999); U.S. Department of State, *U.S. Climate Action Report 2002.*

10. See Intergovernmental Panel on Climate Change, "Climate Change 2001," 72–74.

11. For discussion of adaptation measures, see Mendelsohn, *The Greening of Global Warming;* Pierre Crosson, "Agriculture and Climate Change," in Michael Toman, ed., *Climate Change Economics and Policy: An RFF Anthology* (Washington, D.C.: Resources for the Future, 2001), 61; Roger A. Sedjo and Brent Sohngen, "Forests in Climate Change," in Michael Toman, ed., *Climate Change Economics and Policy,* 75; Intergovernmental Panel on Climate Change, "Climate Change 2001: Impacts, Adaptation, and Vulnerability," 2001, 8. See also N. J. Rosenberg, P. R. Crosson, K. D. Frederick, W. E. Easterling, M. S. McKenny, M. D. Bowes, R. A. Sedjo, J. Darmstadter, L. A. Katz, and K. M. Lemon, "The MINK Methodology: Background and Baseline," in N. J. Rosenberg, ed., *Towards an Integrated Impact Assessment of Climate Change: The MINK Study* (Dordrecht, Netherlands: Kluwer Academic Publishers, 1993); R. M. Adams, B. A. McCarl, D. J. Dudek, and J. D. Glyer, "Implications of Global Climate Change for Western Agriculture," *Western Journal of Agricultural Economics* 13 (1988): 348; Daniel J. Dudek, "Assessing the Implications of Changes in Carbon Dioxide Concentrations and Climate for Agriculture in the United States," in John C. Topping, ed., *Proceedings of the First North American Conference on Preparing for Climate Change: A Cooperative Approach* (Rockville, Md.: Government Institutes, Inc., April 1988), 428–50; Daniel J. Dudek, *Climate Change Impacts upon Agriculture and Resources: A Case Study of California* (New York: Environmental Defense Fund, 1990).

12. Charles D. Kolstad and Michael Toman, "The Economics of Climate Change," Discussion Paper 00-40REV, Resources for the Future, June 2001, 23. For examples of the difficulties in generating aggregate damage estimates, see William Cline, *The Economics of Global Warming* (Washington, D.C.: Institute for International Economics, 1992).

13. Richard Tol, "New Estimates of the Damage Costs of Climate Change, Part I: Benchmark Estimates," *Environmental and Resource Economics* 21 (2002): 47; Richard Tol, "New Estimates of the Damage Costs of Climate Change, Part II: Dynamic Estimates," *Environmental and Resource Economics* 21 (2002): 135.

14. Ibid.

15. See Jason Shogren and Michael Toman, "How Much Climate Change Is Too Much? An Economics Perspective," *Climate Change Issues Brief* no. 25, Resources for the Future, September 2000, 10. A recent study by Nordhaus found about a .5 percent loss in U.S. GDP on the basis of a 2.5 degree Celsius rise in temperature. See William D. Nordhaus and Joseph Boyer, *Warming the World: Economic Models of Global Warming* (Cambridge: MIT Press, 2000), 91.

16. See John Reilly, Mustafa Babiker, and Monika Mayer, "Comparing Greenhouse Gases," Report 77, MIT Joint Program on the Science and Policy of Global Change, July 2001, available at www.mit.edu/globalchange/www/MITJPSPGC_Rpt77.pdf.

17. See Richard Newell and William Pizer, "Discounting the Benefits of Climate Change Mitigation: How Much Do Uncertain Rates Increase Valuations?" Resources for the Future paper for the Pew Center on Climate Change, November 2001.

18. Richard J. Revesz, "Environmental Regulation, Cost-Benefit Analysis, and the Discounting of Human Lives," *Columbia Law Review* 99 (1999): 941; Paul R. Portney and John P. Weyant, eds., *Discounting and Intergenerational Equity* (Washington, D.C.: Resources for the Future, 1999).

19. Luis Gomez-Echeverri, "Most Developing Countries Are Neither Prepared to Address nor Interested in Climate Change," in Luis Gomez-Echeverri, ed., *Climate Change and Development* (New York and New Haven: United Nations Development Program and Yale School of Forestry and Environmental Studies, 2000), 309, 315. At the most recent Conference of the Parties to the climate treaties, Prime Minister Atal Bihari Vajpayee of India firmly declared that developing countries have more pressing concerns regarding health and education and hence cannot be expected to invest in climate protection. See Amy Waldman, "At Climate Meeting, Unlikely Ally for Have-Nots," *New York Times,* November 1, 2002.

20. Alan S. Manne and Richard G. Richels, "The Kyoto Protocol: A Cost-Effective Strategy for Meeting Environmental Objectives?" in Carlo Carraro, ed., *Efficiency and Equity of Climate Change Policy* (Norwell, Mass.: Kluwer Academic Publishers, 2000), 43; Jason Shogren, "Benefits and Costs of Kyoto," in Carlo Carraro, ed., *Efficiency and Equity of Climate Change Policy,* 17; Shogren and Toman, "How Much Climate Change Is Too Much?" A figure of 4 percent is cited by the Council of Economic Advisers, *Economic Report of the President 2002* (Washington, D.C.: Government Printing Office, 2002), 247, which indicates that the present Bush administration believes that the costs of joining the Kyoto Protocol would be quite high.

21. See the text in this chapter accompanying notes 16–18.

22. John P. Weyant, ed., *The Costs of the Kyoto Protocol: A Multimodel Evaluation, Energy Journal* (special issue) (May 1999).

23. In 1998 the Clinton administration's Council of Economic Advisers set forth a very optimistic assessment that assumed full use of flexibility mechanisms (domestic and international emissions trading, joint implementation, and the clean development mechanism), efficient implementation strategies, and a high rate of technological advance. The CEA reported that compliance with the Kyoto Protocol would require a drop in annual GDP of less than .5 percent, with gasoline prices rising about five cents, a drop in electricity prices, and no significant impacts on unemployment or trade. Jason Shogren, *The Benefits and Costs of the Kyoto Protocol* (Washington, D.C.: AEI Press, 1999), 19. The marginal costs under that scenario were $10 to $20 per ton of carbon. A study offered by the Interlaboratory Working Group, a consortium of five federal lab groups in 1997, also found that the Kyoto Protocol could be met at low costs through widespread adoption of more efficient energy systems by consumers and industry. Interlaboratory Working Group, *Scenarios of U.S. Carbon Reductions: Potential Impacts of Energy Technologies by 2010 and Beyond* (Washington, D.C.: U.S. Department of Energy, Office of Energy Efficiency and Renewable Technologies, September 1997). In stark contrast, estimates generated by the private economic consulting firms of WEFA, Inc. and DRI/McGraw-Hill suggested that meeting the Kyoto Protocol would entail a GDP reduction of 3 percent or $250 billion per year (assuming intranational emissions trading). The firms also estimated the loss of 2 million jobs and a 50 percent increase in the price of gas. WEFA, Inc., "Global Warming: The Economic Cost of Early Action, National Impacts," 1997; DRI/McGraw-Hill, "The Impact of Carbon Mitigation Strategies on State Economies," August 1997. A 1998 report by the U.S. Department of Energy, Energy Information Administration, put the cost at $348 per ton of emitted carbon (assuming no international emissions trading). U.S. Energy Information Administration, *Impacts of the Kyoto Protocol on U.S. Energy Markets and Economic Activity* (Washington, D.C.: Government Printing Office, October 1998). A report by Ronald Sutherland found GDP declines of 4.9 percent per year. Ronald Sutherland, "Achieving the Kyoto Protocol in the U.S.: How Great Are the Needed Changes?" *Mitigation and Adaptation Strategies for Global Change* 5 (2000): 123. Meanwhile, Resources for the Future and Charles River Associates found costs falling somewhere in the middle of the range. See Shogren, *The Benefits and Costs of the Kyoto Protocol,* 20. Resources for the Future estimated impacts at 1 percent of GDP or 2 percent at worst. Those losses, however, include a 25 percent increase in energy costs and a thirty-cent rise in the price of gas. Ibid. Charles River Associates put the estimates at a 1.4 to 2.0 percent reduction in GDP in 2020. In total, the worldwide cost estimates are even more shaky. Ibid. The margins of error in such figures may be almost as large as the cost estimate itself. William D. Nordhaus, "Assessing the Economics of Climate Change: An Introduction," in William D. Nordhaus, ed., *Economics and Policy Issues in Climate Change* (Washington, D.C.: Resources for the Future, 1998), 13.

24. Ronald J. Sutherland, "'No Cost' Efforts to Reduce Carbon Emissions in the U.S.: An Economic Perspective," *Energy Journal* 21 (2000): 89.

25. Kolstad and Toman, "The Economics of Climate Change," 17.

26. Ibid.

27. See Sutherland, "'No Cost' Efforts to Reduce Carbon Emissions in the U.S.," 89 (citing Amory B. Lovins and L. Hunter Lovins, *Climate: Making Sense and Making Money* (Old Snowmass, Colo.: Rocky Mountain Institute, November 1997)).

28. Shogren and Toman, "How Much Climate Change Is Too Much?" 13.

29. See Sutherland, "'No Cost' Efforts to Reduce Carbon Emissions in the U.S."

30. Ibid.

31. See Winston Harrington, Richard D. Morgenstern, and Peter Nelson, "On the Accuracy of Regulatory Cost Estimates," *Journal of Policy Analysis and Management* 19 (2000): 297–322.

32. Richard B. Stewart and Jonathan B. Wiener, "A Comprehensive Approach to Climate Change," *American Enterprise* 1 (6) (November–December 1990); U.S. Department of Justice, *A Comprehensive Approach to Global Climate Change* (Washington, D.C.: Government Printing Office, 1991); Richard B. Stewart and Jonathan B. Wiener, "A Comprehensive Approach to Climate Change Policy: Issues of Design and Practicality," *Arizona Journal of International and Comparative Law* 9 (1992): 83, 85; Jonathan B. Wiener, "Something Borrowed for Something Blue: Legal Transplants and the Evolution of Global Environmental Law," *Ecology Law Quarterly* 27 (2001): 1295.

33. For suggestions of improvements on the global warming potential, see U.S. Department of Justice, *A Comprehensive Approach to Global Climate Change;* Stewart and Wiener, "A Comprehensive Approach to Climate Change Policy," 86–101 ; John Reilly and Kenneth Richards, "Climate Change Damage and the Trace Gas Index Issue," *Environmental and Resource Economics* 3 (1993): 41; James K. Hammitt et al., "A Welfare-Based Index for Assessing Environmental Effects of Greenhouse-Gas Emissions," *Nature* 381 (1996): 301–3; Alan Manne and Richard Richels, "An Alternative Approach to Establishing Tradeoffs among Greenhouse Gases," *Nature* 410 (2001): 675; John Reilly, Mustafa Babiker, and Monika Mayer, "Comparing Greenhouse Gases," Report 77, MIT Joint Program on the Science and Policy of Global Change, July 2001, available at www.mit.edu/globalchange/www/MITJPSPGC_Rpt77.pdf. See also chap. 5, n. 36, on improvements to the global warming potential index.

34. See John Reilly et al., "Multigas Assessment of the Kyoto Protocol," *Nature* 401 (October 7, 1999): 549–55.

35. See A. Denny Ellerman, Henry D. Jacoby, and Annelene Decaux, "The Effects on Developing Countries of the Kyoto Protocol and CO_2 Emissions Trading," Report 41, MIT Joint Program on the Science and Policy of Global Change, December 1, 1998; Alan S. Manne and Richard G. Richels, "U.S. Rejection of the Kyoto Protocol: The Impact on Compliance Costs and CO_2 Emissions," Working

Paper 01-12, AEI–Brookings Joint Center for Regulatory Studies, October 2001, available at www.aei.brookings.org/publications/working/working_01_12.pdf. The Energy Modeling Forum studies concluded that global trading would reduce costs to the United States by 53 to 90 percent relative to the costs to the United States of achieving its Kyoto target without any international trading and that trading among Annex I countries alone would reduce costs between 21 to 65 percent with more than half of the models falling in the 50 to 60 percent range. Sarah A. Cline, "Appendix A: The Costs of the Kyoto Protocol," in Michael Toman, ed., *Climate Change Economics and Policy: An RFF Anthology* (Washington, D.C.: Resources for the Future, 2001), 55 (citing John P. Weyant and J. Hill, "Introduction and Overview," in Weyant, *The Costs of the Kyoto Protocol*, vii–xiv). A study by Nordhaus and Boyer found that costs of the Kyoto Protocol, without international trading, were fifteen times the costs of policies allowing for global trade. Nordhaus and Boyer, *Warming the World*, 177. The Clinton administration's Council of Economic Advisers' study, based on a very optimistic scenario that assumed the smooth and full implementation of all flexibility measures including international trading, found that international trading would reduce costs by 75 percent relative to domestic trading only. The extremely high costs found by the Energy Information Administration and the WEFA study assumed domestic trading only. See Shogren, *The Benefits and Costs of the Kyoto Protocol*, 19. Even the engineering-based Interlaboratory Working Group study found that deeper cuts were available under a regime that allowed domestic emissions trading versus one without trading. Rob Coppock, "International Treaties as Possible Alternatives to Kyoto," *Weathervane* (Washington, D.C.: Resources for the Future, 2001), 2, available at www.weathervane.rff.org/features/feature128.html. At least one study also found that policies (such as "supplementarity") capping the percentage of the Kyoto target that could be met through the purchase of emission permits would also raise costs significantly. Manne and Richels, "The Kyoto Protocol," 48.

36. See Shogren, "Benefits and Costs of Kyoto," 17, 28. For example, one prominent analysis found the cost to the United States in 2010 of the Kyoto target to be about 1 percent of GDP with no emissions trading (with a marginal cost per ton of carbon emissions avoided of about $240), about .5 percent of GDP with full emissions trading among industrialized (Annex B) countries plus the clean development mechanism (marginal cost of $100 per ton), and about .25 percent of GDP with full global emissions trading (marginal cost of $70 per ton). Manne and Richels, "The Kyoto Protocol," 48.

37. See Harrington, Morgenstern, and Nelson, "On the Accuracy of Regulatory Cost Estimates," 297.

38. See Alan Manne and Richard Richels, "The Berlin Mandate: The Costs of Meeting Post-2000 Targets and Timetables," *Energy Policy* 24 (1996): 205–10; Richard Richels, Jae Edmonds, Howard Gruenspecht, and Tom Wigley, "The Berlin Mandate: The Design of Cost-Effective Mitigation Strategies," Working Paper 14.3, Energy Modeling Forum, Stanford University, February 1996, 7.

39. See Mustafa H. Babiker, Henry D. Jacoby, John M. Reilly, and David M. Reiner, "The Evolution of a Climate Regime: Kyoto to Marrakech," Report 82, MIT Joint Program on the Science and Policy of Global Change, February 2002, 6–7 and figure 1, available at web.mit.edu/globalchange/www/abstracts. html#a82. The MIT model finds cost savings from comprehensiveness plus trading to be roughly similar in other Annex B countries. The 90 percent savings estimate may be overstated by the assumption of smooth implementation but understated because it omits the further cost savings of enhancing sinks and also omits further cost savings from mechanisms for temporal flexibility such as banking and borrowing and from induced technological innovation.

40. See letter from President George W. Bush to Senator Chuck Hagel, March 13, 2001.

41. Tom Wigley, Richard Richels, and Jae Edmonds, "Economic and Environmental Choices in the Stabilization of Atmospheric CO_2 Concentrations," *Nature* 379 (January 1996): 240–43.

42. See James K. Hammitt, "Evaluation Endpoints and Climate Policy: Atmospheric Stabilization, Benefit-Cost Analysis, and Near-Term Greenhouse-Gas Emissions," *Climatic Change* 41 (1999): 447–68; William D. Nordhaus, "After Kyoto: Alternative Mechanisms to Control Global Warming," paper prepared for a joint session of the American Economic Association and the Association of Environmental and Resource Economics, January 4, 2002, available at www.econ.yale.edu/~nordhaus/homepage/PostKyoto_v4.pdf.

43. See Nordhaus and Boyer, *Warming the World,* 175; Manne and Richels, "The Kyoto Protocol," 59.

44. See Wigley, Richels, and Edmonds, "Economic and Environmental Choices in the Stabilization of Atmospheric CO_2 Concentrations." Compare Stephen H. Schneider and Lawrence H. Goulder, "Achieving Low-Cost Emissions Targets," *Nature* 389 (1997): 13–14.

45. Hammitt, "Evaluation Endpoints and Climate Policy." The marginal abatement costs associated with the optimal path are $10 per ton of carbon in 2000, $40 in 2050, $110 in 2100, and $190 in 2150. by contrast, the marginal abatement costs associated with the least-cost stabilization paths are close to zero through 2010, 2050, and 2070 for stabilization at 550, 650, and 750 parts per million, respectively, and then rise steeply from zero to over $300 per ton of carbon within about fifty years after those dates to accomplish stabilization.

46. A similar result is reached by William D. Nordhaus, "Global Warming Economics," *Science* 294 (November 9, 2001): 1283, figure 1, that shows that an "efficient" climate policy, balancing costs and benefits, would involve less abatement than under the Kyoto Protocol with full participation by the United States (but greater abatement than under the Kyoto Protocol with the United States not participating).

47. See John D. Graham, "Presidential Management of the Regulatory State," speech to Weidenbaum Center Forum, National Press Club, Washington, D.C.,

December 17, 2001, available at www.whitehouse.gov/omb/inforeg/regpol-admin_speeches.html.

48. See Richard B. Stewart, "Environmental Decisionmaking under Uncertainty," *Research in Law and Economics* 20 (2002): 71.

49. Ibid. The limitations of the precautionary principle are especially apparent when precautionary measures would themselves introduce new environmental risks. See Jonathan B. Wiener, "Precaution in a Multirisk World," in Dennis Paustenbach, ed., *Human and Ecological Risk Assessment* (New York: John Wiley and Sons, 2002).

50. The European Commission has articulated a view of the precautionary principle that embraces (indeed requires) cost-benefit balancing. European Commission, *Communication on the Precautionary Principle,* COM (2000)1final (Brussels: European Commission, February 2000).

Chapter 3: Participation by All Major Greenhouse Gas–Emitting Nations in Climate Regulation

1. See Carbon Dioxide Information Analysis Center at Oak Ridge National Laboratory, "National Fossil-Fuel CO_2 Emissions," available at www.cdiac.esd.ornl.gov/trends/emis/tre_coun.htm; Kevin A. Baumert and Nancy Kete, "The U.S., Developing Countries, and Climate Protection: Leadership or Stalemate?" Issue Brief, World Resources Institute (June 2001), 2 and table 1.

2. Developing countries emitted about 2 billion out of the roughly 6 billion tons of carbon emitted in 1998. See A. Denny Ellerman, Henry D. Jacoby, and Annelene Decaux, "The Effects on Developing Countries of the Kyoto Protocol and CO_2 Emissions Trading," Report 41, MIT Joint Program on the Science and Policy of Global Change, December 1, 1998, B3 and table 1.

3. See, for example, Alan S. Manne and Richard G. Richels, "U.S. Rejection of the Kyoto Protocol: The Impact on Compliance Costs and CO_2 Emissions," Working Paper 01-12, AEI–Brookings Joint Center for Regulatory Studies, October 2001, figure 1, available at www.aei.brookings.org/publications/working/working_01_12.pdf (showing developing countries accounting for about 2 billion out of the total 6 billion tons of carbon emitted in 2000 and about 5 billion out of the 10 billion tons projected for 2020).

4. Energy Information Administration, *International Energy Outlook 2001* (March 2001): 160.

5. See David G. Streets et al., "Black Carbon Emissions in China," *Atmospheric Environment* 35 (2001): 4281, 4293 (noting that "raising the profile of black carbon in the climate change debate could draw countries like China closer to joining a global commitment to the reduction of greenhouse gas emissions because they would simultaneously accrue significant local and regional air quality benefits.").

6. Baumert and Kete, "The U.S., Developing Countries, and Climate Protection," 3 and figure 2. There was an apparent decrease in Chinese carbon dioxide and

black carbon (soot) emissions from 1997 to 2000. Ibid., 7 and figure 6; David G. Streets et al., "Recent Reductions in China's Greenhouse Gas Emissions," *Science* 294 (November 30, 2001): 1835 (finding that reduced coal use and other changes in China from 1995 to 2000 reduced China's carbon dioxide emissions by 7.3 percent, its methane emissions by 2.2 percent, its black carbon (soot) emissions by 32 percent, and its sulfur dioxide emissions by 21 percent over that period); Natural Resources Defense Council, "Second Analysis Confirms Greenhouse Gas Reductions in China," October 2001, available at www.nrdc.org/globalwarming/ achinagg.asp (visited December 19, 2001) (finding that China's carbon dioxide emissions fell by 6 to 14 percent over from 1996 to 1999). But that decrease is likely due to a temporary slowdown in China's economic growth in the late 1990s associated with the Asian financial crisis and to policy changes that reduced Chinese coal subsidies. Streets et al., "Recent Reductions in China's Greenhouse Gas Emissions," 1835–36. And the size of the 1997–2000 emissions decrease may have been overstated; a report issued by the U.S. Embassy called the statistical claims greatly exaggerated and concluded that "energy use has probably not fallen in absolute terms, and consequently, neither have greenhouse gas emissions." U.S. Embassy, Beijing, *The Controversy over China's Reported Falling Energy Use* (August 2001), available at www.usembassy-china.org.cn/english/sandt/energy_stats_web.htm. A Japanese scientist funded by the World Bank also questioned the claims; he observed that coal mines ordered shut down by the central government often either remain open or reopen soon thereafter. John Pomfret, "Research Casts Doubt on China's Pollution Claims," *Washington Post,* August 15, 2001. In sum, China's carbon dioxide emissions seem likely to grow again as China's economic growth rebounds. And even from 1997 to 2000, as China reduced its carbon dioxide and black carbon emissions, it also reduced its emissions of sulfur dioxide (a gas that tends to cool the atmosphere) so much that the net effect was to *increase,* not decrease, China's net contribution to global warming. See Streets et al., "Recent Reductions in China's Greenhouse Gas Emissions."

    7. See Philip M. Fearnside, "The Potential of Brazil's Forest Sector for Mitigating Global Warming under the Kyoto Protocol," *Mitigation and Adaptation Strategies for Global Change* 6 (2001): 355, 358; Duncan Austin et al., *Contributions to Climate Change: Are Conventional Metrics Misleading the Debate?* (Washington, D.C.: World Resources Institute, 1998).

    8. See Jonathan Baert Wiener, "Global Environmental Regulation: Instrument Choice in Legal Context," *Yale Law Journal* 108 (1999): 677, 694–97.

    9. Ibid., 695 and n. 70 (citing studies showing leakage rates from 4 to 100 percent); Alan S. Manne and Richard G. Richels, "The Kyoto Protocol: A Cost-Effective Strategy for Meeting Environmental Objectives?" in Carlo Carraro, ed., *Efficiency and Equity of Climate Change Policy* (Norwell, Mass.: Kluwer Academic Publishers, 2000), 52 (finding roughly 10 percent aggregate greenhouse gas emissions leakage in 2010 from industrialized to developing countries due to the

Kyoto Protocol but also finding that the effects on industries in individual countries would be larger and would plausibly spur "acrimonious conflicts").

10. See Richard Schmalensee, "Greenhouse Policy Architectures and Institutions," in William D. Nordhaus, ed., *Economics and Policy Issues in Climate Change* (Washington, D.C.: Resources for the Future, 1998), 146.

11. See Richard B. Stewart, "Environmental Regulation and International Competitiveness," *Yale Law Journal* 102 (1993): 2039. As his article points out, the extent of competitiveness fears is often not justified by the facts, but the worries remain a politically potent force. See "Statement of Senator Robert Byrd," *Congressional Record,* June 8, 2001, S6000, S6001 ("Don't sign it; don't sign that protocol until the major emitters among the developing nations of the world have also signed on and have come into the boat with us. . . . We all have a responsibility. . . . [W]e want the developing countries to get in the same boat with us. . . . We are not saying they have to sign up for precisely the same limits we place on ourselves . . . but they do need to sign on. . . . We don't want our industries to go overseas as a result of an unwise signing of the protocol that would require us to continue to strongly limit ourselves in ways that would encourage manufacturers in this country to go abroad and to establish themselves in the developing countries. Let's all get into the same boat together. There must be a level field insofar as our industries are concerned. Let's don't drive American industries overseas.").

12. See chap. 2, n. 35 (describing findings of the Energy Modeling Forum study); chap. 2, n. 36 (describing findings of the Manne and Richels study). See also Ellerman, Jacoby, and Decaux, "The Effects on Developing Countries of the Kyoto Protocol and CO_2 Emissions Trading," 7 (reporting similar estimates).

13. For example, Russia may act as a monopolist in Annex B trading. See Carlo Carraro, Barbara Buchner, and Igor Cersosimo, "On the Consequences of the U.S. Withdrawal from the Kyoto/Bonn Protocol," FEEM Working Paper 102.2001, December 2001, available at www.papers.ssrn.com/abstract=296930; Mustafa H. Babiker, Henry D. Jacoby, John M. Reilly, and David M. Reiner, "The Evolution of a Climate Regime: Kyoto to Marrakech," Report 82, MIT Joint Program on the Science and Policy of Global Change, February 2002, 12–13, available at web.mit.edu/globalchange/www/abstracts.html#a82; Andreas Löschel and ZhongXiang Zhang, "The Economic and Environmental Implications of the U.S. Repudiation of the Kyoto Protocol and the Subsequent Deals in Bonn and Marrakech," FEEM Working Paper 23.2002, April 2002, available at www.papers.ssrn.com/abstract=299463. In the MIT model, Russia sells 98 percent of the allowances traded in Annex B trading (of which only a third or 111 million tons are from "hot air"; the other 234 million tons are new abatement below the business-as-usual level), at $127; but in full global trading, Russia sells only 23 percent of allowances traded, China sells 47 percent, India 11 percent, and others 19 percent, at $24. See Ellerman, Jacoby, and Decaux, "The Effects on Developing Countries of the Kyoto Protocol and CO_2 Emissions Trading," 5, 7.

14. With respect to adaptation measures, nations probably have a sufficient individual incentive to avoid harm, but there is scope for global cooperation in sharing adaptation technologies and in offering financial assistance to developing countries.

15. See Wiener, "Global Environmental Regulation"; Lloyd Gruber, *Ruling the World* (Princeton: Princeton University Press, 2000).

16. Noncompliance is equivalent to partial withdrawal from the treaty, so that deterring free-riding will deter most noncompliance as well. See Scott Barrett, "A Theory of Full International Cooperation," *Journal of Theoretical Politics* 11 (1999): 519–41. But there might be silent noncompliance without withdrawal, in which case the other parties to the treaty might not realize that partial free-riding is occurring and might not take the steps that would be necessary to deter the free-riding. This emphasizes the need for transparent reporting, monitoring, and review of countries' compliance with their abatement commitments. It also underscores the importance of fashioning an institutional design that reduces noncompliance. A design that makes compliance much less costly (such as emissions trading) can be expected to reduce noncompliance.

17. See Richard Tol, "New Estimates of the Damage Costs of Climate Change, Part I: Benchmark Estimates," *Environmental and Resource Economics* 21 (2002): 47; Richard Tol, "New Estimates of the Damage Costs of Climate Change, Part II: Dynamic Estimates," *Environmental and Resource Economics* 21 (2002): 135 (showing heterogeneity in national impacts of climate change, including persisting benefits in China).

18. Some studies show that the European Union's marginal costs of achieving Kyoto compliance (absent trading) are higher than those of the United States, although less than those of Japan. See, for example, Ellerman, Jacoby, and Decaux, "The Effects on Developing Countries of the Kyoto Protocol and CO_2 Emissions Trading." But the much greater size of the reduction below the business-as-usual level required of the United States by the Kyoto Protocol still leaves the United States bearing a heavier total burden than the European Union. Ibid.

19. Compare the annual per capita GDP (in purchasing power parity terms) in 2000 of several prominent developing (non–Annex B) countries, such as Brazil ($7,320), Chile ($9,110), Costa Rica ($8,250), Korea ($17,340), Mexico ($8,810), Saudi Arabia ($11,050), Singapore ($24,970), and South Africa ($9,180) with the figures for several industrialized (Annex B) countries, such as Bulgaria ($5,530), Latvia and Lithuania (both $6,960), Poland ($9,030), Romania ($6,380), Russia ($8,030), and Ukraine ($3,710) (the latter even lower than China's $3,940, Iran's $5,900, and Kazakhstan's $5,490). See World Bank, *World Development Report 2002: Building Institutions for Markets* (Washington, D.C.: World Bank, 2002), 232–33 and table 1.

20. See Tol, "New Estimates of the Damage Costs of Climate Change, Part I."

21. Reduced economic growth in industrialized countries will mean reduced imports of goods made in developing countries, but at the same time leakage of emissions-intensive activities into unregulated developing countries may bolster

developing country economies. Developing countries that are particularly dependent on greenhouse gas–related exports to industrialized countries, such as the OPEC countries, appear likely to suffer high income losses from the Kyoto limits on greenhouse gas emissions. See Ellerman, Jacoby, and Decaux, "The Effects on Developing Countries of the Kyoto Protocol and CO_2 Emissions Trading." OPEC countries have been seeking financial assistance through the Kyoto talks, under Article 3(14) and Article 4(8) and 4(9); and Decision -/CP.7 at Marrakech proposed Decision -/CMP.1 for the Conference of the Parties serving as the Meeting of the Parties to move ahead on such funding (as part of funding for various developing country needs). But note that in the MIT model, under global trading, even the energy-exporting nations are net gainers (they sell 51 million tons of allowances at a net gain of $.68 billion). See Ellerman, Jacoby, and Decaux, "The Effects on Developing Countries of the Kyoto Protocol and CO_2 Emissions Trading," B3 and table C.

22. See Luis Gomez-Echeverri, "Most Developing Countries Are Neither Prepared to Address nor Interested in Climate Change," in Luis Gomez-Echeverri, ed., *Climate Change and Development* (New York and New Haven: United Nations Development Program and Yale School of Forestry and Environmental Studies, 2000), 309; Amy Waldman, "At Climate Meeting, Unlikely Ally for Have-Nots," *New York Times,* November 1, 2002 (citing Indian Prime Minister Atal Bihiri Vajpayee).

23. Kirk R. Smith, Joel Swisher, and Dilip R. Ahuja, "Who Pays (to Solve the Problem and How Much)?" in Peter Hayes and Kirk Smith, eds., *Who Pays? Science, Economics, and North-South Politics in the Climate Change Convention* (New York: United Nations University Press, 1993).

24. See Randall Lutter, "Developing Countries' Greenhouse Emissions: Uncertainty and Implications for Participation in the Kyoto Protocol," *Energy Journal* 21 (2000): 93, 94–115 (finding that even emissions limits set at the business-as-usual level could be costly for a country whose economy subsequently grows faster than expected).

Chapter 4: U.S. Interests and Global Climate Regulation

1. See Richard Tol, "New Estimates of the Damage Costs of Climate Change, Part I: Benchmark Estimates," *Environmental and Resource Economics* 21 (2002): 47; Richard Tol, "New Estimates of the Damage Costs of Climate Change, Part II: Dynamic Estimates," *Environmental and Resource Economics* 21 (2002): 135; U.S. Department of State, *U.S. Climate Action Report 2002* (Third National Communication to the United Nations Framework Convention on Climate Change) (Washington, D.C.: Government Printing Office, May 2002): chap. 6, available at www.epa.gov/globalwarming/publications/car/index.html (visited June 4, 2002).

2. See U.S. Department of State, *U.S. Climate Action Report 2002,* chap. 6.

3. See Tom Wigley, "The Kyoto Protocol: CO_2, CH_4, and Climate Implications,"

Geophysical Research Letters 25 (1998): 2285–88, cited in Jason Shogren, "Benefits and Costs of Kyoto," in Carlo Carraro, ed., *Efficiency and Equity of Climate Change Policy* (Norwell, Mass.: Kluwer Academic Publishers, 2000), n. 10.

4. See Shogren, "Benefits and Costs of Kyoto," 24.

5. David Pearce, "Economic Development and Climate Change," *Environment and Development Economics* 3 (1998): 389–92, cited in Shogren, "Benefits and Costs of Kyoto," 24 and n. 13.

6. See chap. 2, nn. 35 and 36 (describing Energy Modeling Forum and Manne and Richels estimates). Of course, if it did not participate in the Kyoto Protocol, the abatement costs to the United States would be lower. For example, Manne and Richels estimate that participation in the Kyoto Protocol (with full emissions trading among Annex B countries but not global trading) would cost the United States about .7 percent of GDP in 2010, whereas not participating in the Kyoto Protocol would cost much less, perhaps .1 percent of GDP in 2010 (the number is still positive because of abatement undertaken in anticipation of future emissions controls). Alan S. Manne and Richard G. Richels, "U.S. Rejection of the Kyoto Protocol: The Impact on Compliance Costs and CO_2 Emissions," Working Paper 01-12, AEI–Brookings Joint Center for Regulatory Studies, October 2001, available at www.aei.brookings.org/publications/working/working_01_12.pdf, 8–9 and figure 5. Nordhaus finds that participation in the Kyoto Protocol would cost the United States about $125 billion per year, roughly 1.8 percent of GDP today (or more than $2 trillion over the next 300 years, if one assumes that the Kyoto caps remain in place indefinitely), whereas nonparticipation would save the United States essentially all of that cost. William D. Nordhaus, "Global Warming Economics," *Science* 294 (November 9, 2001): 1283, 1284, and figure 3.

7. See European Commission, *Proposal for a Directive of the European Parliament and of the Council Establishing a Scheme for Greenhouse Gas Emission Allowance Trading within the Community and Amending Council Directive 96/61/EC,* COM(2001)581final (Brussels: European Commission, October 23, 2001). The European Council adopted this proposal in late 2002.

8. See Howard F. Chang, "An Economic Analysis of Trade Measures to Protect the Global Environment," *Georgetown Law Journal* 83 (1995): 2131.

9. See S. 556 (Clean Power Act of 2001), introduced by Senator Jim Jeffords, March 15, 2001, and cosponsored by Senator Joseph I. Lieberman and twenty other senators; the bill was favorably reported out by the Senate Environment and Public Works Committee on June 27, 2002. A companion bill, H.R. 1256, has been introduced in the House. Economic analyses of an ambitious electric utility regulatory program with a four pollutant strategy are presented in U.S. Environmental Protection Agency Office of Air and Radiation, Office of Atmospheric Programs, *Economic Analyses of a Multiemissions Strategy* (Washington, D.C.: Government Printing Office, October 31, 2001); U.S. Department of Energy, Energy Information Program, *Analyses of Strategies for Reducing Multiple*

Emissions from Electric Power Plants with Advanced Technology Scenarios (Washington, D.C.: Government Printing Office, October 2001).

10. Although this intuition seems plausible, we have not yet found an econometric study comparing the costs to industry of a "three pollutant plus carbon dioxide later" bill to a "four pollutant now" bill. The latter could be less costly to industry if the savings from undertaking integrated multipollutant control measures rather than having to install new controls on carbon dioxide a few years later would outweigh the increased cost of having to control an additional pollutant now. That, of course, depends on how much "later" carbon dioxide would be added to the three pollutant regime and what costs there would be from having to control carbon dioxide anew after controls on the other three pollutants had already been installed. If "later" would be fairly soon, and if the added carbon dioxide controls would require discarding or replacing some expensive controls that had already been adopted for the three pollutant regime (but which could have been avoided by an integrated four pollutant control approach), then "four pollutants now" could be less costly to industry than "three pollutants plus carbon dioxide later." See Jim Jeffords, "Unhealthy Air," *New York Times,* June 30, 2002 (arguing in favor of a four pollutant approach). Compare U.S. Environmental Protection Agency, "Comparison of Jeffords-Lieberman and Smith-Voinovich-Brownback," 2001, available at www.epa.gov/air/finalanalyses. pdf (finding that a four pollutant approach could have higher initial costs than a three pollutant approach, but equal longer-run costs, and without comparing the four pollutant approach with the three pollutant plus carbon dioxide later scenario); Mary J. Hutzler, acting administrator, Energy Information Administration, Department of Energy, statement before the Committee on Environment and Public Works, U.S. Senate, Hearing on S. 556, "The Clean Power Act of 2001," November 1, 2001, available at www.senate.gov/~epw/ Hutzler_1101.pdf (testifying that achieving carbon dioxide abatement requirements would reduce the costs of achieving nitrogen oxide–sulfur oxide reductions but without concluding that it would be less costly in total to take a four pollutant approach now rather than to add carbon dioxide later). Allowing interpollutant trading could reduce costs further. See Randall Lutter, "New Clean Air Legislation Should Allow Interpollutant Trading," *Policy Matters* 02-6, AEI–Brookings Joint Center for Regulatory Studies, January 2002; Juan-Pablo Montero, "Multipollutant Markets," *RAND Journal of Economics* 32 (4) (2001): 762–74. An integrated multipollutant approach also has environmental advantages. See Lakshman Guruswamy, "The Case for Integrated Pollution Control," *Law and Contemporary Problems* 54 (1991): 41; Nigel Haigh and Francis Irwin eds., *Integrated Pollution Control in Europe and North America* (Washington, D.C.: Conservation Foundation, 1990); John D. Graham and Jonathan Baert Wiener, *Risk vs. Risk: Tradeoffs in Protecting Health and the Environment* (Cambridge: Harvard University Press, 1995).

11. We suggested credit for early action for this reason in Richard B. Stewart and Jonathan B. Wiener, "A Comprehensive Approach to Climate Change Policy:

Issues of Design and Practicality," *Arizona Journal of International and Comparative Law* 9 (1992): 83, 85, 111. The Bush administration's Clear Skies Initiative proposes credit for early abatement action (see U.S. Department of State, *U.S. Climate Action Report 2002,* chap. 1), but it is unclear how that credit will be calculated or rewarded if the United States has no limits on greenhouse gas emissions and does not participate in the Kyoto Protocol. All early action credit schemes face the problem of setting a business-as-usual baseline against which actions worthy of credit can be distinguished.

12. Another strategic concern might relate to energy security. Especially after September 11, 2001, economic and strategic reasons exist to reduce U.S. dependence on foreign sources of energy. Yet it is far from clear that reducing U.S. purchases of Middle Eastern oil would reduce future terrorist attacks: terrorism may arise for other reasons, and reduced oil purchases may undermine the prosperity that enables social stability in exporting countries. Meanwhile, reducing oil imports would not necessarily reduce greenhouse gas emissions in the United States; that would depend on what mix of conservation and other fuels (for example, coal) is used to replace the foreign oil.

13. But the efficiency costs of compensating particularly affected industries need not be high. See Lawrence H. Goulder, "The Costs of Political Feasibility," presentation at Resources for the Future, Washington, D.C., December 2001 (finding that granting rather than selling 13 percent of emissions allowances to particular industries would compensate their losses, with negligible impact on overall efficiency). Granting emissions allowances as an in-kind side payment to secure participation is the same approach used to engage Russia in the Kyoto Protocol, to engage key states and electric utilities in the 1990 Clean Air Act acid rain emissions trading program, and what we advocate to engage China and other major developing countries in an expanded global greenhouse gas regime.

14. Across both Democratic and Republican administrations (and Senate majorities), the United States has stayed out of several prominent treaties, including the Law of the Sea, the Landmines Ban, the International Criminal Court, the treaty on Children's Rights, the Biodiversity Convention and its Biosafety Protocol, and others.

15. See Robert A. Kagan, "Power and Weakness," *Policy Review* 113 (June 2002), available at www.policyreview.com/JUN02/Kagan.html.

16. See Jonathan Baert Wiener, "On the Political Economy of Global Environmental Regulation," *Georgetown Law Journal* 87 (February 1999): 749, 780–81.

17. See Robert A. Kagan and Lee Axelrad, *Regulatory Encounters: Multinational Corporations and American Adversarial Legalism* (Berkeley: University of California Press, 2000); Robert A. Kagan, *Adversarial Legalism: The American Way of Law* (Cambridge: Harvard University Press, 2001); Richard B. Stewart and Eckard Rehbinder, *Environmental Protection Policy* (New York: Walter de Gruyter, 1985).

18. This well-justified concern often underlies U.S. opposition to tough targets

and notions such as the precautionary principle in international treaties. The concern may be so alien to European and Japanese legal cultures that they perceive it only as U.S. unwillingness to step up to its global responsibilities, a depiction that U.S. environmental groups are happy to reiterate. And efforts by EU delegates during the climate negotiations to reassure the United States that the treaty was "just a bold statement" or "only aspirational" had the opposite of the intended effect: far from reassuring the United States, they gave credence to the U.S. fear of less rigorous domestic implementation in Europe and thus further discouraged U.S. adoption.

19. Many other factors are at work. First, U.S. negotiating delegations may comprise a broader set of agencies than other countries' delegations; the inclusion of economic and energy ministries as well as environmental and foreign affairs ministries may lead U.S. delegations to take costs more seriously, whereas other countries' delegations may negotiate without as much regard for cost or feasibility. Second, different electoral systems may favor different types of political actors. In the United States, the winner-take-all electoral rule inhibits influence by third parties and keeps presidential control over treaties in the hands of moderates. In Europe the proportional representation system fosters third parties; the Green Parties have been especially successful of late, and Green ministers are often appointed environment ministers, with responsibility for climate treaty negotiations. Those Green members of parliament respond more directly to domestic Green constituencies—and more to the symbolic politics of looking "more green" than other countries (especially by blaming the United States for being not green enough)—than do American (unelected) negotiators appointed by moderate presidents. That difference may also help explain the European Union's opposition to flexibility mechanisms as long as the United States was advocating them and then acceptance of those approaches in Bonn and Marrakech once the United States had withdrawn and could simply be blamed for withdrawal. Third, rent seeking may explain some opposition to flexibility mechanisms. Europe may have opposed flexibility because it wanted to "raise rivals' costs." See Wiener, "On the Political Economy of Global Environmental Regulation," 780–81. Developing countries may oppose flexibility because, despite the large potential gains to their societies from selling emissions allowances, the negotiators for developing countries may represent governing elites whose power base would be threatened by the enrichment of the merchant class through emissions trading. Ibid. See chap. 7, n. 19, for further discussion.

Chapter 5: The Elements of Sound Regulatory Design for Climate Policy

1. See Bruce Yandle and Stuart Buck, "Bootleggers, Baptists, and the Global Warming Battle," *Harvard Environmental Law Review* 26 (2002): 177; John R. Bolton, "Should We Take Global Governance Seriously?" *Chicago Journal of*

International Law 1 (Fall 2000): 205; Office of the White House Press Secretary, "President Announces Clear Skies and Global Climate Change Initiatives," February 14, 2002, available at www.whitehouse.gov/news/releases/2002/02/ 20020214-5.html (visited February 14, 2002).

2. Garrett Hardin, "The Tragedy of the Commons," *Science* 162 (1968): 1243.

3. The costs of regulation include both the opportunity cost of resources diverted from other uses into regulatory compliance and the distortions introduced by political biases in regulatory design. Critics often worry that national regulatory law is plagued by rent-seeking distortions. Rent seeking is possible because national law is adopted by majority vote, through which organized special interests can extract rents from the general public. International treaty law, by contrast, is based on consent; no country can be compelled to be bound by a treaty. Hence, rent seeking is more difficult under international law. In that respect, international treaties are more like the tortoise than the hare: slower and steadier than national legislation, more difficult to bring to fruition, but more insulated against the distortions of special interest politics. On the other hand, international treaty making may also be more difficult for the public to monitor than is national legislation and thus more susceptible to unobserved distortion. See Jonathan Baert Wiener, "On the Political Economy of Global Environmental Regulation," *Georgetown Law Journal* 87 (February 1999): 749, 769–71, 782–94.

4. See Jonathan B. Wiener, "Something Borrowed for Something Blue: Legal Transplants and the Evolution of Global Environmental Law," *Ecology Law Quarterly* 27 (2001): 1295.

5. See World Bank, *World Development Report 1992: Development and the Environment* (Washington, D.C.: World Bank, 1992); Norman Myers and Jennifer Kent, *Perverse Subsidies: How Tax Dollars Can Undercut the Environment and the Economy* (Washington, D.C.: Island Press, 2001).

6. See Howard Gruenspecht and Robert Stavins, "A Level Field on Pollution at Power Plants," *Boston Globe,* January 26, 2002.

7. U.S. energy intensity, measured as energy consumption per dollar of GDP, declined at an average annual rate of 2.3 percent between 1970 and 1986 and continued to fall at an annual rate of 1.5 percent from 1987 to 2000. Energy Information Administration, U.S. Department of Energy, "Annual Energy Outlook 2002 with Projections to 2020," March 28, 2002, available at www.eia. doe.gov/oiaf/aeo/#energy (visited May 15, 2002). Over the same 1970–2000 period, total U.S. carbon dioxide emissions increased more than 30 percent. See Carbon Dioxide Information Analysis Center at Oak Ridge National Laboratory, "National Fossil-Fuel CO_2 Emissions," available at www.cdiac.esd.ornl.gov/trends /emis/tre_coun.htm (visited February 8, 2002). Similarly, global energy intensity declined at .7 percent annually over the 1990s. See European Commission, Directorate-General for Energy and Transport, "2000 Annual Energy Review," January 2001, 1,4, available at www.europa.eu.int/ comm/energy/library/summary.pdf (visited May 15, 2002). But total carbon dioxide emissions grew by 8 percent over

the decade. See Carbon Dioxide Information Analysis Center at Oak Ridge National Laboratory, "National Fossil-Fuel CO_2 Emissions."

8. Appropriate use of "when" flexibility also implies that units of abatement can be compared over time; for example, in terms of its effects on climate protection, a ton of greenhouse gas abatement today may be roughly equivalent to a ton of greenhouse gas abatement ten years from now but more valuable than a ton of greenhouse gas abatement fifty years from now. "When" flexibility, if it stretches over large enough time periods, will require some metric for calculating relative abatement equivalence across time. In principle, banking of emissions allowances (early abatement) should earn, and borrowing of emissions allowances (deferred abatement) should be charged, an "interest rate" that renders equivalent the abatement occurring at different times.

9. See Richard B. Stewart and Jonathan B. Wiener, "A Comprehensive Approach to Climate Change," *American Enterprise* 1 (6) (November–December 1990): 75; U.S. Department of Justice, *A Comprehensive Approach to Global Climate Change* (Washington, D.C.: Government Printing Office, 1991); Stewart and Wiener, "A Comprehensive Approach to Climate Change Policy"; Wiener, "Something Borrowed for Something Blue."

10. In addition to the six sets of greenhouse gas already controlled in the Kyoto Protocol, growing evidence exists that other substances affecting net global warming should be included, at least for reporting if not for full regulatory control and tradable abatement credit. They include black carbon (soot) and sulfate aerosols. See James E. Hansen et al., "Global Warming in the Twenty-first Century: An Alternative Scenario," *Proceedings of the National Academy of Sciences* 97 (2000): 9875. For example, omitting black carbon can neglect the dominant cause of reduced global warming from reducing coal combustion, and omitting the cooling effect of sulfur dioxide can yield perverse policies that would increase net warming at least in the near term (the first 50 to 100 years). See David G. Streets et al., "Recent Reductions in China's Greenhouse Gas Emissions," *Science* 294 (November 30, 2001): 1835 (finding that reduced coal use and other changes in China from 1995 to 2000 reduced China's carbon dioxide emissions by 7.3 percent, its methane emissions by 2.2 percent, its black carbon (soot) emissions by 32 percent, and its sulfur dioxide emissions by 21 percent over that period and thereby yielded a projected reduction in global mean temperatures over a 100-year period of –.028 degree Celsius because of the combined reductions in carbon dioxide, methane, and black carbon (with black carbon accounting for .026 of that .028 degree decline) but also yielded a projected increase in global mean temperatures over that 100-year period of .040 degree Celsius because of the reduction in sulfur dioxide, for a total net increase in global mean temperature of .012 degree Celsius (± .020) because of the combined emissions reduction of all four gases over the 1995–2000 period). (Most reports of China's emissions reductions from 1995 to 2000 have focused on carbon dioxide and omitted the other gases.) If over the 1995–2000 period the United States increased carbon dioxide emissions by

6.3 percent (ibid.), while also reducing sulfur dioxide emissions sharply under the 1990 Clean Air Act acid rain title, then the United States has contributed much more to increasing global warming than its carbon dioxide emissions alone would imply.

Good reasons may exist to leave sulfur dioxide and other sulfate aerosols out of the climate change treaties. In light of the significant hazards to human health and acid deposition of sulfur aerosols, it is probably not desirable to increase emissions of them to obtain their net cooling effect. If China's and other developing countries' interest in greenhouse gas abatement is largely due to the local environmental cobenefits of sulfur oxides, nitrogen oxides, and particulate matter, but if those reductions would exacerbate global warming, then including the cooling effect of those reductions in greenhouse gas abatement project evaluations could steer greenhouse gas abatement to other projects that do not yield those local cobenefits and could necessitate higher side payments to attract developing countries' participation. On the other hand, if the local effects of those aerosols were counted in a "full effects" trace gas index (including both warming and nonwarming impacts weighted for their relative importance, as we suggested in Richard B. Stewart and Jonathan B. Wiener, "A Comprehensive Approach to Climate Change Policy: Issues of Design and Practicality," *Arizona Journal of International and Comparative Law* 9 (1992): 83), this index would help guide more optimal policy, including directing some financing to the projects that reduce the local pollutants (sulfur and others), even if they increased projected warming on net. Also, it may be that targeted policies could control the most toxic aerosols and particulates while allowing less toxic aerosols and particulates to exert their cooling effect. At least countries' net emissions of sulfur should be reported to the climate change regime so that the decreased cooling effect can be taken into account in climate forecasts and in policy choices.

11. John Reilly et al., "Multigas Assessment of the Kyoto Protocol," *Nature* 401 (October 7, 1999): 549.

12. Jonathan Baert Wiener, "Protecting the Global Environment," in John D. Graham and Jonathan Baert Wiener, eds., *Risk vs. Risk: Tradeoffs in Protecting Health and the Environment* (Cambridge: Harvard University Press, 1995), chap. 10.

13. Hansen et al., "Global Warming in the Twenty-first Century"; Arlene M. Fiore, Daniel J. Jacob, Brendan D. Field, David G. Streets, Suneeta D. Fernandes, and Carey Jang, "Linking Ozone Pollution and Climate Change: The Case for Controlling Methane," *Geophysical Research Letters* 29 (2002): 1919. Piecemeal regulation of each greenhouse gas separately could also achieve those environmental benefits, although at arbitrary cross-gas weights, and would not achieve the cost savings from flexibility in abatement across the set of greenhouse gases.

14. Stewart and Wiener, "A Comprehensive Approach to Climate Change Policy."

15. The classic case for narrow incrementalism is Charles E. Lindblom, "The Science of 'Muddling Through,'" *Public Administration Review* 19 (1959): 79.

16. See Jonathan Baert Wiener, "Managing the Iatrogenic Risks of Risk Management," *Risk: Health, Safety, and Environment* 9 (1998): 39.

17. On regulatory matches and mismatches, see Stephen Breyer, *Regulation and Its Reform* (Cambridge: Harvard University Press, 1982).

18. See Intergovernmental Panel on Climate Change, Working Group I, "Climate Change 2001: The Scientific Basis—Summary for Policymakers and Technical Summary," 2001, 36–47.

19. See Graham and Wiener, *Risk vs. Risk*.

20. See Winston Harrington, *Acid Rain: A Primer* (Washington, D.C.: Resources for the Future, 1989) (describing increase in solid waste due to restrictions on sulfur air emissions); Robert W. Hahn and Eric H. Males, "Can Regulatory Institutions Cope with Cross-Media Pollution?" *Journal of the Air and Waste Management Association* 40 (1990): 24–31.

21. See Lakshman Guruswamy, "The Case for Integrated Pollution Control," *Law and Contemporary Problems* 54 (1991): 41; Graham and Wiener, *Risk vs. Risk;* Joel A. Tarr, *The Search for the Ultimate Sink: Urban Pollution in Historical Perspective* (Akron, Ohio: University of Akron Press, 1996), especially chap. 1.

22. See Henning Rodhe, "A Comparison of the Contribution of Various Gases to the Greenhouse Effect," *Science* 248 (June 8, 1990): 1217–19.

23. See Wiener, "Protecting the Global Environment," 209–12 (collecting studies from the 1980s and early 1990s finding methane leakage rates of 6 to 9 percent in Russia and 1 to 11 percent in the United Kingdom). Some more recent studies have suggested a decline in Russian methane leakage during the 1990s. See J. V. Dedikov et al., "Estimating Methane Releases from Natural Gas Production and Transmission in Russia," *Atmospheric Environment* 33 (1999): 3291 (finding a leakage rate closer to 1 percent and attributing the decline to improved equipment and the incentives for product conservation created by the shift to a market economy); E. J. Dlugokencky et al., "A Dramatic Decrease in the Growth-Rate of Atmospheric Methane in the Northern Hemisphere during 1992—Reply," *Geophysical Research Letters* 21 (1994): 2447 (not proposing a specific rate of leakage but attempting to explain lower levels of atmospheric methane as resulting from decreased fossil-fuel use, less leakage reported in Siberia, and new market incentives that encourage managers to care about lost methane). Others have argued, however, that those claims of lower leakage rates are based on anecdotal evidence and on extrapolation from nonrepresentative areas. See K. B. Hogan and R. C. Harriss, "A Dramatic Decrease in the Growth-Rate of Atmospheric Methane in the Northern Hemisphere during 1992—Comment," *Geophysical Research Letters* 21 (1994): 2445. Reshetnikov et al. argue that most of the Russian gas system remains in a state of decay and disrepair and attribute any decline in observed methane leakage to declines in total production, a shift to focus on export markets ("the less leaky parts of the system"), and continuing technical improvements that "have reduced [total] leakage by perhaps a third to a half, or more: but this is guesswork." A. I. Reshetnikov, N. N. Paramonova, and A. A. Shashkov, "An Evaluation of Historical

Methane Emissions from the Soviet Gas Industry," *Journal of Geophysical Research—Atmospheres* 105 (D3) (2000): 3517–29.

Given the evidence of actual methane leakage rates in Russia (and elsewhere in Europe), the environmental benefits of the comprehensive approach—which were powerful when we first advanced them in the early 1990s—still remain robust today. First, Russian and other European leakage rates may still be quite high, such that a carbon dioxide–only policy would have perverse effects on total global warming. Second, if Russian leakage has declined because of reduced total gas production, then leakage could increase again if total gas production were to rise to meet new European demand for coal-to-gas fuel switching under a carbon dioxide–only policy. Third, even if Russian methane leakage has declined from 6 to 9 percent to, say, 3 to 6 percent (as suggested by Reshetnikov, Paramonova, and Shashkov), then the comprehensive approach would still be much more environmentally effective than a carbon dioxide–only approach; the 3 to 6 percent leakage would still offset half or all of the effectiveness of the carbon dioxide–only policy. Fourth, a decline in methane leakage during the 1990s may reflect in part the success of the comprehensive approach: the fact that the Framework Convention on Climate Change in 1992 and the Kyoto Protocol in 1997 both adopted the comprehensive approach (including methane) may have been one of the new incentives cited by observers that stimulated investments in reducing leakage. The comprehensive approach to climate policy is part of the move to incorporate greenhouse externalities into market price signals. Fifth, the reduced leakage, if true, shows that methane emissions control and measurement methods are endogenous—responding to incentives—rather than fixed. That rebuts a key assertion by critics of the comprehensive approach, namely that non–carbon dioxide emissions are too uncertain to regulate. Sixth, even if Russian methane leakage rates have declined dramatically and permanently, the comprehensive approach would still be environmentally superior to an energy–carbon dioxide–only policy because it would prevent perverse cross-greenhouse gas shifts in other countries involving other greenhouse gas and would encourage forest conservation.

24. At first glance, replacement of fossil with biomass fuels seems attractive, because it would reduce energy-sector carbon dioxide emissions, while the emissions of carbon dioxide from burning the biomass fuels would, one might presume, be at least partly offset by the sequestration of that same carbon dioxide from the atmosphere by the corn as it grew. That analysis, however, neglects three important categories of emissions. First, the carbon dioxide emissions from the ancillary agricultural operations needed to farm the corn, manufacture fertilizer, irrigate the land, and convert the corn into fuel would likely be very large. Second, growing corn requires large quantities of nitrogen fertilizer, which release nitrous oxide emissions—a greenhouse gas almost 300 times more potent per mass than carbon dioxide. Third, if the corn is grown on cleared forest lands, the carbon liberated from the forest ecosystem (trees, plants, and soils) and the reduced ability of the

unforested land to sequester carbon (compared with the corn field) must be counted as well. Together, those three side effects could make biomass fuel much less attractive, and possibly even perverse, as a climate protection strategy.

25. See note 13.

26. We say "potentially" because, although conserving forests would protect biodiversity, new afforestation projects to sequester carbon might replace biodiverse mature forests with monoculture plantation forests. See Wiener, "Protecting the Global Environment," 218–19. Meanwhile, some emissions of greenhouse gas could aid forests: carbon dioxide emissions help fertilize plant photosynthesis, a beneficial effect that the other greenhouse gases do not offer. See ibid., 214–18 (detailing the plant fertilization effect of elevated carbon dioxide); Evan H. DeLucia et al., "Net Primary Production of a Forest Ecosystem with Experimental CO_2 Enrichment," *Science* 284 (May 14, 1999): 1177–79. Thus, to be fully environmentally comprehensive, a comprehensive climate policy would need to be broadened or accompanied by biodiversity protections and by gas-comparison weights to reflect the greenhouse gases' full ecosystem impacts.

27. See R. Bradley, E. Watts, and E. Williams, *Limiting Net Greenhouse Emissions in the United States, Volume II: Energy Responses* (Washington, D.C.: U.S. Department of Energy, Office of Environmental Analysis, 1991), 8.10–8.12.

28. See World Bank, *World Development Report 1992: Development and the Environment* (Washington, D.C.: World Bank, 1992), box 8.6.

29. See Reilly et al., "Multigas Assessment of the Kyoto Protocol."

30. Ibid., 553–54.

31. See Hansen et al., "Global Warming in the Twenty-first Century." See also Fiore et al., "Linking Ozone Pollution and Climate Change."

32. See David Victor, "Limits of Market-Based Strategies for Slowing Global Warming—The Case of Tradable Permits," *Policy Sciences* 24 (1991): 199. See also Richard Schmalensee, "Greenhouse Policy Architectures and Institutions," in William D. Nordhaus, ed., *Economics and Policy Issues in Climate Change* (Washington, D.C.: Resources for the Future, 1998). The European Commission proposal on trading greenhouse gas emissions within the European Union also focuses on carbon dioxide first and leaves the inclusion of other greenhouse gases for some undecided later date. See European Commission, *Proposal for a Directive of the European Parliament and of the Council Establishing a Scheme for Greenhouse Gas Emission Allowance Trading within the Community and Amending Council Directive 96/61/EC*, COM(2001)581final (Brussels: European Commission, October 23, 2001).

33. Annex Z contains quantity limits on the tons of credit that countries may claim for sink expansion activities.

34. Ironically, advocates of aggressive climate protection often invoke the precautionary principle by urging that scientific uncertainty is no excuse for inaction against serious risks. But then those same advocates assert that scientific uncertainty precludes addressing non–carbon dioxide greenhouse gas and sinks in a

climate protection regime. That is an internal contradiction. See Jonathan B. Wiener, "Solving the Precautionary Paradox: Policy Approaches to Improve Measurement of Greenhouse Gas Sources and Sinks," in J. van Ham et al., eds., *Non–CO₂ Greenhouse Gases* (Dordrecht, Netherlands: Kluwer Academic Publishers, 1994), 527. Ignoring parts of the problem through adoption of a piecemeal approach will not make them go away and, for reasons already discussed, is likely to make them worse.

35. See Stewart and Wiener, "A Comprehensive Approach to Climate Change Policy"; Wiener, "Solving the Precautionary Paradox." A similar approach was used to measure the emissions reductions from energy conservation measures in the U.S. acid rain trading program. See U.S. Environmental Protection Agency, *Conservation Verification Protocols, A Guidance Document for Electric Utilities Affected by the Acid Rain Program* (Washington, D.C.: Government Printing Office, 1993), available at www.epa.gov/airmarkets/arp/crer/cvpsumm.html.

36. The global warming potential index is not perfect and should be improved to account for, among other things, saturation effects as atmospheric concentrations increase, intergas interactions as atmospheric composition changes, the choice of discount rates, the changing social value over time of damages associated with warming, the damages associated with the rate of warming as contrasted with the level of warming, and the full environmental impacts of greenhouse gases including global warming, direct effects on plant growth, ozone depletion, and perhaps regional air pollution issues. We have made such suggestions in the past: see U.S. Department of Justice, *A Comprehensive Approach to Global Climate Change;* Stewart and Wiener, "A Comprehensive Approach to Climate Change Policy," 86–91, 99–101. Recent studies on greenhouse gas indexes have helped reinforce the need for such improvements. See John Reilly and Kenneth Richards, "Climate Change Damage and the Trace Gas Index Issue," *Environmental and Resource Economics* 3 (1993): 41; Alan Manne and Richard Richels, "An Alternative Approach to Establishing Tradeoffs among Greenhouse Gases," *Nature* 410 (2001): 675; John Reilly, Mustafa Babiker, and Monika Mayer, "Comparing Greenhouse Gases," Report 77, MIT Joint Program on the Science and Policy of Global Change, July 2001, available at www.mit.edu/globalchange/www/MITJPSPGC_Rpt77.pdf; James K. Hammitt et al., "A Welfare-Based Index for Assessing Environmental Effects of Greenhouse-Gas Emissions," *Nature* 381 (1996): 301–3. The global warming potential index is not perfect, but it is more accurate than ignoring the non–carbon dioxide gases (implicitly assigning them an index weight of zero); the need for those improvements is not a sound basis to abandon the global warming potential index and omit the non–carbon dioxide greenhouse gases or weight them arbitrarily. The Framework Convention on Climate Change is open to such improvement in the greenhouse gas indexes: Article 4(2)(c) adopts not the global warming potential index per se but the "best available scientific knowledge" on the "respective contributions of such gases to climate change." The body charged with revising greenhouse gas index values should be insulated from political pressures, because its changes will

affect the values of investment in abatement actions. See Reilly, Babiker, and Mayer, "Comparing Greenhouse Gases," 14–15. In addition, as discussed in chap. 2, n. 33, and chap. 5, n. 9, consideration should be given to expanding the group of greenhouse gases included in a greenhouse gas regulatory regime, at least for reporting and analysis purposes.

We share the concern that adopting a flawed global warming potential index may engender some path dependence that locks the climate policy regime into an inefficient gas-comparison approach that is difficult to revise later (because revisions could imply costs to those who have invested on the basis of the initial index). We have cited precisely that kind of concern as a reason for adopting the comprehensive approach in general, rather than starting with an energy–carbon dioxide–only regime and then being unable to expand it later in the face of vested interests that favor the narrow regime. See U.S. Department of Justice, *A Comprehensive Approach to Global Climate Change;* Stewart and Wiener, "A Comprehensive Approach to Climate Change Policy." One advantage of the approach we propose below—the United States engaging China and other major developing countries in a regime parallel to the Kyoto Protocol—would be the opportunity to adopt an improved greenhouse gas index.

37. Measurement of other greenhouse gases and sinks would be necessary even under a carbon dioxide emissions–only policy, if we are to evaluate the true effectiveness of the policy in protecting the climate, including the effects of perverse shifts in greenhouse gas emissions.

38. See Richard Cooper, "Toward a Real Global Warming Treaty," *Foreign Affairs* 77 (2) (1998): 66–79; William D. Nordhaus, "After Kyoto: Alternative Mechanisms to Control Global Warming," paper prepared for a joint session of the American Economic Association and the Association of Environmental and Resource Economics, January 4, 2002, available at www.econ.yale.edu/~nordhaus/homepage/PostKyoto_v4.pdf.

39. See Paul R. Portney and Robert N. Stavins, "Introduction," in Paul R. Portney and Robert N. Stavins, eds., *Public Policies for Environmental Protection,* 2d ed. (Washington, D.C.: Resources for the Future, 2000). For a general discussion of economic incentive systems and command regulatory approaches, see Richard B. Stewart, "Economic Incentives for Environmental Protection: Opportunities and Obstacles," in Richard L. Revesz, Philippe Sands, and Richard B. Stewart, eds., *Environmental Law, the Economy, and Sustainable Development: The United States, the European Union, and the International Community* (New York: Cambridge University Press, 2001), 171.

40. See Stewart, "Economic Incentives for Environmental Protection."

41. Maximizing cost-effectiveness is important because it saves resources that can be used to increase the amount of environmental protection undertaken or for other important social goals. See William J. Baumol and Wallace E. Oates, *The Theory of Environmental Policy,* 2d ed. (New York: Cambridge University Press, 1988), 21–22, 29.

42. See Stewart, "Economic Incentives for Environmental Protection." For example, before 1990, the primary approach to controlling acid rain was a technology-based scheme to require the installation of scrubbers that remove sulfur dioxide from electric power plant smokestacks. That uniform conduct instrument proved costly and discouraged electric utilities from alternative abatement methods such as switching to lower-sulfur fuels or conserving energy. In 1990 Congress adopted a new approach, using tradable allowances. Each electric utility was assigned sulfur dioxide emissions allowances, amounting in total to about a 50 percent aggregate reduction in national sulfur dioxide emissions. Firms could reduce their emissions to meet their allowance limits or go further and sell extra allowances or do less and buy additional allowances. Abatement methods could include scrubbers, lower-sulfur fuels, energy conservation, or other innovations. The result has been an even greater national reduction in sulfur dioxide emissions than required, at roughly half the cost of the prior uniform approach. See Paul L. Joskow, Richard Schmalensee, and Elizabeth M. Bailey, "The Market for Sulfur Dioxide Emissions," *American Economic Review* 88 (1998): 669.

43. See chap. 2, nn. 35–39. See, for example, Mustafa H. Babiker, Henry D. Jacoby, John M. Reilly, and David M. Reiner, "The Evolution of a Climate Regime: Kyoto to Marrakech," Report 82, MIT Joint Program on the Science and Policy of Global Change, February 2002, available at web.mit.edu/globalchange/www/abstracts.html#a82; Alan S. Manne and Richard G. Richels, "U.S. Rejection of the Kyoto Protocol: The Impact on Compliance Costs and CO_2 Emissions," Working Paper 01-12, AEI–Brookings Joint Center for Regulatory Studies, October 2001, available at www.aei.brookings.org/publications/working/working_01_12.pdf; John P. Weyant and J. Hill, "Introduction and Overview," in John P. Weyant, ed., *The Costs of the Kyoto Protocol: A Multimodel Evaluation, Energy Journal* (special issue) (May 1999), vii; A. Denny Ellerman, Henry D. Jacoby, and Annelene Decaux, "The Effects on Developing Countries of the Kyoto Protocol and CO_2 Emissions Trading," Report 41, MIT Joint Program on the Science and Policy of Global Change, December 1, 1998; Peter Bohm, "Joint Implementation as Emission Quota Trade: An Experiment among Four Nordic Countries," *Nord* 1997 (4), (1997), Nordic Council of Ministers, Copenhagen; Alan Manne and Richard Richels, "The Berlin Mandate: The Costs of Meeting Post-2000 Targets and Timetables," *Energy Policy* 24 (1996): 205–10; Jean-Marc Burniaux et al., "The Costs of Reducing CO_2 Emissions: Evidence from GREEN," Working Paper 115, OECD Economics Department, Paris, 1992.

44. Alan S. Manne and Richard G. Richels, "The Kyoto Protocol: A Cost-Effective Strategy for Meeting Environmental Objectives?" in Carlo Carraro, ed., *Efficiency and Equity of Climate Change Policy* (Norwell, Mass.: Kluwer Academic Publishers, 2000), 48–49.

45. See Adam Jaffe and Robert N. Stavins, "Dynamic Incentives of Environmental Regulations: The Effects of Alternative Policy Instruments on Technology Diffusion," *Journal of Environmental Economics and Management* 29 (1995): S-43. For a critique

of the claim that economic incentives provide superior incentives for innovation relative to command-and-control regulation, see Timothy F. Malloy, "Regulation by Incentives: Myths, Models, and Micromarkets," *Texas Law Review* 80 (2002): 531.

46. See n. 42 above and U.S. Environmental Protection Agency, "Acid Rain Program: Overview," available at www.epa.gov/airmarkets/arp/overview.html (visited November 4, 2002).

47. See Breyer, *Regulation and Its Reform,* 278–79 (noting that monitoring the actual environmental performance of technology–based standards is quite difficult).

48. This claim was made regarding U.S. regulation by Howard Latin, "Ideal versus Real Regulatory Efficiency: Implementation of Uniform Standards and 'Fine-Tuning' Regulatory Reforms," *Stanford Law Review* 37 (1985): 1267, and rebutted by Bruce Ackerman and Richard B. Stewart, "Reforming Environmental Law," *Stanford Law Review* 37 (1985): 1333. The claim has recently been renewed by Daniel H. Cole and Peter Z. Grossman, "When Is Command-and-Control Efficient? Institutions, Technology, and the Comparative Efficiency of Alternative Regulatory Regimes for Environmental Protection," *Wisconsin Law Review* 1999 (1999): 887. The argument that R & D and global technology–based standards could be superior to economic incentive systems for international climate policy has recently been made by Barrett and Stavins, "Increasing Participation and Compliance in International Climate Change Agreements."

49. See Jonathan Baert Wiener, "Global Environmental Regulation: Instrument Choice in Legal Context," *Yale Law Journal* 108 (1999): 677 (reviewing the debate over taxes versus trading); Barrett and Stavins, "Increasing Participation and Compliance in International Climate Change Agreements" (comparing post-Kyoto alternatives).

50. Martin L. Weitzman, "Prices vs. Quantities," *Review of Economic Studies* 41 (1974): 477.

51. See William Pizer, "Prices vs. Quantities Revisited: The Case of Climate Change," Discussion Paper 98-02, Resources for the Future, Washington, D.C., October 1997; Richard Newell and William Pizer, "Regulating Stock Externalities under Uncertainties," Discussion Paper 99-10-REV, Resources for the Future, Washington, D.C., May 2000.

52. See Wiener, "Global Environmental Regulation."

53. Ibid. See also Adam Rose and Brandt Stevens, "A Dynamic Analysis of the Efficiency and Equity of Tradable Greenhouse Gas Emissions Permits," in Carlo Carraro, ed., *Efficiency and Equity of Climate Change Policy* (Norwell, Mass.: Kluwer Academic Publishers, 2000), 247, 251, 263.

54. See Wiener, "Global Environmental Regulation."

55. See ibid., 726–27, 755–57; Baumol and Oates, *The Theory of Environmental Policy,* 211–28 (noting that abatement subsidies would reduce emissions at each firm but increase the size of the polluting industry and observing that using subsidies could conceivably increase net emissions); Wallace E. Oates, "Economics,

Economists, and Environmental Policy," *Eastern Economic Journal* 16 (1990): 289, 290 ("[I]n a competitive setting, [abatement] subsidies will lead to an excessively large number of firms and industry output. . . . [I]t is even conceivable that aggregate industry emissions could go up!" (citations omitted)); Robert E. Kohn, "When Subsidies for Pollution Abatement Increase Total Emissions," *Southern Economic Journal* 59 (1992): 77, 84–85; Stuart Mestelman, "Production Externalities and Corrective Subsidies: A General Equilibrium Analysis," *Journal of Environmental Economics and Management* 9 (1982): 186, 191.

56. See Wiener, "Global Environmental Regulation."

57. See Babiker et al., "The Evolution of a Climate Regime"; Ellerman, Jacoby, and Decaux, "The Effects on Developing Countries of the Kyoto Protocol and CO_2 Emissions Trading"; Joaquim Oliveira-Martins et al., "The Costs of Reducing CO_2 Emissions: A Comparison of Carbon Tax Curves with GREEN," Working Paper 118, OECD Economics Department, 1992.

58. Thus, an appropriately designed emissions trading system would meet developing country arguments that they should not be burdened with solving a problem created by the rich countries.

59. Although the European Union and others complain about the United States' buying allowances backed by Russian "hot air," if the United States does not buy those allowances from Russia, then the European Union will itself be using Russian hot air—by replacing European coal emissions with natural gas imported from Russia, so that EU emissions are lower but Russia emits more when it burns coal to replace the natural gas it sold. Banning Russian sales of headroom allowances would increase the costs of the treaty, encourage Russia to withdraw, or encourage Russia to use its headroom allowances at home by emitting more and thus achieving little climate protection at great cost. Perhaps for those reasons, the Bonn and Marrakech accords did not ban sales of Russian headroom allowances.

60. Peter Bohm, "International Greenhouse Gas Emissions Trading—With Special Reference to the Kyoto Protocol," in Carlo Carraro, ed., *Efficiency and Equity of Climate Change Policy* (Norwell, Mass.: Kluwer Academic Publishers 2000), 93, 108.

61. Babiker et al., "The Evolution of a Climate Regime," 11, 15.

62. An earlier run of the MIT model forecast U.S. purchases of somewhat less, $13 billion in Russian and Ukrainian allowances in 2010 under the Kyoto Protocol with Annex B trading (and only $9.27 billion from Russia, China, and others with full global trading). See Ellerman, Jacoby, and Decaux, "The Effects on Developing Countries of the Kyoto Protocol and CO_2 Emissions Trading," B3 and table 1-bis.

63. See Wiener, "Global Environmental Regulation," part 5. International authorities and developing countries might be able to monitor and detect fiscal cushioning and aid displacement moves, but the costs of such monitoring would likely exceed the costs of monitoring compliance with a system of tradable allowance assignments.

64. See ibid., part 4.

65. Baumol and Oates, *The Theory of Environmental Policy,* 279–81.

66. Ibid., 281. See n. 55, above; Oates, "Economics, Economists, and Environmental Policy"; Kohn, "When Subsidies for Pollution Abatement Increase Total Emissions."

67. See Wiener, "Global Environmental Regulation," part 4.

68. David F. Bradford, "Improving on Kyoto: Greenhouse Gas Control as the Purchase of a Global Public Good," Global Public Good Model Version 01, Princeton University and New York University, April 30, 2002 (copy on file with authors).

69. See Wiener, "Global Environmental Regulation," 750–54.

70. See Newell and Pizer, "Regulating Stock Externalities under Uncertainties." But experience with quantity limits in environmental regulation, particularly limits combined with emissions trading systems, shows that costs are often less than anticipated. See Winston Harrington, Richard D. Morgenstern, and Peter Nelson, "On the Accuracy of Regulatory Cost Estimates," *Journal of Policy Analysis and Management* 19 (2000): 297–322.

71. For example, in the MIT model, moving from no trading to full global trading reduces the price per ton of abatement from $127 to $24. See Ellerman, Jacoby, and Decaux, "The Effects on Developing Countries of the Kyoto Protocol and CO_2 Emissions Trading."

72. See Rose and Stevens, "A Dynamic Analysis of the Efficiency and Equity of Tradable Greenhouse Gas Emissions Permits," 261, 269.

73. See Raymond Kopp, Richard Morgenstern, and William Pizer, "Something for Everyone: A Climate Policy That Both Environmentalists and Industry Can Live With," *Weathervane* (Washington, D.C.: Resources for the Future, September 1997); Raymond Kopp, Richard Morgenstern, William Pizer, and Michael Toman, "A Proposal for Credible Early Action in U.S. Climate Policy," *Weathervane* (Washington, D.C.: Resources for the Future, February 1999); Joseph E. Aldy, Peter R. Orszag, and Joseph E. Stiglitz, "Climate Change: An Agenda for Global Collective Action," Pew Center on Global Climate Change, October 2001, available at www.pewclimate.org/media/stiglitz.pdf; David Victor, *The Collapse of the Kyoto Protocol and the Struggle to Slow Global Warming* (Princeton: Princeton University Press, 2001).

74. Some advocates of the safety valve respond to the fear of emissions escalation by earmarking the safety valve revenues for investment in abatement efforts overseas. But if such abatement opportunities were available at or below the safety valve trigger price, presumably private actors would already have made such purchases through emissions trading or the clean development mechanism. If abatement opportunities would cost more than the safety valve trigger price, then the safety valve would be allowing emissions to rise by selling allowances at the trigger price and then purchasing less-than-offsetting units of abatement overseas.

75. Compare Victor, *The Collapse of the Kyoto Protocol and the Struggle to Slow Global Warming* (advocating a safety valve with extra allowances sold by national governments), with Aldy, Orszag, and Stiglitz, "Climate Change" (advocating a safety valve with extra allowances sold by a central international agency).

76. See Henry D. Jacoby and A. Denny Ellerman, "The 'Safety Valve' and Climate Policy," Report 83, MIT Joint Program on the Science and Policy of Global Change (February 2002), available at web.mit.edu/globalchange/www/abstracts.html#a83.

77. See Council of Economic Advisers, *Economic Report of the President 2002* (Washington, D.C.: Government Printing Office, 2002), 246–47.

78. See Andrew C. Revkin, "Bush Offers Plan for Voluntary Measures to Limit Gas Emissions," *New York Times,* February 15, 2002; Office of the White House Press Secretary, "President Announces Clear Skies and Global Climate Change Initiatives," February 14, 2002, available at www.whitehouse.gov/news/releases/2002/02/20020214-5.html (visited February 14, 2002).

79. See Gloria Helfand, "Standards versus Standards: The Effects of Different Pollution Restrictions," *American Economic Review* 81 (1991): 622.

80. The program is voluntary. It relies on emissions registration, tax breaks, and a vague promise of affording credits against future regulatory requirements to motivate voluntary early reductions. There are no sanctions for exceeding the emissions intensity goals nor any plans for assigning emissions intensity allowances to individual firms. The program is wholly domestic (not yet including mechanisms to engage developing countries, except for the idea of intensity-based targets) and does not address the full domestic economy (indeed, voluntary registrants could claim to reduce emissions while spinning off emitting units into separate corporations that are unmeasured by the registry). It is, however, worth noting that the Bush proposal may be expanded as it is elaborated and implemented. See R. Glenn Hubbard, "Testimony before the Committee on Commerce, Science, and Transportation," U.S. Senate, July 11, 2002, available at www.commerce.senate.gov/hearings/071102hubbard.pdf. And the Bush plan (if actually accomplished) would yield a total emissions reduction below the business-as-usual level in 2010 that is quite similar to the degree of total emissions reduction recommended by optimal path models. The Bush plan proposes to achieve an emissions intensity in 2010 (or 2012) of .151 tons of carbon per dollar of GDP, which would be 18 percent below the 2002 emissions intensity of .183 and 4.5 percent below the business-as-usual 2010 emissions intensity of .165. To calculate the impact of that plan on total emissions, we assume U.S. business-as-usual total greenhouse gas emissions of 1670 million metric tons of carbon equivalent in 1990, 1906 million metric tons of carbon equivalent in 2000, and 2214 million metric tons of carbon equivalent in 2010; U.S. GDP of $5.88 trillion in 1990, $9.96 trillion in 2000, and $13.4 trillion in 2010; and thus U.S. business-as-usual emissions intensity of .284 tons of carbon equivalent per dollar in 1990, .191 in 2000, .183 in 2002, and .165 in 2010. Hence, the Bush plan to achieve

an emissions intensity of .151 would amount to total emissions of 2023 million metric tons of carbon equivalent in 2010, for a 191 million metric tons of carbon equivalent reduction or an 8 percent reduction below the business-as-usual total emissions in 2010. In his testimony Hubbard estimates a reduction of 100 million metric tons of carbon equivalent and a 4.5 percent reduction in total emissions below the business-as-usual level in 2010. So the Bush plan would yield somewhere between a 4 to 8 percent reduction below business-as-usual total emissions in 2010. By contrast, the U.S. target under the Kyoto Protocol is about a 30 percent reduction below the business-as-usual level in 2010 (or 7 percent below 1990). The least-cost path to stabilize concentrations would require a 0 percent reduction below the business-as-usual level in 2010 (but much sharper reductions later). See chap. 2, nn. 43–46; Tom Wigley, Richard Richels, and Jae Edmonds, "Economic and Environmental Choices in the Stabilization of Atmospheric CO_2 Concentrations," *Nature* 379 (January 1996): 240–43. Hammitt's optimal path would require a 3 percent global emissions reduction below the business-as-usual level in 2010, with sharper reductions in later years. See James K. Hammitt, "Evaluation Endpoints and Climate Policy: Atmospheric Stabilization, Benefit-Cost Analysis, and Near-Term Greenhouse-Gas Emissions," *Climatic Change* 41 (1999): 447. Nordhaus's optimal path would involve a .8 to 1.5 percent reduction below the business-as-usual level in 2010. See Nordhaus, "After Kyoto," 8 and figure 3. Thus, in terms of aggregate emissions, the Bush emissions intensity target is actually fairly close to the optimal path in 2010 (although the Bush plan does not yet address the years after 2010), more stringent than the least-cost stabilization path (in the near term), and less stringent than the Kyoto target for 2010.

81. Robert W. Hahn, "Market Power and Transferable Property Rights," *Quarterly Journal of Economics* 99 (1984): 753.

82. See Manne and Richels, "The Kyoto Protocol," 51–52. See also Andreas Löschel and ZhongXiang Zhang, "The Economic and Environmental Implications of the U.S. Repudiation of the Kyoto Protocol and the Subsequent Deals in Bonn and Marrakech," FEEM Working Paper 23.2002, April 2002, available at www.papers.ssrn.com/abstract=299463; Manne and Richels, "U.S. Rejection of the Kyoto Protocol." But see Babiker et al., "The Evolution of a Climate Regime" (suggesting that East European countries interested in joining the European Union might undercut Russian attempts to charge monopoly prices).

83. See Daniel J. Dudek and Jonathan Baert Wiener, *Joint Implementation, Transaction Costs, and Climate Change,* OECD/GD (96) 173 (1996), 20–21, available at www.oecd.org/pdf/M00007000/M00007875.pdf. Transaction costs under a tradable allowance system would involve searching for trade partners, negotiating the transaction, monitoring performance, and enforcing the deal, among other things. Taxes have some transaction costs as well, including the costs of monitoring and reporting taxable activities, collecting taxes, and enforcing against nonpayment.

84. Ibid. For further discussion, see Stewart, "Economic Incentives for Environmental Protection."

85. See Cooper, "Toward a Real Global Warming Treaty," 66, 70–72, 74, 78; Victor, *The Collapse of the Kyoto Protocol and the Struggle to Slow Global Warming.*

86. See Robert W. Hahn, *The Economics and Politics of Climate Change* (Washington, D.C.: AEI Press, 1998), 43.

87. See Ronald H. Coase, "The Problem of Social Cost," *Journal of Law and Economics* 3 (1960): 1.

88. Of course, the visibility of the wealth transfers involved in an emissions trading system could create negotiation problems where players are nations with domestic political constituencies. But a system of direct financial assistance to developing countries (bilaterally or through a central fund) would entail even more visible wealth transfers (and out of taxpayers' pockets) than an emissions trading system in which allowances are allocated and then the wealth transfer occurs through myriad individual, decentralized, competitive allowance purchases. A pure command regulatory system would not involve financial transfers and for that reason would be unable to enlist participation by most developing countries.

89. A related concern is that developing countries may sell their low-cost abatement opportunities to industrialized countries and then have only more expensive abatement opportunities left in the future. But developing countries are unlikely to act irrationally by selling allowances at a price lower than the value to the developing country of retaining the allowance. In other words, developing countries are likely to sell allowances only at prices that earn a profit, when taking into account the option value of retaining the allowance for the future. The risk of underpricing can be addressed by issuing (leasing) allowances for only limited periods to prevent lenders from doing long-term harm and by training developing country representatives to participate competently in an allowance market.

90. See Wiener, "Global Environmental Regulation," 788; Robert W. Hahn and Robert N. Stavins, *What Has the Kyoto Protocol Wrought? The Real Architecture of Tradable Permit Markets* (Washington, D.C.: AEI Press, 1999).

91. See Anne Smith, *Implications of Inconsistent and Nonmarket Domestic Greenhouse Gas Strategies* (Cambridge: Charles River Associates, May 2001).

92. The consequences of climate change can be seen as falling along a spectrum from pure adaptation (no preventive action to limit emissions or climate change; investment entirely in adaptive measures such as relocation of development from low-lying areas, development of drought-resistant crops, public health measures to combat disease) to pure prevention (relying totally on actions to curtail emissions with the ultimate goal of eliminating any risk of future climate change). Either end of the spectrum would be excessively costly in relation to marginal benefits. The optimal policy will fall somewhere in the middle ground, minimize the sum of adaptation costs plus prevention costs, and thus maximize net benefits.

93. Article 2 of the Framework Convention on Climate Change provides: "OBJECTIVE: The ultimate objective of this Convention and any related legal instruments that the Conference of the Parties may adopt is to achieve, in accordance with the relevant provisions of the Convention, stabilization of greenhouse gas concentrations in the atmosphere at a level that would prevent dangerous anthropogenic interference with the climate system. Such a level should be achieved within a time-frame sufficient to allow ecosystems to adapt naturally to climate change, to ensure that food production is not threatened and to enable economic development to proceed in a sustainable manner."

94. Hammitt, "Evaluation Endpoints and Climate Policy." See also Nordhaus, "After Kyoto." See the discussion in chap. 2, accompanying nn. 43–46.

Chapter 6: Assessing and Correcting the Kyoto Protocol's Flaws

1. In addition, under Articles 3.1 and 4.1, two or more countries may choose to fulfill their obligations jointly, which could provide the foundation for emissions trading among the countries participating in such an arrangement.

2. See Jonathan B. Wiener, "Something Borrowed for Something Blue: Legal Transplants and the Evolution of Global Environmental Law," *Ecology Law Quarterly* 27 (2001): 1295 (describing evolution of those ideas in American and international climate policy). The early documents advocating those ideas include "Memorandum from Assistant Attorney General Richard B. Stewart to Chairman of the Domestic Policy Council Working Group on Global Change D. Allan Bromley," December 18, 1989; "U.S. Submission to Intergovernmental Panel on Climate Change Working Group III," December 29, 1989; Richard B. Stewart and Jonathan B. Wiener, "A Comprehensive Approach to Climate Change," *American Enterprise* 1 (6) (November–December 1990): 75; U.S. Department of Justice, *A Comprehensive Approach to Global Climate Change* (Washington, D.C.: Government Printing Office, 1991); Richard B. Stewart and Jonathan B. Wiener, "A Comprehensive Approach to Climate Change Policy: Issues of Design and Practicality," *Arizona Journal of International and Comparative Law* 9 (1992): 83, 85.

3. Emissions credit trading programs like the joint implementation program authorized under Article 6 of the Kyoto Protocol and the clean development mechanism authorized under Article 12 pose greater difficulties of measurement and efficacy, but they can be managed by default measurement rules that are gradually made more sophisticated over time.

4. See, for example, Kenneth Richards, "Coercion and Enterprise in the Provision of Environmental Public Goods: The Case of Carbon Sequestration in the United States," *Critical Reviews in Environmental Science and Technology* 27 (special issue) (1997): S293–S307 (on institutional uncertainties and sink costs).

5. See Jonathan Baert Wiener, "On the Political Economy of Global Environmental Regulation," *Georgetown Law Journal* 87 (February 1999): 749, 778–80. The

EU stance may reflect a classic "Baptists and bootleggers" alliance to distort regulatory policy for parochial ends. See ibid., 778–80; Bruce Yandle and Stuart Buck, "Bootleggers, Baptists, and the Global Warming Battle," *Harvard Environmental Law Review* 26 (2002): 177; Bruce Yandle, "Bootleggers and Baptists in the Market for Regulation," in Jason F. Shogren, ed., *The Political Economy of Government Regulation* (Boston: Kluwer, 1989), 29–54 (tracing the label "Baptists and bootleggers" to the odd bedfellows who supported bans on Sunday liquor sales: moral purists who sought to prevent sin and illegal alcohol producers whose sales would rise from suppressing their competitors). Environmental absolutists—in nongovernmental organizations and in the Green Parties helping to make up the ruling coalitions of some key European governments—could denounce the flexibility mechanisms as lacking environmental integrity, while European and developing country representatives could piously endorse that view because it served their underlying economic interest in imposing higher costs on their trade rivals, principally the United States, Japan, and Canada. Developing countries have opposed emissions trading and their own accession to such a system in part because they fear the costs of emissions caps (even with substantial headroom to grow and to sell allowances at a profit), in part because they fear being at a competitive disadvantage when participating in emissions trading markets, and in part because their domestic politics may pit governing elites against the market sector so that the revenues from market-based emissions trading look like a bane rather than a boon to the officials who negotiate the climate treaties. See Wiener, "On the Political Economy of Global Environmental Regulation," 775–81.

6. Ibid., 780–81. See also chap. 4, nn. 17–18.

7. The Marrakech Accords, Draft Decision -/CMP.1, Part J.5, "Modalities for the Accounting of Assigned Amounts under Article 7, Paragraph 4, of the Kyoto Protocol," para. 16, 107.

8. The Marrakech Accords, Part J.3, "Modalities and Procedures for a Clean Development Mechanism as Defined in Article 12 of the Kyoto Protocol, Decision -/CP.7 (Article 12)," para. 7(b), 70.

9. It is unclear from the Bonn and Marrakech documents when, on what criteria, and at whose decision such eligibility would be restored.

10. Kyoto Protocol Article 12(3)(b) provides that clean development mechanism credits earned beginning in 2000 may be used by Annex I countries against their first commitment period limitations obligations.

11. See Mustafa H. Babiker, Henry D. Jacoby, John M. Reilly, and David M. Reiner, "The Evolution of a Climate Regime: Kyoto to Marrakech," Report 82, MIT Joint Program on the Science and Policy of Global Change, February 2002, 12–13, available at web.mit.edu/globalchange/www/abstracts.html#a82; Andreas Löschel and ZhongXiang Zhang, "The Economic and Environmental Implications of the U.S. Repudiation of the Kyoto Protocol and the Subsequent Deals in Bonn and Marrakech," FEEM Working Paper 23.2002, April 2002, available at www.papers.ssrn.com/abstract=299463; Alan S. Manne and Richard G. Richels, "The Kyoto Protocol: A Cost-Effective Strategy for Meeting Environmental

Objectives?" in Carlo Carraro, ed., *Efficiency and Equity of Climate Change Policy* (Norwell, Mass.: Kluwer Academic Publishers, 2000), 54.

12. See chap. 3, n. 9 (citing leakage studies). Leakage will also render the developing countries' economies more greenhouse gas–intensive over time and thus will make it more costly and less attractive for them to join the treaty in the future. Richard Schmalensee, "Greenhouse Policy Architectures and Institutions," in William D. Nordhaus, ed., *Economics and Policy Issues in Climate Change* (Washington, D.C.: Resources for the Future, 1998), 146.

13. Alan and Richels, "The Kyoto Protocol," 52–53; Byrd-Hagel Resolution, S. Res. 98, *Congressional Record* 143 (July 25, 1997): S8113–39; "Climate Change: Senate Approves Resolution to Require Binding Controls on Developing Nations," *Environment Reporter* 28 (BNA) (August 1, 1997): 621; "Statement of Senator Robert Byrd," *Congressional Record,* June 8, 2001, S6000, S6001 (see chap. 3, n. 11, for an extract of Byrd's statement).

14. See Jacob Werksman and James Cameron, "The Clean Development Mechanism: The 'Kyoto Surprise,'" in Luis Gomez-Echeverri, ed., *Climate Change and Development* (New York and New Haven: United Nations Development Program and Yale School of Forestry and Environmental Studies, 2000), 249, 257; Malik Amin Aslam, Jos Cozijnsen, Svetlana Morozova, Mark Stuart, Richard B. Stewart, and Philippe Sands, *Greenhouse Gas Market Perspectives: Trade and Investment Implications of the Climate Change Regime, Recent Research on Institutional and Economic Aspects of Carbon Trading,* UNCTAD/DITC/ TED/Misc.9 (Geneva: UNCTAD, 2001).

15. See Jonathan Baert Wiener, "Global Environmental Regulation: Instrument Choice in Legal Context," *Yale Law Journal* 108 (1999): 677, 726–27, 755–57. See chap. 5, nn. 55 and 66.

16. See James K. Hammitt, "Evaluation Endpoints and Climate Policy: Atmospheric Stabilization, Benefit-Cost Analysis, and Near-Term Greenhouse-Gas Emissions," *Climatic Change* 41 (1999): 447. The least-cost path to stabilize emissions at 750, 650, or 550 parts per million would require essentially zero reduction below the business-as-usual level through 2025 but steeper reductions later. See Tom Wigley, Richard Richels, and Jae Edmonds, "Economic and Environmental Choices in the Stabilization of Atmospheric CO_2 Concentrations," *Nature* 379 (January 1996): 240–43.

17. For example, with high climate sensitivity, Hammitt's optimal path requires an 8 percent reduction in emissions below the business-as-usual level in 2010 and remains 40 percent above 1990 levels through 2100 before declining—well above the Kyoto targets.

Chapter 7: U.S. Lead in Reconstruction

1. "[A] U.S. demand for imposing a cap on China's future emissions is absolutely unacceptable for China, at least until its per capita income catches up with the level of middle-developed countries." ZhongXiang Zhang, "Can China Afford to Commit Itself to an Emissions Cap? An Economic and Political Analysis," *Energy*

Economics 22 (2000): 587, 606. See also Deborah E. Cooper, "The Kyoto Protocol and, China," *Georgetown International Law Review* 11 (1999): 401 (reviewing China's consistent opposition to emission limitations obligations).

2. For discussion of this literature and its application to the climate change treaties, see Jonathan B. Wiener, "Something Borrowed for Something Blue: Legal Transplants and the Evolution of Global Environmental Law," *Ecology Law Quarterly* 27 (2001): 1295, 1296–1371.

3. The Montreal Protocol could have evolved even more efficiently (more environmental benefits at less cost) if it had employed the approach we favor— a cap-and-trade regime with headroom tradable allowances for developing countries—instead of giving developing countries a significant lag time (but no tradable allowances) before their obligations arose. See Peter Bohm, "Efficiency Issues and the Montreal Protocol on CFCs," in Partha Dasgupta and Karl-Goran Maler, eds., *The Environment and Emerging Development Issues*, vol. 2 (New York: Clarendon Press, 1997), 308, 327.

4. See Jonathan Baert Wiener, "Global Environmental Regulation: Instrument Choice in Legal Context," *Yale Law Journal* 108 (1999): 677, 743–55; Lloyd Gruber, *Ruling the World: Power Politics and the Rise of Supranational Institutions* (Princeton: Princeton University Press, 2000).

5. The problem of initial treaty parties' attempting to block new entrants is addressed in Richard B. Stewart, Jonathan B. Wiener, and Philippe Sands, *Legal Issues Presented by a Pilot International Greenhouse Gas Trading System* (Geneva: UNCTAD, 1996). See also ZhongXiang Zhang, "The Design and Implementation of an International Trading Scheme for Greenhouse Gas Emissions," *Environment and Planning: Government and Policy* 18 (2000): 321, 332 (advocating enlargement of the emissions trading system to include developing countries but worrying that Annex B parties might try to block developing country accession to preserve market power in allowance sales). For example, one can envision that Russia might vote to block China's accession lest China compete with Russian allowance sales.

6. Byrd-Hagel Resolution, S. Res. 98, *Congressional Record* 143 (July 25, 1997): S8113–39; "Climate Change: Senate Approves Resolution to Require Binding Controls on Developing Nations," *Environment Reporter* 28 (BNA) (August 1, 1997): 621.For Senator Byrd's more recent statement, see chap. 3, n. 11.

7. John M. Broder, "Clinton Adamant on Third World Role in Climate Accord," *New York Times*, December 12, 1997. As noted in chap. 1, n. 9, one year later a *New York Times* editorial asserted that Senate ratification would be "out of the question" until large developing countries such as India and China were brought on board. "Remember Global Warming?" November 11, 1998.

8. An alternative strategy is simply to assist poorer countries now, rather than limit greenhouse gas emissions, on the view that poorer countries would rather have present help than future help. See Thomas C. Schelling, *Costs and Benefits of Greenhouse Gas Reduction* (Washington, D.C.: AEI Press, 1998). That objective is accomplished to a significant extent under our

proposal to engage developing countries via assignment of valuable headroom allowances.

9. In our view, relative future net benefit, not historical causal responsibility, should guide countries' relative contributions to climate protection. See Wiener, "Global Environmental Regulation."

10. See chap. 3, nn. 9–11.

11. See Byrd-Hagel Resolution. Similarly, the fear of leakage to developing countries in response to the Montreal Protocol made it a high priority for the industrialized country parties to secure the participation of China, Russia, and India. See Tony Brenton, *The Greening of Machiavelli: The Evolution of International Environmental Politics* (London: Earthscan, 1994), 142.

12. The European Union has compounded that error by insisting (perhaps because of domestic political conditions that have created a "lock-in") on going ahead with the Kyoto Protocol without a further effort to engage the United States and major developing countries. Likewise, U.S. administrations and advocacy groups intent on creating a viable international climate protection regime erred in focusing their negotiating efforts on the European Union while neglecting China, India, Brazil, and other major emitting developing countries. The European Union (and the United States) should have been working to attract China and other nations and thereby to engage the United States as well.

13. See Richard Tol, "New Estimates of the Damage Costs of Climate Change, Part I: Benchmark Estimates," *Environmental and Resource Economics* 21 (2002): 47; Richard Tol, "New Estimates of the Damage Costs of Climate Change, Part II: Dynamic Estimates," *Environmental and Resource Economics* 21 (2002): 135 (finding that China would reap a benefit from moderate global warming of approximately 2 percent of GDP over the next century); Zhou Xin, "The Benefits of Climate Change? China's Take on Global Warming," *Weathervane* (Washington, D.C.: Resources for the Future, February 2, 1997), available at www.weathervane.rff.org/features/feature012.html (reporting that Chinese researchers have concluded that a warmer climate will benefit China and other developing countries). A similar perception may exist in Russia, which helps explain why Russia needed to receive extra headroom allowances to attract Russia's participation in the Kyoto Protocol. See Michael Hoel, "How Should International Greenhouse Gas Agreements Be Designed?" in Partha Dasgupta et al., eds., *The Economics of Transnational Commons,* 172, 181 (New York: Oxford University Press, 1997) ("[O]ne could argue . . . that significant parts of the former U.S.S.R. would benefit from a warmer climate."); A. L. Hollick and R. N. Cooper, "Global Commons: Can They Be Managed?" in *The Economics of Transnational Commons,* 141, 168 ("[S]ome countries may be expected to benefit from at least a modest amount of warming (e.g., . . . the [former] Soviet Union), and this possibility may also induce reluctance to contribute to an international [abatement] effort."); Oran R. Young, "The Politics of International Regime Formation: Managing Natural Resources and the Environment," *International Organization* 43 (1989): 349, 367–68 (similar).

14. A. Denny Ellerman, Henry D. Jacoby, and Annelene Decaux, "The Effects on Developing Countries of the Kyoto Protocol and CO_2 Emissions Trading," Report 41, MIT Joint Program on the Science and Policy of Global Change, December 1, 1998, B3 and tables B and C. (Rounding may affect some of the numbers.) Those estimates do not account for allowance sales based on sink enhancement or abatement of non–carbon dioxide greenhouse gases. Those figures assume that the United States participates under its Kyoto target; the MIT model shows the United States purchasing 390 million tons of allowances in the global allowance trading market (almost half of the 935 million tons traded). If the United States did not participate, presumably China's allowance sale revenues would be significantly lower. That reinforces our belief that China would not join the cap-and-trade regime without the United States.

15. Ellerman, Jacoby, and Decaux, "The Effects on Developing Countries of the Kyoto Protocol and CO_2 Emissions Trading," B3 and tables B and C. The industrialized countries would purchase more allowances under global trading than under Annex B trading because allowance prices would be lower—$24 rather than $127 per ton. Ibid.

16. See Scott Barrett, "Transfers and the Gains from Trading Carbon Emission Entitlements in a Global Warming Treaty," in *Combating Global Warming: Study on a System of Tradable Carbon Emission Entitlements* (Geneva: UNCTAD, 1992); Joaquim Oliveira-Martins et al., "The Costs of Reducing CO_2 Emissions: A Comparison of Carbon Tax Curves with GREEN," Working Paper 118, OECD Economics Department, 1992 (finding that under a policy capping global aggregate carbon dioxide emissions at their 1990 levels by the year 2050, by cutting emissions sharply in the OECD member states while letting emissions grow (though more slowly than in the baseline forecast) in developing countries, allowance trading would yield resource flows (in constant 1985 dollars) to China, India, and the former Soviet Union of about $14 billion in 2000, about $86 billion in 2020, and about $206 billion in 2050, while also reducing global costs and OECD–member costs by about 50 percent or more compared with a no-trading regime).

17. See Zhang, "Can China Afford to Commit Itself to an Emissions Cap?"; Randall Lutter, "Developing Countries' Greenhouse Emissions: Uncertainty and Implications for Participation in the Kyoto Protocol," *Energy Journal* 21 (2000): 93

18. See Jayant Sathaye et al., "Costs of Reducing Carbon Emission from the Energy Sector: A Comparison of China, India, and Brazil," *Ambio* 25 (June 1996): 262 (finding that technological change and energy policy in both India and Brazil can maintain or even increase the nation's GDP while simultaneously reducing carbon emissions); Madhu Khanna and David Zilberman, "Adoption of Energy Efficient Technologies and Carbon Abatement: The Electricity Generating Sector in India," *Energy Economics* 23 (2001): 637 (finding that policy reforms that introduce energy efficiency in the electricity generating sector in India can reduce carbon emissions by 6 percent while allowing aggregate electricity output to

increase 9 percent relative to the base level in 1990, even in the absence of an emissions tax).

19. Another factor that may influence developing country opposition to emissions trading may be domestic rivalry within developing countries. Although emissions trading would benefit their economies as a whole, it could benefit the market class at the (relative) expense of the governing class, and the representatives of those countries in the climate treaty negotiations may represent the governing class that would prefer to receive direct government-to-government financial transfers and not to have emissions trading enrich its domestic rivals. See Jonathan Baert Wiener, "On the Political Economy of Global Environmental Regulation," *Georgetown Law Journal* 87 (February 1999): 749, 780–81. A formal model of such strategic behavior by government elites to hold back national economic progress is presented by Daron Acemoglu and James A. Robinson, "Economic Backwardness in Political Perspective," Massachusetts Institute of Technology, Department of Economics, February 2002, available at econ-www.mit.edu/faculty/acemoglu/files/papers/backward8.pdf (drawing in turn on Alexander Gerschenkron, *Economic Backwardness in Historical Perspective* (Cambridge: Harvard University Press, 1962)). If such behavior is indeed blocking participation in global emissions trading, advocates of global emissions trading will need to help foster the transition to market economies and promarket government policies in developing countries, help publicize the net benefits to developing countries of participation in allowance trading, and perhaps help arrange for developing country governing elites to receive some of the benefits of allowance trading.

20. See chap. 3, n. 6.

21. See Barbara A. Finamore and Tauna M. Saymanski, "Taming the Dragon Heads: Controlling Air Emissions from Power Plants in China," *Environmental Law Reporter* 32 (December 2002): 11439; Richard D. Morganstern et al., "Demonstrating Emissions Trading in Taiyuan China," *RFF Resources* 148 (Summer 2002): 7; Christina L. Dobridge, Tam Pui Ying, and So Hoi Ying, *Emissions Trading in China: Opportunities and Constraints* (Hong Kong: Civic Exchange, 2001). Such optimism should not be exaggerated. See William P. Alford and Yuanyuan Shen, "Limits of the Law in Addressing China's Environmental Dilemma," *Stanford Environmental Law Journal* 16 (1997): 125, 136–37 ("[T]he establishment of a workable system of tradable discharge permits [in China] presume[s] more in the way of market mechanisms . . . than is now available in China or likely to be in the foreseeable future. . . . [M]any Chinese economic entities continue to operate in ways inconsistent with such market principles. Large national state-owned enterprises still occupy a prominent role in the economy [and] . . . such enterprises include many of China's biggest polluters."). The mass privatization announced at the Fifteenth Communist Party Congress in September of 1997 may have accelerated the transition to markets, but it remains to be seen whether that privatization will include sectors relevant to global environmental problems, such as the energy sector. See Shao Shiwei Lu, Zhengyong Berrah,

Noureddine Tenenbaum, and Bernard Zhao Jianping, eds., "China: Power Sector Regulation in a Socialist Market Economy," World Bank Discussion Paper 361, March 31, 1997, xiii, 3–6 (noting that the Chinese electric power sector remains centrally organized and state-run and lacks well-defined property rights or market incentives for efficiency).

22. See Agriculture and Meteorology Institute, Chinese Academy of Agricultural Science, "Impact of Climate Change on Chinese Agriculture and Possible Adaptive Measures" (last updated February 2001), available at www.ami.ac.cn/climatechange2/85/crop/preface_2.htm (visited December 23, 2001) (translated by Zheng Zhou, Duke University) ("Agriculture is going to be the hardest hit sector by climate change (in China)" (para. 6, last sentence); "Considering the expansion of desert and semidesert areas due to global warming, the productive potential of agricultural crops will be lowered by an average of 10 percent as a result of climate change. But the highest production can still reach 720–930 million tons and may still satisfy the peak demand for food (650 million tons), with much greater difficulties of course. The difficulties need to be overcome by an increased governmental investment in agriculture" (para. 7)).

23. See Avery Goldstein, "The Diplomatic Face of China's Grand Strategy: A Rising Power's Emerging Choice," *China Quarterly* 168 (December 2001): 835, 845.

24. Ellerman, Jacoby, and Decaux, "The Effects on Developing Countries of the Kyoto Protocol and CO_2 Emissions Trading," B3 and table B. Put another way, to meet Kyoto targets from the business-as-usual level in 2010, the United States would abate 572 million tons (466 million tons domestically, plus 106 million tons allowance purchases), the former Soviet Union would be allowed to increase 111 million tons of headroom above its business-as-usual level, and the rest of Annex B would abate 740 million tons (495 million tons domestically, plus 245 million tons allowance purchases). Ibid., tables 1 and B. There is still domestic abatement: 466 million tons by the United States, 201 million tons by the European Union, 49 million tons by Japan, 128 million tons by other industrialized nations, and 124 million tons by Eastern Europe. Ibid.

25. Ibid., figure 8.

26. On the other hand, allowance prices in Annex B trading may not fall so much because of U.S. withdrawal if Russia decides to bank its allowances to have them to sell to the United States in the second commitment period. See Alan S. Manne and Richard G. Richels, "U.S. Rejection of the Kyoto Protocol: The Impact on Compliance Costs and CO_2 Emissions," Working Paper 01-12, AEI–Brookings Joint Center for Regulatory Studies, October 2001, available at www.aei.brookings.org/publications/working/working_01_12.pdf. Such a move would depend on Russia's prediction that the United States would join in the second commitment period and also that China would not join the cap-and-trade regime. If the United States failed to join, or if China also joined (or sold large numbers of clean development mechanism credits), Russia would gain much less from banking allowances to sell in the second commitment period.

27. "Without the U.S. in the market, the supply of excess emission reductions ("hot air") from the Annex I countries with economies in transition could be equal to most or all of the remaining demand for emission reductions by the other Annex I countries." Ned Helme, "The Marrakech Accords: Where Will the Trade Winds Blow?" *In the Air* (Washington, D.C.: Center for Clean Air Policy, December 2001), 1.

28. See William D. Nordhaus, "Global Warming Economics," *Science* 294 (November 9, 2001): 1283, 1284.

29. See Babiker et al., "The Evolution of a Climate Regime"; Carlo Carraro, Barbara Buchner, and Igor Cersosimo, "On the Consequences of the U.S. Withdrawal from the Kyoto/Bonn Protocol," FEEM Working Paper 102.2001, December 2001, available at www.papers.ssrn.com/abstract=296930; Andreas Löschel and ZhongXiang Zhang, "The Economic and Environmental Implications of the U.S. Repudiation of the Kyoto Protocol and the Subsequent Deals in Bonn and Marrakech," FEEM Working Paper 23.2002, April 2002, available at www.papers.ssrn.com/abstract=299463.

30. See Manne and Richels, "U.S. Rejection of the Kyoto Protocol," figures 4 and 5. As a result, they find that costs to the European Union and other Annex B parties would fall significantly and costs to Russia would rise (from net benefit to net cost). But Manne and Richels note that if the former Soviet Union (Russia and Ukraine) anticipates U.S. accession in a second commitment period, the former Soviet Union may withhold most of its allowances in 2010 and bank them for later sale when the United States enters the market; if so, the allowance price in 2010 would drop very little. Ibid., figure 4. (On the other hand, they do not model the possibility of Chinese accession in the second commitment period, which would presumably reduce allowance prices and therefore lead Russia not to bank so many allowances, that is, to sell more in 2010.) A further consideration is that if the former Soviet Union could exercise market power in the Annex B trading system, it might maintain relatively high prices for allowances even without U.S. participation. Ibid., 10 and figure 8.

31. If Kyoto allowance prices turn out to be quite low, it is possible that Russia would prefer accession by just the United States, or by the United States and only a few developing countries, or developing countries with restrictions on their sales to keep the allowance price higher. If Kyoto allowance prices turn out to be very expensive for the European Union and Japan (for example, because of an effective Russian monopoly), the European Union and Japan might prefer accession by some developing countries without the United States. Under uncertainty about future prices, Russia, the European Union, and Japan might all prefer, or might reach a bargain providing for, joint accession by the United States and China and other developing countries.

32. Those examples are drawn from James K. Hammitt, "Evaluation Endpoints and Climate Policy: Atmospheric Stabilization, Benefit-Cost Analysis, and Near-Term Greenhouse-Gas Emissions," *Climatic Change* 41 (1999): 447–68. William

D. Nordhaus, "After Kyoto: Alternative Mechanisms to Control Global Warming," paper prepared for a joint session of the American Economic Association and the Association of Environmental and Resource Economics, January 4, 2002, available at www.econ.yale.edu/~nordhaus/homepage/PostKyoto_v4.pdf, generates roughly similar optimal targets. The point here is the principle of setting targets based on net benefits, not the specific percentage reductions reported by particular economic models.

33. Overly ambitious targets set too close to the present are too difficult to achieve and therefore invite repeated violation and deferral in a process that makes the initial targets lack credibility and inculcates public cynicism about the regulatory regime. A similar cycle of unrealistic targets followed by deferral and cynicism has characterized several major U.S. environmental laws, such as the national ambient air quality standards under the Clean Air Act amendments of 1970, 1977, and 1990 and the best technology standards under the Clean Water Act amendments of 1972, 1977, and 1987. See William F. Pedersen, "Turning the Tide on Water Quality," *Ecology Law Quarterly* 15 (1988): 69; R. Shep Melnick, "Pollution Deadlines and the Coalition for Failure," *Public Interest* 75 (1984): 123. On the other hand, targets set too many years hence may fail to motivate changes in business investments and may themselves lack credibility because there is so much time available to debate and revise them. A middle course is to set not a single target for one out-year or period but a stepwise schedule of emissions limitation targets, beginning with smaller reductions from the business-as-usual level and tightening over time. That approach was successful in the "lead phasedown" from the 1970s through the late 1980s and was approximated in the acid rain title of the 1990 Clean Air Act amendments and in the Montreal Protocol on chlorofluorocarbons. In the climate context, such targets could be set in accordance with emissions pathways developed under net benefits–maximizing criteria.

34. The Marrakech Accords, Part J.3, "Modalities and Procedures for a Clean Development Mechanism as Defined in Article 12 of the Kyoto Protocol," Decision -/CP.7 (Article 12), para. 7(b), 70. The only justification for retaining that restriction would be to create an incentive for developing countries to join the international cap-and-trade system.

35. See the Marrakech Accords, Part J.4, "Modalities, Rules, and Guidelines for Emissions Trading," and its annex paragraphs 6–10, Decision -/CP.7 (Article 17), 96–100 (unedited version of November 10, 2001, downloaded from www.unfccc.int on November 14, 2001). That restriction applies to assigned amount units, emission reduction units, certified emission reduction credits, and emission removal units. Some commenters have speculated that the effects of the commitment period reserve on allowance selling would be "minor," but they have not modeled it quantitatively. See Babiker et al., "The Evolution of a Climate Regime," 10. Others have expressed concern that the commitment period reserve requirement would raise costs. See Johan Eyckmans, Denise Van Regemorter, and Vincent van Steenberghe, "Is Kyoto Fatally Flawed? An Analysis with MacGEM,"

Working Paper 2001-18, Energy, Transport, and Environment Working Paper Series, Faculty of Economics and Applied Economic Sciences, Center for Economic Studies, Catholic University at Leuven, September 2001, 12–16, available at www.econ.kuleuven.ac.be/ew/academic/energmil/publications/ete-wp01-18.pdf (under "this restriction . . . [the] supply of permits is limited and hence, the equilibrium price rises from 10.033 to 13.783 $/t carbon dioxide. While world total compliance costs increase only marginally from 0.0082 percent to 0.0083 percent 2010 GDP, Annex B excluding USA total costs increase by about 30 percent, from 0.029 percent to 0.038 percent 2010 GDP."); Peter Bohm, "Improving Cost-Effectiveness and Facilitating Participation of Developing Countries in International Emissions Trading," University of Stockholm, September 2001, 15–18, available at www.rieti.go.jp/jp/events/02031901/bohm.pdf ("To sum up, if effective, the CPR [commitment period reserve] reduces cost-effectiveness. In addition, it has distributional effects. It hits seller countries, typically poorer countries, but not buyer countries, which are all wealthier countries."); Richard Baron, "The Commitment Period Reserve," Information Paper, OECD Environment Directorate and International Energy Agency, COM/ENV/EPOC/IEA/SLT(2001)13, October 2001, available at www.oecd.org/pdf/M00020000/M00020141.pdf ("Analyses suggest that the quantity of restricted sales might be limited, when compared to [sic] the overall trading that would be allowed during the commitment period. In addition, trading tools such as forward and futures contracts could remedy this problem without increasing the risk of overselling—albeit with an additional cost related to this more complex type of transaction.").

36. If countries adopt domestic trading systems (as most probably will), they will issue allowances to private or public entities that will own and have the right to sell or transfer them. International sales and transfers of allowances by such entities would be recorded in a central register and matched by bookkeeping transfers of tradable emissions units assigned to their respective nations. See Stewart, Wiener, and Sands, *Legal Issues Presented by a Pilot International Greenhouse Gas Trading System.* If nations do not adopt domestic trading systems, they would sell or otherwise transfer units directly.

37. See Annie Petsonk, "The Kyoto Protocol and the WTO: Integrating Greenhouse Gas Emissions Allowance Trading into the Global Marketplace," *Duke Environmental Law and Policy Forum* 10 (1999): 185–220.

38. See Eleanor M. Fox, "Toward World Antitrust and Market Access," *American Journal of International Law* 91 (1997): 1, 3.

39. See Stewart, Wiener, and Sands, *Legal Issues Presented by a Pilot International Greenhouse Gas Trading System;* David Victor, *The Collapse of the Kyoto Protocol and the Struggle to Slow Global Warming* (Princeton: Princeton University Press, 2001); ZhongXiang Zhang, "The Liability Rules under International Greenhouse Gas Emissions Trading," *Energy Policy* 29 (2001): 501–8. Under buyer as well as seller liability, there must be effective monitoring, reporting, and review arrangements that will enable compliance to be determined on a consistent and credible basis.

40. For discussion of potential problems with that practice, see chap. 5, n. 73.

41. The United States has recently advocated such an approach. See Amy Waldman, "At Climate Meeting, Unlikely Ally for Have-Nots," *New York Times,* November 1, 2002; Andrew C. Revkin, "Climate Talks Shift Focus to How to Deal with Changes," *New York Times,* November 3, 2002.

42. See Robert J. Lempert and Michael E. Schlesinger, "Adaptive Strategies for Climate Change," in Robert G. Watts, ed., *Innovative Energy Strategies for CO_2 Stabilization* (New York: Cambridge University Press, 2002).

43. Such a method would be revenue-neutral—no increase in cost to the average motorist. It would shift insurance premiums from a fixed annual cost to a variable cost and thereby discourage marginal driving. It would also capture uninsured motorists in the insurance system and thereby potentially reduce costs to insured motorists.

44. See chap. 4, n. 11 (regarding proposals for early action credit).

45. See Raymond Kopp, Richard Morgenstern, and William Pizer, "Something for Everyone: A Climate Policy That Both Environmentalists and Industry Can Live With," *Weathervane* (Washington, D.C.: Resources for the Future, September 1997); Axel Michaelowa and Marcus Stronzik, "Early Crediting of Emissions Reductions—A Panacea or Pandora's Box?" in Carlo Carraro, ed., *Efficiency and Equity of Climate Change Policy* (Norwood, Mass.: Kluwer Academic Publishers, 2000), 185.

46. See chap. 4, n. 10; Juan-Pablo Montero, "Multipollutant Markets," *RAND Journal of Economics* 32 (4) (2001): 762–74 (analyzing conditions under which multipollutant trading markets are more efficient than separate markets).

47. By contrast, the European Commission proposal for an EU carbon dioxide trading system calls for negotiated access to the EU system for allowances (or other tradable units) issued by other governments. It is envisaged that access agreements would be negotiated by the commission with other countries on a country-by-country basis. Before concluding such an agreement, the commission would assure itself "that the environmental quality of allowances issued elsewhere is satisfactory and the monitoring compliance and national registry provisions are robust." European Commission, *Proposal for a Directive of the European Parliament and of the Council Establishing a Scheme for Greenhouse Gas Emission Allowance Trading within the Community and Amending Council Directive 96/61/EC,* COM(2001)581final (Brussels: European Commission, October 23, 2001), 16. We believe it far preferable to provide for automatic recognition of allowances issued by another nation participating in an international cap-and-trade agreement, with monitoring and enforcement provided by the general requirements of environmental integrity and compliance assurance established pursuant to the international agreement among all parties. See Stewart, Wiener, and Sands, *Legal Issues Presented by a Pilot International Greenhouse Gas Trading System.*

48. See Lawrence H. Goulder, "The Costs of Political Feasibility," presentation at Resources for the Future, Washington, D.C., December 2001.

Chapter 8: Conclusion

1. See Robert W. Hahn, *The Economics and Politics of Climate Change* (Washington, D.C.: AEI Press, 1998) (advocating policy experiments).

Index

About the Authors

Richard B. Stewart is University Professor and Emily Kempin Professor of Law at the New York University School of Law and director of NYU's Center on Environmental and Land Use Law. An internationally recognized expert on environmental law and policy and administrative law and regulation, he has published more than ten books and seventy articles and essays.

From 1989 to 1991 Mr. Stewart served as assistant attorney general for environment and natural resources at the U.S. Department of Justice, where he headed a staff of 400 lawyers in the representation of the United States in all environmental cases in court. Among other matters, he had principal responsibility for representing the United States in the Exxon Valdez oil spill litigation, which resulted in a $1 billion settlement of civil and criminal charges against Exxon.

From 1977 to 1989 Mr. Stewart served as a trustee of the Environmental Defense Fund (now Environmental Defense), a leading national environmental organization, and as its chairman from 1982 to 1984. He currently serves as advisory trustee of Environmental Defense and as a member of its Litigation Review Committee. He is also a director of the Health Effects Institute, a nonprofit organization jointly funded by the Environmental Protection Agency and industry to conduct policy-relevant research on the health effects of air pollutants.

Following his graduation from Harvard Law School in 1966, he served as law clerk to Justice Potter Stewart of the United States Supreme Court. From 1967 to 1971 he practiced law with the Washington, D.C., firm of Covington and Burling. From 1971 to 1989 Stewart was a member of the Harvard Law School faculty and became Byrne Professor of Administrative Law and associate dean. He was also a member of the Kennedy School of

Government faculty at Harvard. He left Harvard in 1989 to assume his position at the Justice Department and joined the NYU law faculty in 1992 following completion of his government service. Mr. Stewart has been a visiting professor of law at the University of Chicago, the University of California at Berkeley, the European University Institute, the University of Bologna, the University of Rome, and Georgetown University. He also served as special counsel to the Senate Watergate Committee.

Mr. Stewart is a graduate of Yale University, Harvard Law School, where he was a member of the *Harvard Law Review*, and Oxford University, where he was a Rhodes Scholar. He is a member of the American Bar Association and the American Law Institute. He is a fellow of the American Academy of Arts and Sciences and holds an honorary doctorate from Erasmus University, Rotterdam.

Jonathan B. Wiener is professor of law at Duke Law School, professor of environmental policy at the Nicholas School of the Environment and Earth Sciences at Duke University, and the faculty director of the Duke Center for Environmental Solutions. He is also a University Fellow of Resources for the Future in Washington, D.C. In 1999 he was a visiting professor at Harvard Law School. Mr. Wiener was elected to the governing council of the International Society for Risk Analysis in 2001, and he has been a member of the editorial board of *Risk Analysis: An International Journal* since 1998. His research addresses the science, economics, and law of risk regulation, both in the United States and internationally. The design of climate change policy has been a central focus of his work.

Before joining the Duke faculty in 1994, he served in both the first Bush and Clinton administrations, as senior staff economist at the White House Council of Economic Advisers in 1992 and 1993; as policy counsel to the director of the White House Office of Science and Technology Policy in 1992; and as special assistant to the head of the Environment and Natural Resources Division of the U.S. Department of Justice (Richard Stewart) from 1989 to 1991. In those positions he helped to formulate U.S. climate policy and to negotiate the international climate change treaties.

Mr. Wiener clerked for Judge (now U.S. Supreme Court Justice) Stephen G. Breyer on the U.S. Court of Appeals in Boston (1988 –1989) and for Chief Judge Jack B. Weinstein on the U.S. District Court in New York (1987–1988). He attended Harvard College (A.B. in economics in 1984) and Harvard Law School (J.D. in 1987), where he was an editor of the *Harvard Law Review.*